# STORE
# TRAFFIC
# IS A GIFT

## 🛒 Also by Mark Ryski

*When Retail Customers Count*
*Conversion: The Last Great Retail Metric*

The Retailer's Guide to
Converting Visits into Sales

# STORE
# TRAFFIC
# IS A GIFT

## Mark Ryski

GREENLEAF
BOOK GROUP PRESS

Published by Greenleaf Book Group Press
Austin, Texas
www.gbgpress.com

Distributed by Greenleaf Book Group

For ordering information or special discounts for bulk purchases,
please contact Greenleaf Book Group at PO Box 91869, Austin, TX
78709, 512.891.6100.

Design and composition by Greenleaf Book Group
Cover design by Greenleaf Book Group

Publisher's Cataloging-in-Publication data is available.

Print ISBN: 979-8-88645-376-8

eBook ISBN: 979-8-88645-376-8

To offset the number of trees consumed in the printing of our books,
Greenleaf donates a portion of the proceeds from each printing to
the Arbor Day Foundation. Greenleaf Book Group has replaced over
50,000 trees since 2007.

Printed in the United States of America on acid-free paper

25 26 27 28 29 30 31 32    10 9 8 7 6 5 4 3 2 1

First Edition

*For Ellen*

&

*For the hardworking and
dedicated people who
work in retail stores*

# Contents

# Foreword

Every recipe depends on one indispensable ingredient—without which, the dish fails. In retail, that ingredient is foot traffic. Until a shopper crosses the threshold, no sale can happen. Without sales, no store can survive.

Yet traffic, like any crucial ingredient, must be handled with care: measured precisely, seasoned with the right in-store experience, and never wasted. Mastering the art of monitoring and converting foot traffic into sales requires data-driven discipline and diligence—knowledge that Mark Ryski's *Store Traffic Is a Gift* delivers in abundance.

The title, borrowed from a veteran retail executive, could not be more apt. In an era of boundless choice—where consumers effortlessly jump between channels, locations, and brands and where time is short and attention spans shorter—every person who walks through a shop's door is indeed a gift.

Traffic, however, is only the starting point, the proverbial top of the funnel. Knowing how to guide that traffic through various stages of the purchase journey to the ultimate goal of a sale is what really matters. Again, managing and monitoring this is far more challenging than it used to be because the pathways to purchase are not linear, nor are they simple.

It is also fair to say that in the current economic climate, people have become far more discerning. Compared to 2019, consumers are browsing an average of two more stores when shopping for everyday apparel. They're also taking an average of twelve minutes longer to complete a purchase, mainly because they're considering and comparing more things across different retailers. The same pattern holds true across many other categories.

In this more competitive, complex environment, having a firm grasp on the metrics around traffic and conversion matters. They're more than mere numbers in a spreadsheet; they signal what's working and what needs to be changed, what delights and disappoints. They allow retailers to optimize many aspects of the store proposition in a way that is aligned with consumer demand.

Of course, there will be some who insist that traffic to physical stores is far less important than it once was, who argue that the future is really all about online. The hard numbers show this not to be true. In 2024, 76.2% of core retail sales were made in stores, and even by 2030, that proportion will still be well over 70%. What's more, stores play an invisible role in supporting online; last year, over 30% of online retail sales were driven, in some way, by physical stores.

Naturally, the connectedness of online and stores adds yet another layer of challenge when it comes to interpreting foot traffic. However, Mark neatly addresses this point and explains how omnichannel has simply changed the nature of measurement and interpretation, making traffic data even more critical rather than making it redundant.

The other bogeyman is the tired old buzzword "retail apocalypse." This springs up every now and again, especially when store closures are announced. What's interesting is that over the past year or so, the vast majority of store closures and retail bankruptcies have not been caused by the rise of online or the might of Amazon. Rather, the root cause is a failure by individual retailers to adapt or deliver for the customer. As a result, they lost business to other, usually physical, retailers. Notably, these are dynamics that foot traffic and its associated measurements could have predicted and, with the right action, prevented.

Understanding the right course of action comes from proper interpretation, and this is where the book comes into its own. In an industry awash with dashboards and KPIs, Mark's perspective stands out for its practicality. He translates traffic analytics into everyday language that everyone—from shop-floor associates to C-suite executives—can understand and act on. That makes *Store Traffic Is a Gift* a critical read for everyone in retail.

**—Neil Saunders**
Managing Director Retail, GlobalData
April 2025

*\* All data and statistics sourced from GlobalData*

# Introduction

I n mid-March 2020, I literally watched a retailer who usually received hundreds of thousands of store visits per day dwindle to virtually zero visits overnight. It was alarming and surreal. I couldn't believe my eyes. It was beyond comprehension. When the COVID-19 pandemic became a full-scale crisis by the end of March that year, how retailers and shoppers responded to that existential threat left the retail industry permanently altered. Never in the more than two decades that I have spent collecting and analyzing brick-and-mortar store visit trends has there ever been such an intense focus on store traffic as there was during the pandemic.

When I published my second book, *Conversion: The Last Great Retail Metric*, in 2011, retailers were focused on e-commerce and integrating their online efforts with their brick-and-mortar store operations. These retailers experienced many growing pains as they tried to create a seamless experience for shoppers.

"Big Data" and the use of actionable analytics were also

getting a lot of attention in 2011 as retailers worked to harness the mountains of data they were amassing. Store traffic and shopper conversion analytics were lumped in with a vast array of data from countless systems, including point-of-sale, workforce management and labor scheduling systems, customer experience platforms, financial systems, marketing platforms, merchandising systems, and, at the time, a torrent of new data from all varieties of social media. But retailers struggled to extract meaningful and actionable insights from that information.

However, the challenges retailers faced in 2011 paled in comparison to the existential struggle virtually all retailers faced in 2020. You see, the COVID-19 pandemic did not discriminate. It impacted *every* store—regardless of the retailer's size, category, or past success.

Retailers who were considered "essential" were allowed to remain open, as their offerings were deemed critical to daily life and the basic functioning of society, including food, medicine, and, as it turned out, toilet paper. These retailers that dodged the closure bullet found themselves scrambling to comply with a litany of new and continuously changing regulations intended to minimize disease transmission. Store traffic capacity limits were imposed, forcing retailers to literally guard their front entrances and limit the number of shoppers who were allowed to enter in any given hour. This resulted in long lines of dazed, confused, and frustrated—to the point of physical violence—mask-wearing shoppers.

But even when the patient shoppers finally got the opportunity to enter the store, many were forced to have their body temperature unceremoniously taken as it was believed that an elevated temperature was an indicator of infection. Once past the indignity of a temperature check and other screening protocols, shoppers found themselves in an *Alice in Wonderland* store environment where up was down and down was up.

The term *social distancing* became part of the zeitgeist, which in retail stores translated into one-way-only aisles and floor stickers marking the paths shoppers could safely travel. Retailers went to extraordinary lengths to comply with the numerous anti-retailing regulations to try to protect the health and welfare of their shoppers and frontline staff.

And if this all wasn't enough, frontline store workers looked more like biohazard cleanup crews with face masks and rubber gloves busily focused not on customer service, but rather on disinfecting surfaces. Cashiers were encased in plexiglass and also wore surgical masks, making it very difficult to communicate with customers, let alone breathe. Every protocol was antithetical to creating an enjoyable store experience.

Store traffic volumes spiked for the "essential" retailers, as shopper visits were concentrated to the stores that remained open. But more store traffic didn't translate into the sales windfall that you might expect. As the president of a general merchandise chain confided in me at the time, "You need to sell a lot of toilet paper to make up for the sale of a single television."

Soon store traffic became something retailers had to manage instead of serve—a lose-lose proposition for the retailer and the shopper.

And what of the large swath of retailers that found themselves in the unfortunate group deemed "nonessential" by government policymakers? These retailers were forced to close their doors and sell their goods online, regardless of their ability to do so. Many of these retailers scrambled to become e-commerce businesses virtually overnight, and the ones that weren't able to do it faced profound financial hardship or simply failed and went out of business.

## The Key Lesson for Retailers:
## Store Traffic Is a Precious Gift

With the pandemic now years in the rearview mirror, the lessons learned should not be lost on retailers. Some continue to feel the effects of the COVID-19 pandemic, as their store traffic counts are still down from pre-pandemic levels and may never return. Furthermore, the nature and intention of store visits has changed because demand for services like buy online, pick up in store and curbside pickup accelerated during the pandemic and have become baseline services that shoppers today expect.

However, the shift to online shopping has abated, and for many retailers, shoppers have returned to their stores at levels consistent with, and in some cases above, pre-pandemic levels. Retailers are once again focusing on the importance of the physical store. The resiliency of physical retail is undeniable.

As one retail executive put it: "Store traffic is a gift." He's right, it is a gift, and it's a gift that countless retailers squander every hour of every day.

It's mind-boggling that in this age of data and artificial intelligence (AI), so many retailers don't actually track the number of visits their stores receive. Beyond point-of-sale data, I wonder, could there be more basic and vital data for retailers than store traffic counts?

Even more remarkable are the retailers who do collect store traffic data but have chosen to not use it! I asked the former head of data science for a very large and well-known retailer how their executives thought about store traffic data, and her response shocked me: "Our C-level executives don't really think about store traffic . . . it's just not on our radar."

Retailers who don't accurately and consistently count store visits—or choose not to use the traffic data they already have—have no idea how many shoppers they'll need to serve, the time of day the shoppers are likely to visit, or how their store traffic is trending over time.

But that's just the beginning.

When you analyze store traffic data for a living as I have for more than two decades, you come to understand how this basic data can reveal profound and surprising insights about your retail operation—insights that you could never acquire without store traffic data.

But what makes store traffic so valuable is that it contextualizes everything that happens in the store. It is the ultimate "demand signal" that informs myriad decisions, including staffing, marketing, customer service, merchandising, and finance. In fact, you would be hard-pressed to find any operational decision that doesn't connect to store traffic in some way.

No retailer with physical stores can afford to take their store traffic for granted. And if you're not looking at it now, I guarantee that you are missing sales and opportunities to improve your labor scheduling and measure the impact of your marketing spend, to name just two at the top of the list.

## Tell Me Something I Don't Know

With so much data at any retailer's disposal, it's hard to imagine that there could be anything new or valuable to learn about store traffic. But my encounters with retailers belie this.

As a store traffic analytics practitioner, I will not only share the reasons why store traffic insights matter, but more importantly, I will also share how to put these insights into practice to drive better store sales and make more-informed, data-driven decisions.

Virtually any retailer can do this. All it takes is store traffic counts and the determination to want to improve results.

And here's another bold promise that I can confidently make. Once you come to understand the value of store traffic insights and how to apply them in your retail business, you will forever change how you operate your stores and make decisions.

Before we begin, I need to clarify my use of terminology in the book. Retailers are all unique, and that includes the terminology they use. This is one area that makes a book like this challenging— using terminology that everyone will understand.

To ensure that all readers are on the same page, I offer the following definitions for key terms that you will find throughout the book.

**Store Traffic:** The number of individuals who enter a store. This includes buyers and non-buyers. In North America, *store traffic*, or simply *traffic*, is the most common term. In the United Kingdom and Europe, it is more commonly referred to as *footfall*.

**Sales Transactions:** The number of sales receipts generated. Throughout this book, I refer to them as transactions. Since some retailers still call their sales transaction counts "customer counts," this term needs to be clarified. Sales transaction count only represents the number of discrete sales that are completed and does not include the people who visited the store and left without making a purchase.

**Conversion Rate:** The percentage of sales transactions completed relative to total store traffic visits. Conversion rate is calculated by dividing the sales transaction count by the store traffic count. Some retailers refer to conversion rate as close rate, sales conversion rate, customer conversion rate, footfall conversion rate, and in-store conversion rate.

**Average Sale:** The average dollar amount of each sales transaction completed. Average sale is also commonly referred to as average ticket, average dollar sale, average transaction value, average basket, and average order size.

**Field Leaders:** Any personnel who has decision-making authority and responsibility for physical stores. Field leaders include regional managers, zone managers, and district managers who are responsible for more than one store, while store managers and assistant store managers are responsible for only one store.

**Store Team:** This term refers to all other store-level personnel who are responsible for serving store visitors and preparing the store for sales, including sales associates, customer service representatives, merchandisers, and cashiers. Collectively, these people are considered frontline workers.

Throughout this book, I use real-world examples based on actual work I have done with some of the leading retailers in North America and beyond. However, all data has been anonymized and retailer names excluded to preserve confidentiality. Chapter 1 opens with what may be a controversial argument about the connection between sales and store traffic. The connection isn't exactly what most people believe it is, and I have data to prove it. Chapter 2 dives into what drives shopper conversion. I present five quick tips that any retailer can implement. Chapter 3 goes deep on store labor— what I call the physical retailers' conversion secret weapon. I'll also talk about labor productivity and offer a new approach for how retailers should measure it.

Chapters 4 and 5 introduce the idea of Super Converting stores and how retailers can identify and leverage their best performing stores. I present retailers a four-step methodology for conducting Conversion Rate Optimization (CRO) in their physical stores. Chapter 6 focuses on one of the most important success factors in driving shopper conversion: winning over the store team.

Chapter 7 focuses on how store traffic and conversion results can be used to assess the impact of virtually any initiative implemented in the store, how to financially quantify the impact, and how to build an ROI model using this data. Chapters 8 and 9 dive deeper into merchandising and marketing and how store traffic and conversion data are vital inputs to these decisions.

Chapter 10 discusses how services like buy online, pick up in store (BOPIS) impact store traffic and conversion, as well as the impact of self-checkout and other technologies. I'll also touch on the role Amazon has played as both a competitor and partner to physical retailers.

Chapter 11 delves into the challenges of capturing and maintaining your store traffic data and provides suggestions on how retailers should do this. Chapter 12 examines the other ways shopper traffic is being captured, such as smartphone tracking, and how retailers should interpret this data.

Chapter 13, the final chapter, touches on the use of AI and automation by retailers and how these technologies connect to store traffic and conversion.

My goal for this book is the same as for my previous two books—I want to help retailers improve store sales, make data-informed decisions, and create store experiences that shoppers will appreciate. I want retailers to succeed, grow, and thrive. Making the most of every store visit will help do that, and *Store Traffic Is a Gift* will show you how.

Writing a book that is relevant to the entire retail industry is a challenge, especially when you consider how expansive and diverse "retailing" is. But while there are innumerable permutations as to how the concepts in this book can apply to any given retailer, the key point is that they do, regardless of the retailer's category, size, or analytic sophistication.

My sincere hope is that readers find this book filled with useful information, compelling insights, and practical advice.

Remember, your store traffic is a gift. The ideas in this book will help you unwrap it.

# CHAPTER 1

# The Surprising Connection Between Store Traffic and Store Sales

Every retailer wants more store traffic. More store traffic means more sales, right?

Conceptually this seems undeniable, but when you actually analyze store traffic patterns, you realize this is not always true. Stores can receive *more* store traffic and have *lower* sales!

But here's the real kicker—sales can also go up even when store traffic is down!

Impossible, you say? It's not at all once you come to understand how store traffic and sales outcomes are related, and I'll share a simple example of this at the end of the chapter.

For now, let's start at the beginning—store traffic. Before a sale becomes a sale, a shopper visits the store. Once in the store, the shopper has a shopping experience of some kind, and if it's a positive experience, then it turns into a sale. The shopper found what they were looking for, made it through the checkout process, and consummated the store visit with a sale.

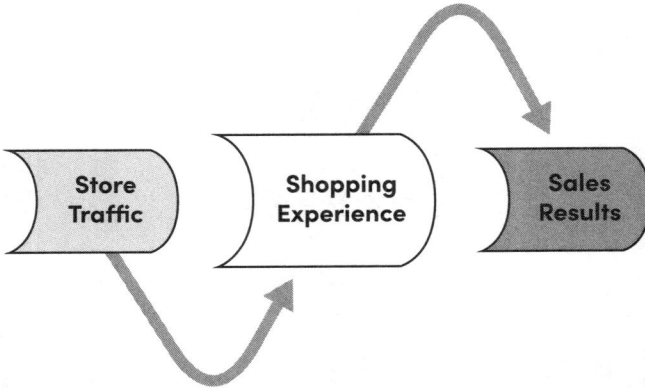

If we break down sales results into the underlying drivers, we can clearly see how the sales are being produced.

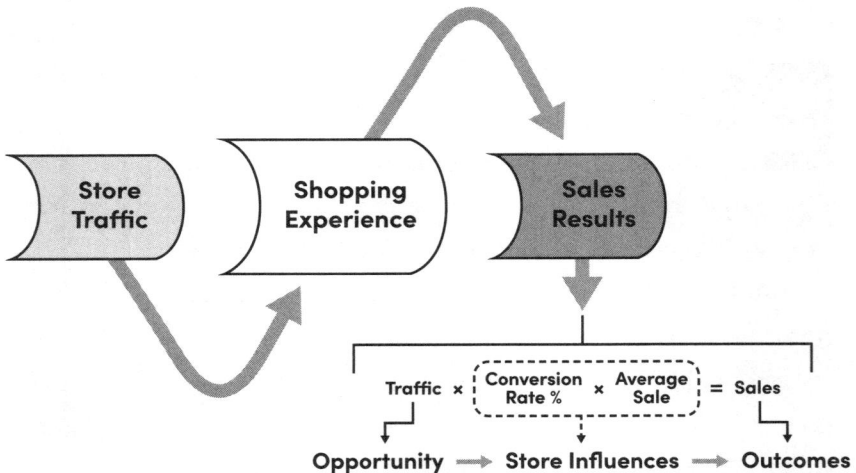

Store sales are a function of only three things: [1] store traffic, the number of visits or traffic a store receives; [2] conversion rate, the percentage of traffic (shoppers) that gets converted into a sales transaction; and [3] average sale, the average value of each sale or the amount each buyer actually spends. You can always calculate your sales outcomes simply as follows:

[Store Traffic Count] × [Conversion Rate %] × [Average Sale $] = Sales

Store traffic is important because it defines the size of the store's sales opportunity. Each store has a unique traffic opportunity, so it's vital to know how much traffic each store receives and if the traffic is trending up or down. Traffic can greatly impact sales, but it's the one variable the store teams don't directly influence. Yes, store teams serve the store traffic they receive, but generally, those teams have little or no ability to drive more traffic into their store. Their goal is to convert as many store visitors into buyers as possible.

So how do store teams influence sales?

They must focus on serving the shoppers who are in the store in a way that maximizes their conversion rates. As the preceding formula shows, there are only two ways for store teams to influence sales outcomes: by increasing conversion rates and by increasing average sale values. That's it.

Breaking out the store's sales results into the underlying sales drivers provides the store manager and store team with a clearer understanding of what they need to do to drive sales outcomes. For example, if the store has lower conversion rates, they should focus on improving conversion rates. If their average sale values are low, they should focus on average sales. As you will see, store traffic data not only enables the store team to understand exactly what's driving sales, but it will also pinpoint—down to the exact hours of the day—where sales are being missed. More on this in the next chapter.

Beyond the store manager and frontline team, it's imperative that all field leaders—including regional, district, and zone managers—have a clear view of what's driving sales outcomes in the stores they oversee. The field leaders need to work with the store managers and store teams, encouraging them to focus on the areas that will deliver the best sales outcomes in their store.

I cannot stress how important it is to get a clear line of sight from the store floor to field leaders, but it shouldn't stop there. Head office functional teams and ultimately senior leadership should also be aware of what's driving results.

When all stakeholders are looking at the insights the same way, you can start to make meaningful change and produce better sales outcomes.

## Traffic Counts Versus Transaction Counts

We can't talk about improving sales outcomes with store traffic data unless we agree on the definition of what store traffic actually represents. As it turns out, not all retailers define store traffic the same way.

Before electronic store traffic counters were widely available, some retailers used sales transaction counts as a proxy for store traffic. To these retailers, the only count that actually mattered was the customer count, which they defined as the number of sales transactions. These retailers would simply tally up all the sales transactions for the day and then use that transaction count as their "traffic" count.

And while it is reasonable to refer to transaction counts as customer counts, since that's exactly what these are, the problem is you can't calculate conversion rates without actual store traffic counts. Remember: Improving conversion rates is one of only two ways store teams can influence sales outcomes, so it's critically important to accurately measure store traffic!

Conversion rate is easily calculated by dividing total sales transaction counts by total store traffic count. For example, if 400 people enter a store during the day, and there were 100 sales transactions completed during the day, that means the store successfully converted 25% of its store traffic into a sale.

- Sales Transaction Count = 100
- Store Traffic Count = 400
- Conversion Rate = Transaction Count/Store Traffic Count = 100/400 = .25 or 25%

When you compare transaction counts to store traffic counts, you will almost always see a significant gap between these two numbers. Store traffic counts are always higher—and more often than not, significantly higher—than transaction counts. The following real-world examples will help illustrate why.

The following chart shows the results for twenty stores that make up a single district of an apparel retail chain. Collectively, the district completed 20,000 sales transactions in one month. This seems like a lot until you realize that the store traffic count for this same period was 100,000.

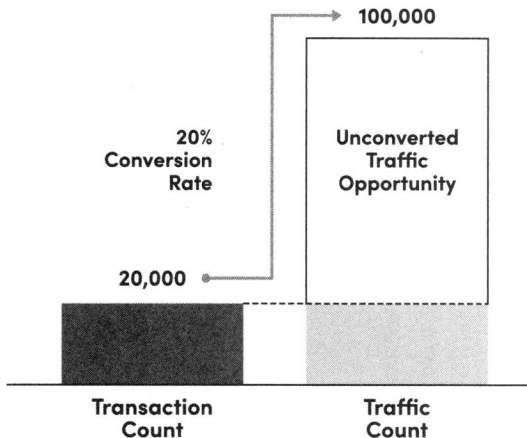

With a 100,000 store traffic count and a 20,000 sales transaction count, this district had a conversion rate of 20%. That's a lot of missed sales.

Seeing store traffic counts for the first time can be surprising and even shocking for retailers who only look at sales transaction counts.

Store traffic count is the only way to accurately measure a store's sales opportunity size and calculate its conversion rate. That's why it's so important to accurately measure it in *every store* and monitor trends over time.

The following chart shows four pairs of stores from a specialty chain, where each pair has virtually the same sales transaction count for the month.

## Transaction Count vs Traffic Count by Store

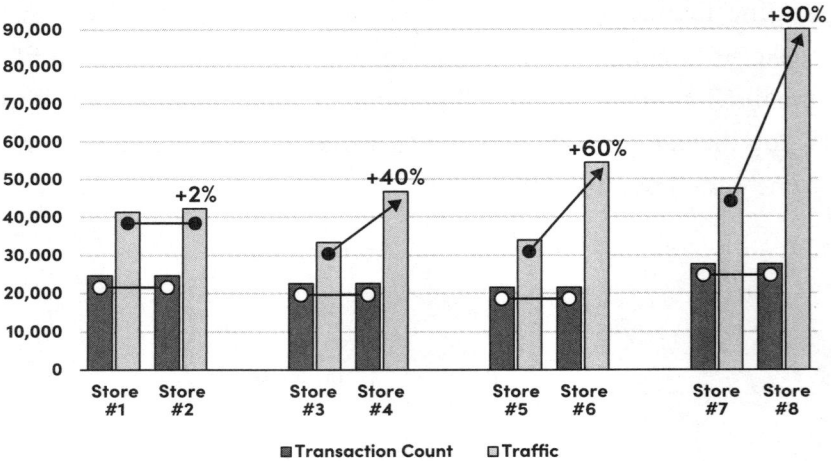

From a sales transaction count perspective, each of the four pairs of stores produces essentially the same number, but when you compare the sales transaction count to the store traffic count, you immediately see how different each store is and how comparable, or not, they actually are. For example, Store #1 and Store #2 had the same sales transaction count, and their store traffic counts were also very close to the same. In this case, sales transaction count provided a reasonable relative measure of activity levels between the two stores.

Now looking at the other store pairings, you can clearly see how different the stores are from a traffic perspective, and most dramatically when comparing Store #7 and Store #8. These stores generated the same number of sales transactions, but Store #8 had 90% more traffic!

Every retailer that's interested in improving sales outcomes should be focused on improving conversion rates by turning more of their store visits into sales, not just driving more traffic into the store. As you can see from the preceding example, more store traffic doesn't always result in higher sales.

But if the retailer doesn't have store traffic counts, then they're flying blind and have no idea what their store's sales potential is, how much of their traffic is being successfully converted into a sale, and, even more importantly, how many sales they are missing out on.

When you count how much traffic leaves a store without being converted, you begin to realize just how large the missed sales opportunity is and how even a small improvement in conversion rate can produce a significant increase in sales.

## How Store Sales Can Increase Even When Store Traffic Decreases

Allow me to state the obvious: No store traffic means no sales. However, what's less obvious is that even when a store's traffic is decreasing, its sales don't always follow. And the opposite is also true. Store traffic can be increasing, but store sales don't always increase.

This may seem counterintuitive, but a simple example will help illustrate how this can happen. Based on my extensive experience analyzing this type of data, it happens much more frequently than retailers ever realize.

| | Store A | | | Store B | | |
|---|---|---|---|---|---|---|
| | Last Year | This Year | YoY % Change | Last Year | This Year | YoY % Change |
| Store Traffic Count | 50,000 | 45,000 | -10% | 48,000 | 53,000 | 10% |
| Conversion Rate | 25% | 30% | 20% | 25% | 20% | -20% |
| Average Sale | $50 | $50 | 0% | $50 | $50 | 0% |
| Sales | $625,000 | $675,000 | 8% | $600,000 | $530,000 | -12% |

At Store A, traffic count is down 10% from last year. Because there is less opportunity in the store, one might assume that store sales will also be down. However, despite having less traffic, the store team did a better job of converting the traffic it did get into sales. Conversion rate increased from 25% last year to 30% this year—that's a 20% year-over-year (YoY) increase in conversion performance. Even though average sale values remained the same at $50, overall sales for the year were up 8% compared to the prior year.

At Store B, traffic was up 10% compared to last year. Here the sales opportunity got 10% larger, but because conversion rates declined by 20%—going from 25% last year to only 20% this year— overall sales were down by 12%.

Store traffic is needed to make a sale, but what the store team does with the traffic is ultimately what determines if a store visit turns into a sale.

Generally, retailers generate store traffic through promotions, advertising, and marketing, but before they spend precious budget to increase store traffic, they should focus on converting the store traffic they're already getting. I'll touch on driving store traffic in chapter 9.

To be clear, it's the job of marketing to generate store traffic opportunities, and it's the store team's job to convert that store traffic into sales. Improving conversion rates and increasing average sale values are the only two ways store teams can influence sales.

Thinking about store sales this way is truly transformational because it shines a very bright light on the sales outcomes stores are producing based on the variables the store team can directly influence (i.e., conversion rate and average sale) instead of sales outcomes, which are influenced by store traffic—a variable they don't influence.

The following table shows a real-world example of YoY results for a sample of stores from a specialty homeware chain. If store traffic always drove store sales, then it should follow that any store that had an increase in YoY traffic should also see an increase in YoY sales, and any store with a decrease in store traffic should see a decrease in sales.

| Store | Average Daily Traffic | | | Conversion Rate % | | | Average Sale $ | | | Average Daily Sales | | |
|---|---|---|---|---|---|---|---|---|---|---|---|---|
| | This Year | Last Year | YoY % Change | This Year | Last Year | YoY % Change | This Year | Last Year | YoY % Change | This Year | Last Year | YoY % Change |
| 1 | 192 | 169 | 13.5% | 27.5% | 29.0% | -5.4% | $18 | $15 | 18.2% | $954 | $752 | 26.9% |
| 2 | 312 | 330 | -5.7% | 34.8% | 30.1% | +15.6% | $23 | $21 | +11.2% | $2,498 | $2,054 | +22.0% |
| 3 | 313 | 305 | 2.4% | 33.2% | 28.8% | 15.5% | $22 | $21 | 5.5% | $2,269 | $1,812 | 25.2% |
| 4 | 280 | 267 | 5.2% | 32.0% | 29.2% | 9.5% | $19 | $19 | 2.1% | $1,708 | $1,453 | 17.6% |
| 5 | 365 | 343 | 6.6% | 37.2% | 35.7% | 4.3% | $22 | $21 | 3.7% | $2,951 | $2,559 | 15.3% |
| 6 | 192 | 193 | -0.6% | 24.9% | 23.1% | 7.9% | $22 | $21 | 7.5% | $1,070 | $929 | 15.3% |
| 7 | 183 | 174 | +5.1% | 28.0% | 26.9% | +4.2% | $19 | $18 | +8.2% | $968 | $844 | +15.3% |
| 8 | 321 | 323 | -0.8% | 30.4% | 28.6% | 6.5% | $24 | $23 | 6.4% | $2,368 | $2,105 | 12.5% |
| 9 | 381 | 370 | 2.8% | 18.9% | 19.1% | -1.4% | $21 | $19 | 10.7% | $1,536 | $1,369 | 12.2% |
| 10 | 78 | 70 | 10.8% | 46.6% | 48.6% | -4.2% | $19 | $18 | 5.5% | $688 | $615 | 12.0% |
| 11 | 315 | 317 | -0.5% | 23.4% | 26.1% | -9.9% | $19 | $20 | -5.0% | $1,400 | $1,654 | -15.3% |
| 12 | 278 | 253 | +10.0% | 23.5% | 26.1% | -9.9% | $19 | $20 | -5.0% | $1,241 | $1,322 | -6.0% |
| 13 | 132 | 135 | -1.9% | 38.5% | 37.5% | 2.8% | $24 | $23 | 6.8% | $1,233 | $1,147 | 7.5% |
| 14 | 151 | 150 | 0.6% | 27.4% | 27.5% | -0.3% | $22 | $20 | 6.7% | $893 | $835 | 7.0% |
| 15 | 125 | 135 | -7.4% | 37.0% | 35.1% | 5.7% | $24 | $22 | 7.0% | $1,089 | $1,039 | 4.8% |
| 16 | 350 | 419 | -16.3% | 26.8% | 23.7% | 12.7% | $20 | $18 | 9.4% | $1,885 | $1,827 | 3.2% |

*Values have been rounded.

### Traffic x Conversion Rate x Average Sale $ = SALES

But often that's not what actually happens.

For example, Store #2 had a 5.7% decline in store traffic versus the prior year, yet YoY sales are up a whopping 22.0%. By breaking out results this way, we can clearly see that while traffic was down, conversion rates and average sale values were both up, and improvements in these metrics drove YoY sales higher despite the store traffic decline.

At Store #7, store traffic was up only 5.1% versus last year, but sales were up 15.3%. In this case, the store delivered significantly higher sales than the store traffic increase. At Store #12, store traffic was up 10.0% versus the prior year, but despite the traffic increase, sales were down 6.0%. Again, by breaking the results into the underlying drivers, we can see that decreases in both conversion rate and average sale value explain why sales are down—and it had nothing to do with store traffic.

Now that the groundwork is laid and we have a shared understanding of store traffic and conversion rate, we will focus on how retailers can use store traffic insights to improve sales performance and make better, data-informed decisions.

## 🛒 Chapter Takeaways

- Three key variables drive sales: store traffic, conversion rate, and average sale value.

- More store traffic does not always equate to higher sales. Sales outcomes depend on how effectively a store team converts traffic into purchases, even if store traffic is static or declining.

- Accurate store traffic counts are essential for calculating conversion rates and identifying missed sales opportunities. You cannot rely on sales transaction counts alone.

- Modest improvements in conversion rates and average sale values can lead to significant sales increases even when store traffic is down.

### PRACTITIONER'S ADVICE

- Concentrate the store team's focus on improving conversion rates and increasing average sale values, as these are the variables they directly influence.

- Focus on converting existing traffic before launching new marketing campaigns to increase traffic.

- Continuously measure conversion rates and average sale values, then adjust strategies accordingly for better sales performance. The focus at store level should be on hourly conversion rates, since every hour of every day, shoppers leave without buying.

# CHAPTER 2

## How to Convert More Store Visitors into Buyers

The first thing you should understand about conversion rates is that physical stores achieve significantly higher conversion rates than online retailers—even higher than Amazon.

Comparing conversion rates in physical stores versus e-commerce across select categories makes it absolutely clear that while people prefer to browse for goods online, the vast majority—about 80% depending on your source—prefer to complete the sales transaction in a physical store.[1]

Online stores convert about 3% of their traffic into sales, and even Amazon, the online leader by far, only converts about 10% of its traffic into a sale.[2] Conversion rates in physical stores can vary across store types and categories, and in some categories, like jewelry, conversion rates can be less than 10%. However, for most other categories, conversion rates range from 20%-plus in apparel and specialty stores to as high as 70%-plus in general merchandise stores.[3] Physical stores have a significant conversion advantage over online.

When asked why shoppers prefer to buy in physical stores, the answers are hardly surprising: immediate gratification of getting to bring the merchandise home, having the ability to touch and feel the merchandise, preference to interact with store staff, and the list goes on. But the motivations for why people choose to make purchases in-store are less important than the fact that they do.

This inherent preference consumers have for purchasing in-store gives all retailers with physical stores the incentive to improve their conversion rate performance. In my experience, the conversion performance of any physical store can be improved.

## What Should My Conversion Rate Be?

Conversion rates in physical stores vary considerably across categories, which stands to reason, but what is really surprising is how much conversion rates can vary by store *within* the same chain. Forget about so-called industry averages. If you want to improve conversion performance in your stores, you need to view each store individually.

While some of this variation can be a result of differences in store format—for example, mall stores versus off-mall stores and geographic location—there are many factors that can impact conversion rates, including product mix, inventory levels, merchandising, and most importantly, the store personnel who serve the shoppers.

Here's a real-world example to illustrate how much conversion rates can vary within the same chain.

The following chart shows the average daily store traffic versus the conversion rate for each location in an eight-hundred-store apparel chain. Not surprisingly, stores that have higher store traffic tend to have lower conversion rates than stores that have lower store traffic. For example, a store located in a busy mall will almost always have much higher traffic and a lower conversion rate than a free-standing store that doesn't get as much incidental store traffic.

## Traffic and Conversion Rate by Store

While we understand that there are variations in store traffic and conversion rates across stores, what's extraordinary is just how widely these rates can range within the same chain. In the previous example, conversion rates ranged from a low of 15% to a high of 50%.

When it comes to improving conversion performance, it's important to realize that each and every brick-and-mortar store is unique. In order to optimize conversion rates, these unique characteristics need to be considered on a store-by-store basis.

It's helpful to think of each physical store as a unique conversion algorithm.

The algorithm ingests shopper traffic and produces sales as the outcome. Everything that happens from the moment the shopper enters the store to the moment they transact the sale is part of the conversion algorithm. The store layout, merchandising, inventory, store staff, and the checkout process are all part of the store's conversion algorithm.

In the online world, most e-commerce firms focus considerable and continuous effort on optimizing their conversion rates through a methodology referred to as Conversion Rate Optimization, or CRO for short. CRO is a system for increasing the percentage of visitors that convert into customers. In the online world, conversion is a result of the offers presented, website design, and navigation. In physical stores, conversion is a result of specific interactions and experiences shoppers have when they visit a store—from the minute they enter the store to the moment they either transact a sale or leave without buying.

But how do retailers know what influences conversion rates the most? The short answer is by doing testing and experimentation, just like online retailers. But the first step is to understand why shoppers visit but leave without buying.

## Why Shoppers Don't Buy

Given the challenging business conditions so many brick-and-mortar retailers continue to face, it's baffling to me that improving in-store conversion rates hasn't become more of a focus, if not an obsession. Even retailers that are performing well could be doing even better by applying these insights.

Too many retailers today still believe that the path to higher sales is in generating more store traffic, despite the fact that every hour of every day, people leave without buying, even when they had intended to buy. There are many reasons shoppers leave without buying.[4] If you want to know why they decide to leave, you have to ask them.

That is exactly what we did when we were trying to understand why people were leaving a general merchandise retailer without making a purchase. To collect this information, we had interviewers positioned just outside the front entrance of the store, and we approached any shopper who was leaving the store without a purchase. These folks were easy to spot since they didn't have a shopping bag.

We asked only two simple questions: [1] Did you intend to make a purchase today? and [2] What was the main reason you did not make a purchase? The responses were surprising.

Of the hundreds of shoppers surveyed in this study, 77% of respondents said they had intended to purchase. Think about that result. What this simple survey revealed was the tremendous conversion opportunity this retailer was missing.[5]

When asked why these unconverted shoppers didn't purchase, the results were also surprising. The two most-cited reasons were: [1] They couldn't find anyone to help, and [2] They didn't want to wait in the checkout line. What was especially interesting about this finding was the impact frontline staff had on conversion rates, even in a general merchandise store that's largely considered self-serve or low service. Just imagine what impact staff have on conversion rates in high-assist or high-touch sales environments.

## Why didn't you make a purchase today?

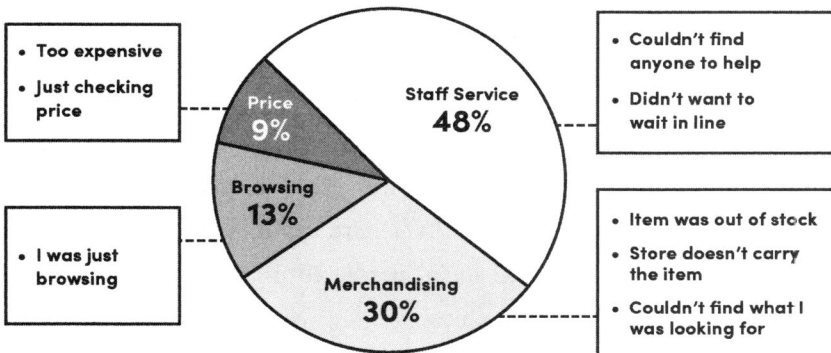

- Too expensive
- Just checking price

Price
9%

Staff Service
48%

- Couldn't find anyone to help
- Didn't want to wait in line

Browsing
13%

- I was just browsing

Merchandising
30%

- Item was out of stock
- Store doesn't carry the item
- Couldn't find what I was looking for

After staff-related issues, the second most common reason shoppers didn't buy was related to merchandising and product availability. Simply not finding what they were looking for was a key reason people walked out, even though the retailer actually had what the shopper wanted to buy. This was another lost sales opportunity that could have been captured.

Based on this example and many others from retailers in different categories, it's clear that conversion rate optimization should begin with an assessment of why shoppers are leaving your store without buying. Though every retail category is different, and every store is unique, any retailer can acquire insight into the conversion barriers in their stores.

## Identifying Conversion Barriers—Social Media, Surveys, and Observation

Every retailer should do exit surveys of non-buyers to identify conversion barriers. This is a simple way to gain invaluable insight into why shoppers are leaving without making a purchase in any given store. However, you can also identify conversion barriers by examining shopper reviews on social media, reviewing your customer satisfaction surveys (if you conduct any), and even simply through observation of shopper behavior in your stores.

### SOCIAL MEDIA

Social media reviews may not always provide meaningful insight if there are too few reviews or if they are too dated. And some disgruntled shoppers may use social media to unfairly heap scorn on a retailer. However, those reviews are still worth examining because they can include useful insight into conversion barriers.

When you read enough reviews, you start to see patterns emerge. For example, a major general merchandise retailer was interested in increasing their conversion rate performance, and as part of the process, we set out to understand their conversion barriers by examining some of the thousands of social media posts on the review site Yelp.

It's remarkable how detailed and specific some of these reviews are, and that's another reason why they are worth reviewing—the high level of detail and specificity can make them more actionable.

In the case of the large general merchandiser, we discovered that one of the key conversion barriers was at checkout. Many shoppers expressed displeasure at having to wait in a long checkout line, only to have the cashier try to "sell" each shopper on the virtues of the chain's loyalty program. In this case, despite the long checkout line, the cashier continued to pitch the loyalty card to every shopper, which caused checkout delays, resulting in some shoppers simply abandoning their shopping carts and leaving the store in frustration.

Not only does this represent an immediate lost sale, but it's also far worse. This shopper posted their experience on at least one social media site, which will leave a permanent scar on the retailer's brand, and given the plethora of choices for alternative places to shop online and in brick-and-mortar stores, there's a good chance that this shopper may not return.

This is a good example of how a reasonable approach to encouraging shoppers to sign on to a loyalty program can create an unintended conversion barrier. There is nothing wrong with having cashiers inform shoppers of a loyalty program, but if the cashier does not have the presence of mind to adjust his behaviors based on the length of the checkout line, sales will be lost, and conversion rates will sag.

## CUSTOMER SURVEYS

Retailers have been using customer satisfaction surveys (CSAT) for many decades. However, the sad fact is that often these surveys provide very little insight into conversion barriers. As one executive from a specialty chain said to me, "All my stores have CSAT scores in the 80% plus range, so all my store managers believe that they are doing a good job . . . there's nothing to action in these survey results, and that's why we stopped doing them."

If you really think about it, conversion rate is a far more reliable measure than CSAT scores or sales alone. Do satisfied customers leave without making a purchase? Perhaps, but I'd argue that, in most cases, there is no better indicator of customer satisfaction than making a sale, and conversion rates measure this precisely relative to the volume of traffic the store receives, making conversion rates a more reliable measure of satisfaction than conducting random customer surveys.

But high CSAT scores should translate into better sales, right? That's not what I discovered. To see how well CSAT scores connect to sales performance, we compared the results for a group of stores in a major specialty chain. The findings were surprising and counterintuitive.

First, we compared the CSAT scores for the top ten performing stores based on their year-over-year (YoY) sales improvement. Our hypothesis was that stores that had the highest YoY sales gains should also be the stores with some of the best CSAT scores. Makes sense, doesn't it?

While some of the top selling stores did have among the highest CSAT scores, two had CSAT scores of only 50%, which was dramatically lower than the chain average CSAT score of 78%.

Only five out of the top ten selling stores had CSAT scores above the chain's 78% average CSAT score. As surprising as this result was, it was even more curious when we compared CSAT scores to sales of the bottom ten stores based on their YoY sales results.

Overall CSAT scores were actually *higher* among this bottom ten group of stores as compared to the chain average—despite having the largest YoY sales declines. Only three of the bottom ten stores had CSAT scores that were below the chain average of 78%, and two of these stores had CSAT scores of 100%!

How can this be possible? While it's reasonable to conclude that customer satisfaction scores and sales performance are correlated, that's not what the data revealed. In this exercise, we found virtually no connection between customer satisfaction scores and YoY sales performance.

I'm not suggesting that retailers shouldn't conduct customer satisfaction surveys, but I am suggesting that they need to be very careful in how they interpret the results, especially in how they attribute sales outcomes to customer satisfaction. At the best of times, collecting customer satisfaction data is fraught. How survey data is collected, when the data is collected, and what questions are asked all contribute to a bias that will always be inherent in any surveying exercise.

For example, some retailers try to encourage customer feedback by way of online surveys, with the details for how to participate printed on the sales receipt. But what about the shoppers who visited and left without buying? These are the shoppers the retailer needs to hear from. However, because they didn't make a purchase, they don't get asked.

The amount of traffic a store receives influences sales outcomes, but store teams do not have the ability to generate traffic. As a result, a store that is delivering poor service and has a low CSAT score may still see their sales increase because it received more store traffic, which has nothing to do with the service the store team is providing shoppers.

The opposite is also true. A store may have poor YoY sales results because traffic volume declined, despite delivering exceptional customer service as evidenced by high CSAT scores.

The conclusion is that customer satisfaction surveys are not a reliable way to assess a store's ability to deliver sales. Recall, sales are a function of the amount of traffic a store receives, the store's conversion rate (i.e., the percentage of visitors who convert into buyers), and the average sale values it can generate from each sale.

## OBSERVATION

Another way retailers can identify conversion barriers is to spend time observing shoppers in the store. Every store manager should invest an hour or two a week doing this simple activity.

The trick here is to resist the temptation to intervene and assist shoppers. While this may result in a few shoppers leaving without getting served, it will provide valuable insight into what caused them to leave or the source of the conversion barrier and enable the store manager to adjust processes or behaviors to minimize the conversion barrier going forward.

# Spotting Missed Conversion Opportunities

Retailers commonly talk about reducing shopper "friction," or the things that cause shoppers to leave without buying. Conversion rate is a critical measure of shopper friction. When shopper friction is high, conversion rates are lower, and when shopper friction is low, conversion rates are higher.

There are many reasons why shoppers visit a store but leave without purchasing, and identifying the reasons specific to each store is important if you want to improve conversion performance. Even if you simply think about the times you as a shopper visited a store with the intention to buy but left without buying, you'll come up with a list of issues.

Long, slow-moving checkout lines, stock-outs, poor merchandising, and poor service resulting from understaffing or disengaged frontline staff are some of the obvious causes of shopper friction that translate directly into lower conversion performance. But before we get to solving the conversion challenges, let's start by looking at exactly when they are occurring.

## Spotting Conversion Opportunities

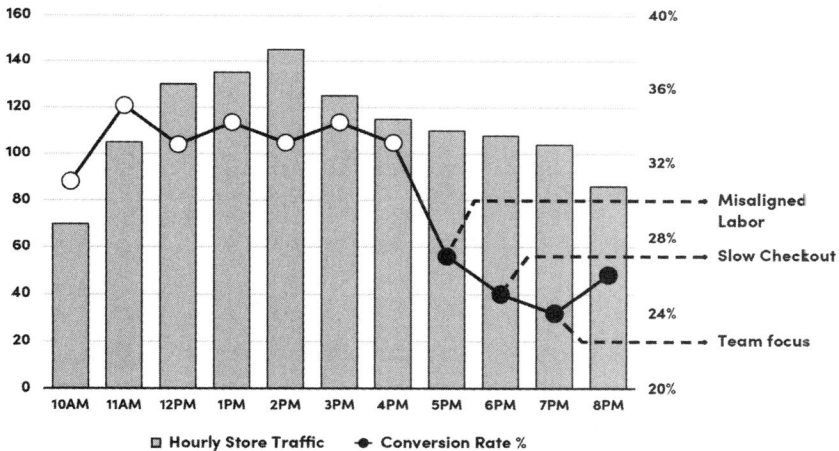

The following chart shows the hourly store traffic count and corresponding conversion rate for each hour of the day on a specific day. Collecting data in this way enables you to pinpoint when the conversion issues are happening right down to the hour of the day.

## Hourly Store Traffic Conversion

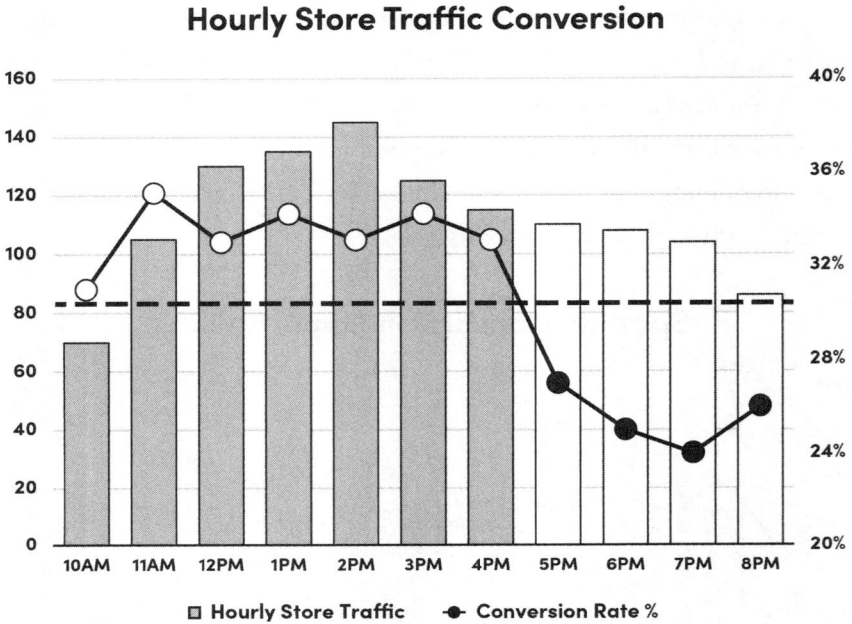

By presenting the data this way, you can see when conversion rates are low and when sales opportunities are being missed. In this real-world example, conversion rates start to decline during the 5 p.m. hour and remain low until the end of the day. This conversion rate "sag" indicated in black dots shows you precisely where to look. Analyzing store traffic and conversion rates can't tell you why this is occurring, but it will show you exactly when it's occurring. And once you know where to look, you can start to dig into why these conversion barriers are occurring and take steps to capture more of these lost sales opportunities.

## CONVERSION BARRIERS—CONTROLLABLE AND NONCONTROLLABLE

When you think about conversion barriers, think of them as being controllable or noncontrollable by the frontline store team. The store team has the greatest ability to influence conversion rates, but the reality is that some conversion barriers are simply beyond their control.

One easy way to know if a conversion barrier is controllable or noncontrollable is to ask: *Could the shopper have made a purchase today?*

If the answer is no, then it's a noncontrollable conversion barrier. However, if the answer is yes, the shopper could have made a purchase—even if it wasn't the exact item they came to the store for—then it's a controllable factor, and the store team is accountable.

Store labor is, without a doubt, the single most important factor that explains a store's conversion performance. It, too, can be both a controllable and noncontrollable conversion barrier, depending on how much say store managers have in requesting and assigning the labor they get. However, it's typically the head office who decides how much labor a store gets, and this labor allocation is almost always driven by the sales volume the store achieves—not the amount of store traffic the store receives and must serve.

There are numerous dimensions to how frontline store labor influences conversion rates. The amount of labor hours a store gets allocated, when the labor is scheduled, and the skills, knowledge, and motivation of this labor are all part of the mix. Labor is so critical to conversion performance that I devote an entire chapter to it (see chapter 3).

For now, let's turn our attention to the impact inventory and merchandising have on conversion.

## NONCONTROLLABLE CONVERSION BARRIERS

One of the most common noncontrollable conversion barriers is related to product mix and inventory levels. Some examples will help explain why.

Stock-outs of fast-moving, high-demand products can certainly lead to conversion rate sags. Going back to pandemic times, it was not uncommon for shoppers to visit stores looking for disinfectant wipes or toilet paper only to find these goods out of stock. Some of these shoppers left without purchasing anything, and this outcome was clearly seen in the store's traffic and conversion results.

In this case, there wasn't anything the frontline store team could do. These items were simply not available to sell, and there were no substitutes. It was an uncontrollable factor for the store team.

Here's another example. A large chain of shoe stores was trying to understand why conversion rates were lower in stores located in California compared to stores of similar size and store traffic volume in other geographic areas.

Upon further investigation, they determined that the cause of the low conversion rate performance was, in part, related to how shoe inventory was shipped to the stores. All stores received shoe inventory in "packs" of sizes, and every store got the same number of each size in the pack.

The problem was that in California, where there is a higher Asian and Latino population than in other areas, the demand for smaller shoe sizes is greater. The shoe packs did not account for this demographic difference, and as a result, these stores frequently stocked out of the sizes they needed, negatively impacting conversion rates.

In this example, the conversion barrier was noncontrollable to the store team because they didn't determine what shoe sizes were included in the packs in the inventory shipments. However, this is a controllable conversion barrier that the head office could influence by adjusting the mix of shoe sizes included in the packs delivered to the California stores.

You should not hold your store team accountable for the things they do not control. While stock-outs and inventory levels are obvious noncontrollable barriers, others include the weather, promotional activity, and even the actions of an aggressive competitor.

Notwithstanding these noncontrollable factors, the fact is that the frontline store team can greatly influence conversion performance, and many conversion barriers are controllable. As one apparel chain executive succinctly put it to me, "Every shopper should leave with a bag." She's right to have this expectation, and it starts with the assumption that every time someone visits the store, it creates a sales opportunity.

## CONTROLLABLE CONVERSION BARRIERS

One of the most frequent noncontrollable conversion barriers is related to product mix and inventory levels, but even when inventory levels are good and the product mix is right, conversion rates can sag—and this time frontline staff can control it.

Let's look at inventory again. If shoppers can't find what they're looking for, they will leave without buying. This can be especially challenging in large-format stores that are tens of thousands of square feet in size.

In the best-case scenario, the product is merchandised neatly on clearly marked shelves. Good merchandising contributes to conversion performance. However, if product is poorly displayed, hard to find, or simply sitting in the backroom instead of on the salesfloor, the store team is responsible because it's their job to ensure that shoppers can find what they're looking for. The following pictures are from a shoe store and an apparel retailer. How much effort are shoppers going to invest in finding what they are looking for when product is displayed in such a disorganized way?

Poor merchandising is a controllable conversion barrier.

Tidying up merchandising is easy to fix, but even stock-outs can be mitigated if frontline store teams know which substitute products to offer. Remember, frontline store teams must assume that every person who enters the store is there to buy something. They need to make the process easy for shoppers.

I know this sounds so simple and obvious, and that's because it is. However, until you examine your store traffic and conversion rates, you won't realize the impact that sloppy merchandising has on the store's conversion performance and, consequently, sales.

Improving conversion rates is an ongoing process. You will never arrive at a conversion rate destination; rather, store teams need to stay focused on improving conversion rate performance. Conversion rates fluctuate hour-to-hour and day-to-day, so what every store team should do is focus on improving their conversion performance. When you talk to store managers about store traffic and conversion, almost without fail the first question they ask is: How do I improve my conversion rate?

These store managers just want to know what they can do to move the conversion performance needle in a positive direction. For these managers, I offer five of the most impactful conversion improvement tips that will apply to virtually any retail environment.

## 5 Tips for Converting More Store Visitors into Buyers

### Tip #1: Make the Insights Easy to Spot

Can you see any insights in this?

Even skilled data analysts would have a hard time finding a trend in data presented like this. Sadly, this is the way traffic and conversion insights are often presented to field managers—tabular, numeric data.

When data is presented simply, clearly, and visually, managers can spot missed conversion opportunities, and they have a significantly higher probability of acting on it.

*continued*

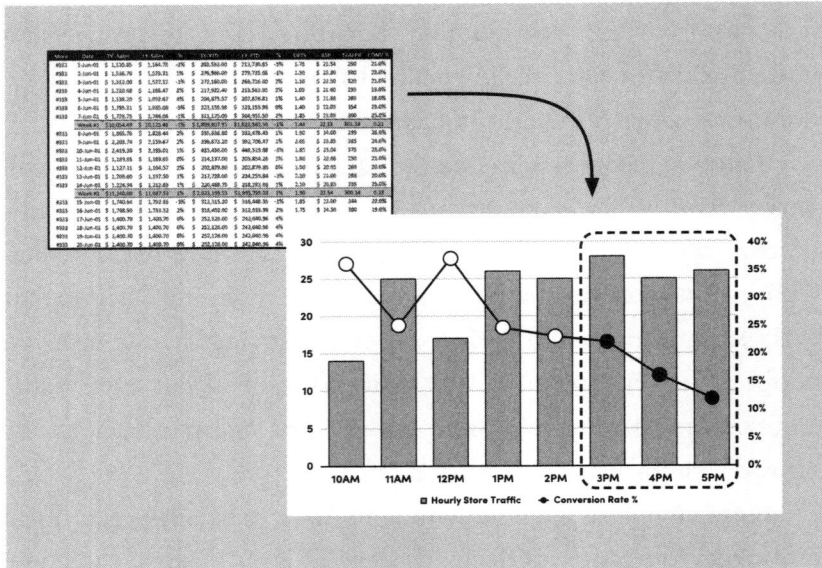

Modern retailing has a data problem. There's too much of it, and it's often challenging if not impossible to interpret and put into practical use by the store team.

I have seen reporting packages that go out to store managers that would require an advanced degree in finance to understand. If the data is not presented in a way that is easy to interpret or spot a trend from, then store teams will not be able to action the insight, and your results won't improve.

Even if a retailer has store traffic data, it's often only accessible to store teams via an online data portal that requires users to log on and then search for the insight. Often this numeric data is presented in dense tabular form, and as a result, spotting a trend or pinpointing exactly where conversion rate sags are occurring is almost impossible.

Remember, some people are visual learners, so presenting insights graphically as well as numerically can make a big difference for busy store managers.

## Tip #2: Focus on Hourly Conversion Rates

Every hour of every day, shoppers visit the store and leave without purchasing.

Store managers and frontline teams need to win conversion every hour, not just during the busiest hours of the day. Each hour needs a focus and a strategy informed by traffic. When stores win each hour, results roll right up the chain.

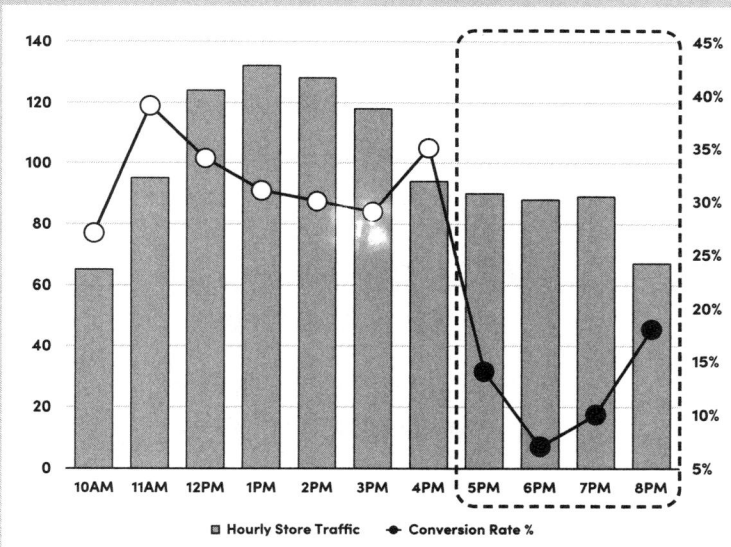

Hourly Store Traffic ◆ Conversion Rate %

Looking at daily totals does not provide the precision managers need to pinpoint where conversion sags are occurring. Providing hourly store traffic and conversion results tells the store team exactly where to look—and knowing where to look is half the battle of improving conversion performance.

In some retail segments, like jewelry, furniture, and high-end specialty stores where store traffic can be very low and sales transactions may not occur every hour, focusing on total daily conversion rates is the better approach. But even if you present conversion results at the daily level, you should still show hourly store traffic so the store manager knows how to best align labor schedules with store traffic opportunity.

Though conversion rates can spike or sag during any hour, sometimes these spikes or sags are merely a function of timing. For example, it's common to see a spike in conversion rates during the last operating hour of the day since some of the store visitors may have entered the store in the hour prior to closing but didn't transact the sale until the last hour of the day.

Store teams should disregard these spikes or sags and focus their attention on the main operating hours of the store.

## Tip #3: Set Conversion Goals and Recognize Wins

Conversion goals are typically set for the chain, region, or district—if they are set at all. Surprisingly, many retailers don't even set conversion goals.

Because no two stores are alike, even within the same chain, it's not precise enough to set a conversion target for all mall stores or street stores. These targets need to be set for each individual store.

Store managers should be challenged to improve against their unique conversion goals for the store, and then they should challenge their store teams to improve conversion against daily and even hourly goals.

Setting conversion targets is critical, but so too is recognizing conversion wins. Managers should be encouraged to celebrate wins with their store teams, which will help foster a positive environment and help make conversion a welcome KPI instead of one that store managers fear.

In this example, the store team had strong conversion performance during the 2 p.m. peak traffic hour and strong conversion in the evening hours.

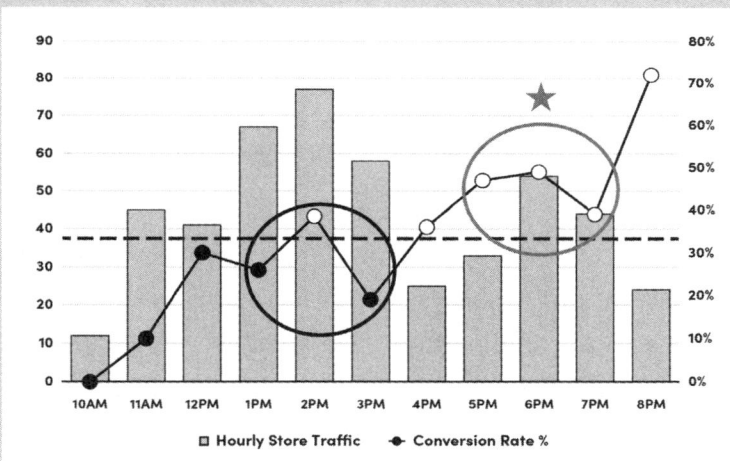

Almost all retailers have sales targets for their stores. But sales targets alone are inadequate because the store team doesn't control the traffic. They do influence conversion rate. However, most retailers I have encountered do not have conversion targets, and without a target to shoot for, it can be a challenge for store teams to stay focused on it day after day and hour after hour.

There are right and wrong ways to set conversion targets, and one of the biggest mistakes is to set a generic conversion rate target across all stores. The CEO of a sporting goods chain once said to me, "Every one of my stores should have at least a 40% conversion rate!" And he said it like a command, as if saying it forcefully would make it more attainable.

But the reality was that only a few of his top-performing stores were achieving this conversion rate. Most stores converted at 30%, and some stores were well below. Setting conversion goals too high will demoralize the store team and ultimately be counterproductive.

Not only should conversion goals be store-specific and aspirational, but they should also be achievable relative to a store's past conversion rate performance.

## Tip #4: Connect Conversion Results to Behaviors

Frontline staff have the single largest ability to influence conversion rates in physical stores. Often conversion rate sags are directly attributable to actions and behaviors of the store manager and frontline team, like scheduling breaks during peak traffic hours. But just as their actions can create conversion sags, they can also drive conversion lifts when they make smart decisions informed by traffic data—behaviors and actions drive conversion rate.

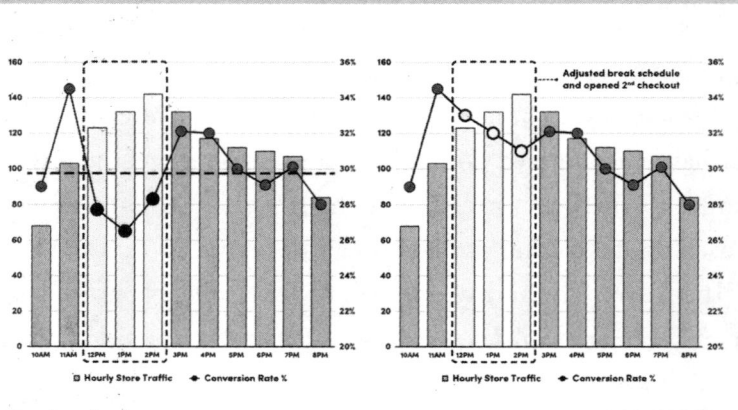

It's remarkable how a relatively small change in a store procedure or behavior can have a big impact on conversion performance.

While it's nice to see conversion rates improve, store managers must be able to connect conversion results to the behaviors and actions that caused or contributed to those better results. This will also enable the store manager to share their learnings in a very specific and practical way so that other store managers can try to replicate it in their own store.

But conversion wins shouldn't just be for store managers. Ultimately, it takes a collective effort to serve shoppers, so the conversion wins should be treated as an accomplishment by the entire store team. Seeing a quantifiable impact from the decisions or actions the store team took is inspiring, and they will come to realize that they do influence conversion rates.

## Tip #5: Staff for Conversion

Scheduling labor to store traffic is among the most important ways retailers can optimize conversion rates. Understaffing during busy periods results in conversion sags; overstaffing during low traffic hours wastes precious labor budget.

As reluctant as some retailers are to add more labor hours, sometimes it's necessary—this is clear in chart A.

However, more labor doesn't always deliver higher conversion rates as chart B clearly shows. There appears to be ample labor in the store, yet conversion rates still sag.

Too much staff can create a sense of complacency. If staff is focused on tasking instead of serving customers, conversion rates will suffer. So before even one more labor hour is allocated, retailers need to make sure they are making the most out of the labor they already have.

*continued*

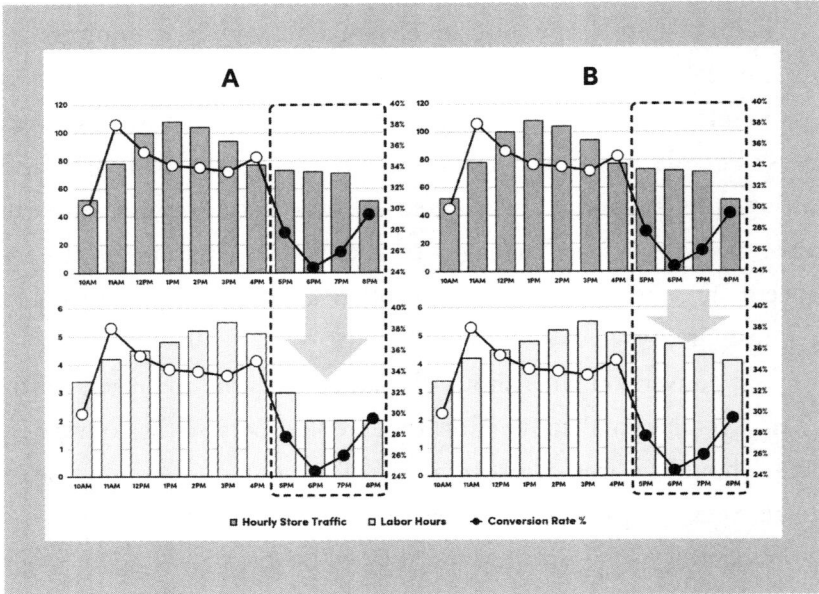

As previously mentioned, I devote an entire chapter to the importance of labor and its impact on conversion rates, but here's a basic idea that every retailer should intuitively understand.

You must schedule your labor relative to when shoppers are actually in your store. I know, this is obvious. But it's not obvious if you don't have store traffic data, and it's even worse if you're relying on sales transaction counts as a proxy for store traffic. Without store traffic counts, there is no meaningful way to schedule your labor, and I can guarantee that you are either over- or understaffing your stores without even knowing it.

However, scheduling your labor to store traffic is only step one. You still might not see improvements in conversion rates if that labor—even properly scheduled—isn't focused on driving conversion performance.

## 🛒 Chapter Takeaways

- Physical stores, where 80% of sales transactions are completed, enjoy significantly higher conversion rates compared to online retailers.

- Treat each store as a unique conversion algorithm where factors like store layout, merchandising, inventory, staff interactions, and checkout processes all contribute to conversion outcomes.

- Conversion goals can keep the store team focused; however, you should avoid relying on industry averages or a chain-wide conversion goal and instead set store-specific, achievable conversion targets based on each store's historical performance.

- Barriers to conversion can be controllable and noncontrollable for store teams. You should differentiate between barriers within the store team's control (e.g., merchandising) and those that are not (e.g., inventory shortages). Don't hold store teams accountable for noncontrollable barriers.

### PRACTITIONER'S ADVICE

- Identify conversion barriers by conducting exit surveys, monitoring social media, and observing shopper behavior to understand why visitors leave without buying. Address issues like staff availability, checkout efficiency, and product merchandising.

- Ensure that store managers have access to actionable insights presented in a clear, easy-to-interpret format. Hourly traffic and conversion data are crucial for pinpointing when conversion opportunities are missed.

- Schedule labor based on actual store traffic patterns rather than sales results. Properly aligned labor schedules can significantly impact conversion rates.

- Recognize and share successful conversion improvement strategies with the store team and with other store managers in the district and chain to motivate and foster a sense of accomplishment. Conversion improvements should be a collective goal.

- Continuously monitor conversion trends and refine conversion strategies. Improving conversion rate is an ongoing process, requiring consistent attention and adaptation.

# CHAPTER 3

---

# Store Labor— Conversion Secret Weapon

n my experience, most retailers don't allocate the right amount of labor to their stores, nor do they schedule the labor that they do allocate to maximize conversion performance. It's a double whammy that leads to reduced sales, poor store experience, and higher labor costs.

Store managers and the store team have the greatest ability to influence conversion performance in the store, so getting your labor right is critical. In fact, I would argue that the allocation and deployment of labor in stores is a secret conversion weapon for retailers—if they know how to use it.

Store labor is one of the largest controllable expenses any retailer will encounter.[1] Not only is labor expensive, but it's getting even more expensive post-pandemic as retailers increase pay to attract and retain frontline workers in an ever-increasingly competitive labor market.

Unfortunately, most retailers that I encounter continue to view labor as an expense that needs to be minimized. In fact, some store managers receive bonuses for having labor costs lower than their budget, which incentivizes understaffing decisions. While reducing operating expenses—including labor—is a worthy goal, the question you must ask is: At what cost?

If I reduce my labor expenses, thereby reducing service levels and having conversion rates drop, was it a good trade-off? No, often it is not a good trade-off, and store traffic and conversion rate data will enable you to quantify it. In fact, understaffing could very well be stunting store sales and causing long-term damage as shoppers choose other stores over yours.

## Scheduling Labor to Store Traffic— Uncommon Sense?

The idea of scheduling labor to store traffic is as old as the hills. Virtually every retailer I've encountered understands it conceptually, but surprisingly, many still don't do it. And as I discovered, there are plenty of reasons (excuses) why they don't.

Store traffic should drive your store's labor schedule. But store traffic is not typically how labor schedules are set. To a great extent, retailers still allocate labor to stores based on their sales results. Sell more, get more labor; sell less, get less labor. But this can often be a chicken-and-the-egg situation.

One of the most obvious reasons retailers don't use store traffic data in their labor decisions is that they simply don't have store traffic data, or in some cases, the retailer doesn't trust the accuracy of the store traffic data they do have. Instead, many of these retailers use sales transaction counts. But as we learned in chapter 1, these counts are often significantly lower than store traffic counts, so basing labor schedules on sales transaction counts is not a good idea and will ensure that you understaff your store.

A real-world example will help illustrate. The following chart shows the store traffic and conversion rate by hour for an apparel store.

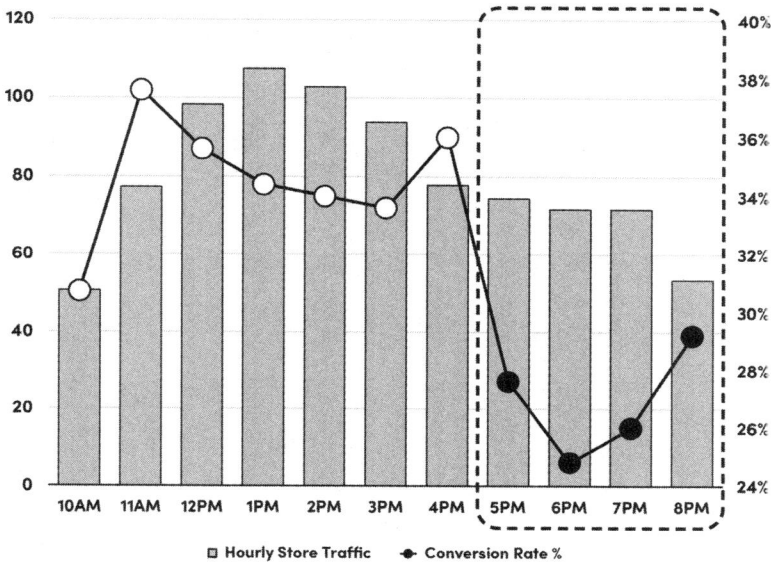

☐ Hourly Store Traffic  ● Conversion Rate %

At this store, conversion rates sag dramatically between 5 p.m. and 9 p.m., as indicated by the black dots. The hour shown at the bottom of each bar represents the starting hour. So the 8 p.m. hour represents the number of visits the store received between 8 p.m. and 9 p.m. Conversion rates during these hours are about eight percentage points lower than they are between 11 a.m. and 4 p.m. Remember, without store traffic data, this retailer could not calculate conversion rates and therefore couldn't spot this conversion rate sag.

Now one of the first questions the store manager should ask is: How is my store team labor scheduled?

The updated chart that follows shows the store traffic and conversion rates by hour but now includes a second chart showing how labor is scheduled by hour versus conversion rate by hour.

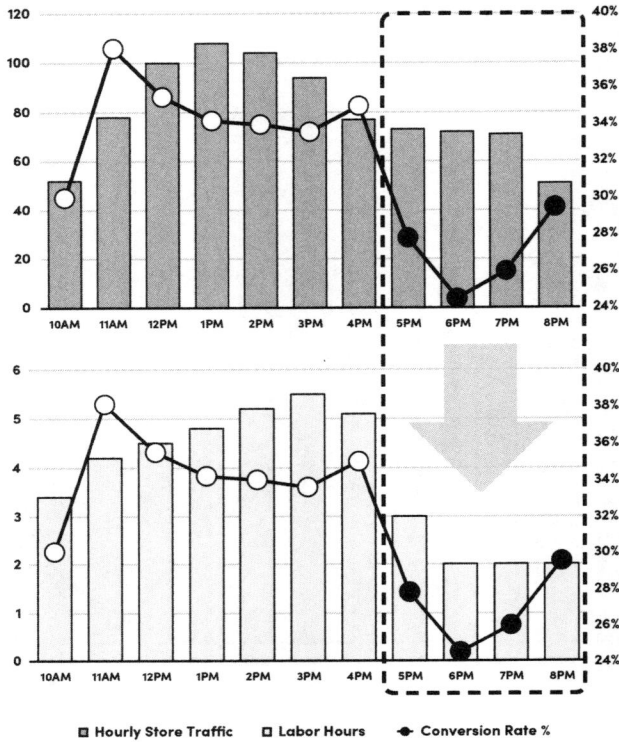

☐ Hourly Store Traffic   ☐ Labor Hours   ◆ Conversion Rate %

What this simple chart makes clear is that from 5 p.m. to 9 p.m., store labor is reduced even though plenty of shoppers are still in the store. This misalignment in labor to store traffic is likely the cause of the conversion rate sag between 5 p.m. and 9 p.m., and that's why sales are soft during these hours—not because there aren't enough shoppers in the store, which is the incorrect conclusion most retailers would immediately make based on sales results.

What do you think the store experience is like for the shoppers visiting this store between 5 p.m. and 9 p.m.? Probably not great, and the conversion rate sags pinpoint to the hour where lost sales are occurring.

When you have store traffic and conversion rate data, it's easy to spot these misalignments so you can schedule your store labor when shoppers are visiting the store. If you can align store labor to store traffic, you will increase your probability of converting more of the visitors to sales.

As a workforce management expert once said to me, "Store traffic data gives you the best, most unbiased future forecast to base your staff scheduling on." I couldn't agree with him more. However, there must also be a second step in your assessment, because you may discover that conversion rates haven't improved even if you do have your store labor aligned with store traffic.

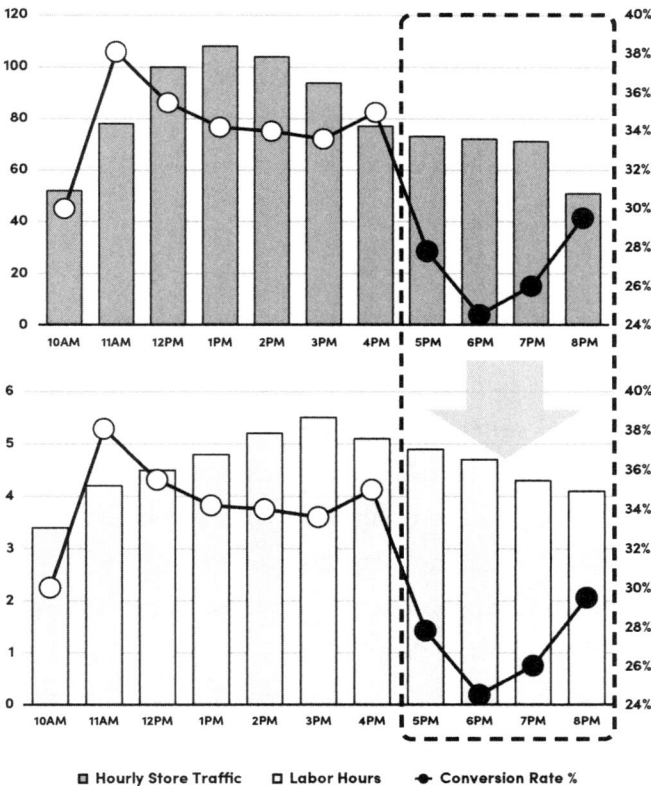

□ Hourly Store Traffic    □ Labor Hours    ● Conversion Rate %

It may seem counterintuitive to say that you can schedule your labor precisely to the store traffic by hour and conversion rates might still be down. The preceding chart illustrates the point.

In this case, store labor was only modestly reduced between 5 p.m. and 9 p.m. as compared to earlier in the day, and yet conversion rates still sagged. How's that possible? Because the labor that is scheduled isn't focused on serving customers.

While getting your store labor scheduled relative to store traffic is the right approach, you also need to ensure that the labor is being deployed to focus on converting shoppers. If they are just doing tasking, you will end up in the same place—sagging conversion rates and higher labor cost!

The fact is that more store labor doesn't always deliver higher conversion rates, so store managers and labor decision-makers need to be very clear about how the store labor should be deployed. It's not just about getting the alignment right.

Another way to think about this is to ask: How productive is my store team labor?

## Measuring Store Labor Productivity

One of the most common ways to assess store labor productivity is to examine sales generated per labor hour.[2]

"Sales per labor hour" is a useful metric, but it's not perfect because it relies on sales results as a basis for assessing labor productivity. Here's an example to illustrate.

To understand the productivity of labor in two stores, a retailer assembled the following data:

|  | Store A | Store B |
|---|---|---|
| Store Sales | $9,000 | $7,700 |
| Store Labor Hours | 50 | 50 |
| Sales per Labor Hour | $180 | $154 |

From a sales per labor hour standpoint, Store A clearly outper-formed Store B. Each store had fifty labor hours to work with, and Store A generated $180 in sales for every labor hour, while Store B only generated $154 in sales for every labor hour. That's $26 or over 17% more sales per labor hour.

Based on this measure, Store A clearly has higher labor produc-tivity than Store B. Case closed. Or is it?

We know that the amount of traffic a store receives influences sales results, and since store teams don't control store traffic, then it follows that sales per labor hour is a metric that is influenced by a noncontrollable variable.

If we compared the sales performance of these two stores based on the variables that the store teams control, then we will have a more accurate reflection of how productive the labor in each store actually was. The following table includes store traffic, conversion rate, and average sale results for the two stores.

|                      | Store A | Store B |
|----------------------|---------|---------|
| Store Sales          | $9,000  | $7,000  |
| Store Labor Hours    | 50      | 50      |
| Sales per Labor Hour | $180    | $154    |

|                  | Store A | Store B |
|------------------|---------|---------|
| Store Traffic    | 600     | 350     |
| Conversion Rate  | 30%     | 40%     |
| Average Sale     | $50     | $55     |

|                        | Store A | Store B |
|------------------------|---------|---------|
| Sales per Store Visitor | $15    | $22     |

Store A received a lot more traffic—600 visits versus only 350 visits to Store B. And this larger traffic opportunity is part of why their sales results are higher. But we can see that from a conversion rate and average sale perspective, Store B outperformed Store A, converting 40% of their visits to sales compared to only 30% at Store A. Furthermore, Store B had a higher average sale value of $55 versus only $50 at Store A.

So how do you make sense of what appears to be contradictory insights? The answer lies in how store traffic influences sales results.

Sales per store visitor, which can also be called sales per traffic count, is a much more reliable measure of labor productivity because it neutralizes the store traffic effect on the results. By calculating the sales generated per store traffic count, we level the playing field and narrow the comparison to the two variables the store teams can influence—conversion rate and average sale.

You can calculate sales per visitor by simply dividing total sales by total store traffic or by multiplying the conversion rate by average sale.

In this example, the sales per visitor at Store A is only $15, whereas it's $22 at Store B—$7 in sales per visitor more than Store A. Since both stores had the same fifty labor hours to work with, I would argue that Store B had much higher labor productivity than Store A, despite having lower sales. Further, Store B had less traffic but converted more of their traffic into sales transactions, and each of those transactions was also $5 higher on average than in Store A.

As you can see, when it comes to measuring store labor productivity, store traffic data and conversion rates are essential.

So how do retailers acquire this insight without store traffic data? They don't, and as a result, they have a big blind spot when it comes to assessing their store labor productivity. But measuring labor productivity is only one use-case for this very versatile metric. Sales per store visit insights can also be used to help you create the right financial incentives for store teams and as a mechanism to efficiently allocate labor across stores.

Let's start with allocating labor across a group of stores.

## Allocating Labor Across Stores Using Store Traffic Data

For most retailers, labor is allocated to stores based on sales budgets.[3] Stores that have higher sales get more labor, and stores that have lower sales get less. But as we just learned, allocating labor based on sales alone can lead to labor misallocations.

Labor misallocations can either be from overstaffing or understaffing, and neither is good. Having too many staff is not only more expensive, but worse, it also deprives other stores from getting the labor they legitimately need since labor budgets ultimately roll up to the total chain.

But there's another problem with overstaffing—complacency. You might think that by overstaffing conversion rates should soar, but often that is not the case. As one retail executive said, "We tested store labor versus conversion rates and found that conversion rates improved by adding labor, but only up to a point, after which conversion rates flattened out."

This executive went on to say that their analysis concluded that store team complacency was part of the reason why. With plenty of staff on the floor, the store team didn't have the same urgency to serve shoppers as when they had fewer staff.

The main point is that driving conversion performance is not merely about throwing more labor at the store.

Overstaffing can be a problem, but given how tight the labor market is and how frugal most retailers are with expenses—especially labor—the more insidious problem is understaffing.

The obvious problem with understaffing is lower conversion rates. These are the lost sales from shoppers who visited, didn't get served, and then left without buying. And if the lost sale isn't bad enough, some of these underserved shoppers may never return or may write a scathing review on social media that will leave a long-term scar on the retailer's reputation that is impossible to quantify. It's also worth noting that understaffing can also contribute to incomplete tasking and merchandising, which can further exacerbate conversion performance issues.

So then, how do you know if you are allocating labor effectively across all your stores when labor allocations can vary dramatically by store?

The first step is to compare the volume of traffic a store receives to the labor it has available to serve the traffic. You can do this by calculating the traffic-to-labor ratio for each store and then comparing those ratios across all stores.

In my experience, this is a largely underutilized but important metric that normalizes labor allocations by comparing the ratio of store traffic to labor hours available in the store. The following example will help illustrate how this works.

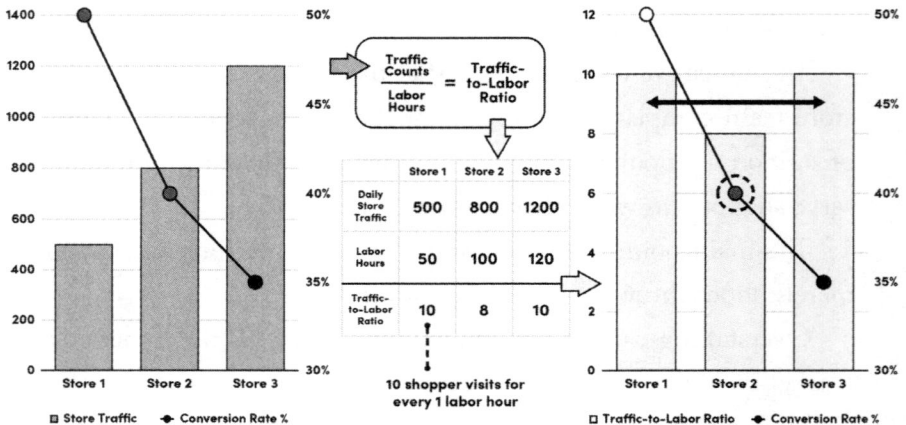

$$\frac{\text{Traffic Counts}}{\text{Labor Hours}} = \text{Traffic-to-Labor Ratio}$$

| | Store 1 | Store 2 | Store 3 |
|---|---|---|---|
| Daily Store Traffic | 500 | 800 | 1200 |
| Labor Hours | 50 | 100 | 120 |
| Traffic-to-Labor Ratio | 10 | 8 | 10 |

10 shopper visits for every 1 labor hour

Store 1 had the lowest traffic and highest conversion rate, and Store 3 had the highest traffic and lowest conversion rate. Traffic-to-labor ratios are calculated by dividing the store's traffic counts by the labor hours it gets. Store 1 receives 500 traffic counts on average per day and has 50 labor hours per day; Store 3 receives 1,200 traffic counts on average per day and has 120 labor hours per day.

When you calculate the traffic-to-labor ratios, you can see that they are the same in Store 1 and Store 3—each store has one labor hour for every ten traffic counts it receives. Said another way, these stores have the same relative labor allocation based on their store traffic, so we can rule out the amount of labor as the likely cause of the poor conversion performance in Store 3.

Curiously, Store 2 had the most favorable traffic-to-labor ratio at eight traffic counts for every one labor hour, yet its conversion rate performance was lower than Store 1. This finding tells us that Store 2 has plenty of labor—in fact, this store has more than the other stores relative to the traffic it receives—but the labor is not being directed in a way that results in conversion.

This insight could only have been acquired by comparing traffic-to-labor ratios, and that's why it's such an important store traffic–based metric.

When you calculate traffic-to-labor ratios and overlay conversion results across all stores in the chain, as illustrated in the following real-world example, important insights about how effectively labor is being allocated to stores become clear. Stores with more favorable traffic-to-labor ratios generally have higher conversion rates than the stores that have less favorable traffic-to-labor ratios. That's no accident.

When the traffic-to-labor ratio is low, it means the number of shoppers the store team needs to serve is lower relative to the labor they have. Consequently, they should be able to serve the shoppers more quickly and effectively—and this should translate into higher conversion rates.

In the following example, the store with the most favorable traffic-to-labor ratio serves just over six shoppers for every labor hour the store has available. This store also has the highest conversion rate at over 40%. While we can't say for certain that the high conversion performance was a direct result of this store having a more favorable traffic-to-labor ratio, it's certainly likely that it was.

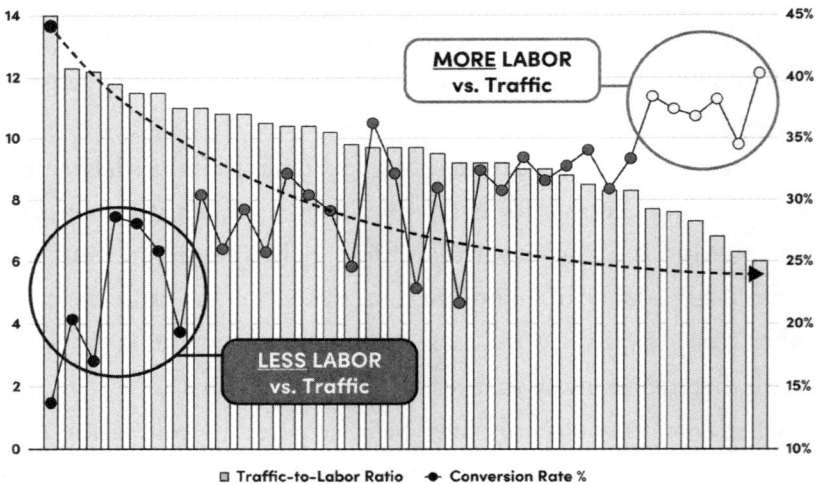

Traffic-to-Labor Ratio        Conversion Rate %

The opposite is also true. In this example, the store with the highest traffic-to-labor ratio needed to serve fourteen shoppers for every labor hour it had available. That's more than twice the traffic-to-labor ratio of the store with the most favorable ratio. In addition to having the least favorable traffic-to-labor ratio, this store also had the lowest conversion rate performance at well under 15%.

While every retailer is different and results will vary, in general, as the traffic-to-labor ratio decreases, conversion performance tends to increase. This tendency makes perfect sense, since stores that have a more favorable traffic-to-labor ratio have fewer shoppers to serve for every labor hour they have to service the traffic. Therefore, workforce management and labor scheduling decision-makers must look at traffic-to-labor ratios and conversion rate performance when determining how to efficiently allocate precious and increasingly expensive store labor resources across stores.

However, this is only the start. As it turns out, this same metric can also be used to diagnose labor productivity issues. Because even when the labor is allocated efficiently and consistently based on traffic-to-labor ratios, conversion rate performance may still be low, which is a telltale sign that there's a labor productivity issue.

## Spotting Labor Productivity Issues with Conversion Rates

When stores have similar traffic-to-labor ratios, like the four stores indicated by the box in the following chart, this tells us that each of the stores has virtually the same labor allocated relative to the traffic it receives. If stores have the same or very similar traffic-to-labor ratios, it's reasonable to expect that these stores should deliver similar conversion rate performances.

But curiously, as you closely examine the traffic-to-labor ratios compared to conversion rates, you will discover that some stores have the same or substantially similar traffic-to-labor ratios but drastically different conversion rate performances.

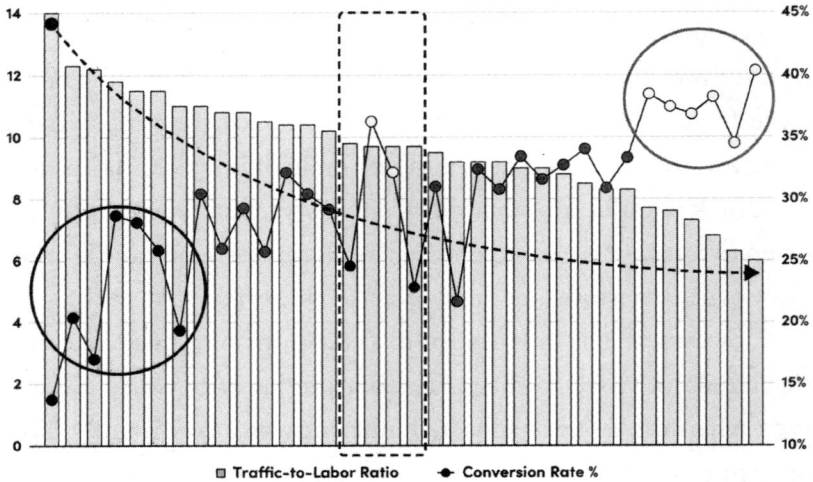

□ Traffic-to-Labor Ratio     ● Conversion Rate %

Looking at the four stores in the example, we can see that each has a traffic-to-labor ratio of about ten shoppers for each labor hour (i.e., a ratio of 10:1), but two stores have higher conversion rates of 32% to 36%, while the other two stores have lower conversion rates at just under 25%.

What this finding tells us is that all four stores have the same amount of labor allocated based on the store traffic they receive, but clearly something else must be occurring that's causing the variations in conversion rate performance.

To understand why conversion rate performance varies across stores that have the same labor allocation requires further investigation. While traffic-to-labor ratios inform how much labor a store should receive, this metric alone does not address other factors that may be negatively impacting a store's conversion performance.

Several factors could explain the lower conversion performance, and I would start with the most obvious one: How is the store team being deployed?

If store teams are too focused on tasking instead of serving shoppers, this could certainly explain why conversion rates are lower. Other conversion barriers such as slow checkout lines, poorly trained staff, or unmotivated staff could also be part of the reason. And let's also not forget that noncontrollable factors at the store, such as stock-outs of fast-selling goods, may also impact conversion rate performance.

Regardless of what's causing the low conversion rate performance in these two stores, the important takeaway is that now this retailer knows it's not related to the amount of labor being allocated to the stores, which is a valuable insight.

Armed with this insight, the district manager or head office workforce management team can continue to investigate in order to uncover the conversion rate performance challenges in the two stores in question.

## Incentivizing the Right Behaviors— Conversion Rates and Pay

Most retailers today still compensate and incentivize their store teams and field leaders based on achieving sales goals.[4]

And while sales goals are useful, underperforming managers may be getting rewarded and recognized because their stores received more store traffic, not because they had superior execution or customer service. Conversely, store managers who may be very effective at generating sales per visitor may not be getting rewarded or recognized because their low store traffic stunts their ability to drive sales volume.

An example will help illustrate.

All the stores in this two-hundred-store chain were ranked based on average daily sales and sales per visitor. The results for the top three stores are shown next.

| Store | Average Daily Sales | Rank | Sales per Visitor Rank |
|---|---|---|---|
| Store A | $3,400 | 1 | 46 |
| Store B | $2,400 | 2 | 60 |
| Store C | $2,250 | 3 | 122 |

Stores A, B, and C were the top-performing stores based on average daily sales, ranking 1, 2, and 3 respectively. However, when we compare the average daily sales rank to the sales per visitor rank, we see a huge discrepancy. Store A is ranked first in the chain based on average daily sales but only 46th based on sales per visitor.

Store C is even more dramatic, ranking third in average daily sales but only 122nd in sales per visitor!

This insight tells us that these top-selling stores are achieving their results because they receive a lot more store traffic, not because of exceptional performance by the store teams.

Considering these modest sales per visitor rankings, what do you think about the performance of these top-ranked stores now? Not so great, despite their high sales rankings. Based on average daily sales, Stores A, B, and C are indeed the stars of the chain, but on a sales per visitor basis—which removes the impact of store traffic by focusing only on conversion rate and average sale—these stores are far from stars.

Next, all stores were ranked based on sales per visitor. Recall, sales per visitor is not concerned with sales volume; rather, it focuses on how much in sales the store is producing for every store visit it gets. This enables us to compare sales per visitor performance across all stores, regardless of how much store traffic a store receives. This view provides a more accurate assessment of a store's performance relative to the traffic opportunities it receives.

As you see in the following table, the top performing sales per visitor stores are delivering only modest performance based on average daily sales.

| Store | Sales per Visitor | Rank | Average Daily Sales Rank |
|-------|-------------------|------|--------------------------|
| Store D | $33.00 | 1 | 69 |
| Store E | $31.00 | 2 | 149 |
| Store F | $28.00 | 3 | 71 |

For example, Store E had the second highest sales per visitor rank in the entire chain, but with an average daily sales rank of only 149th, this store team will likely not get the credit they deserve because their sales volume is low.

All three of these stores are top performers, making the most of every shopper visit their stores receive. Yet based on their average daily sales, these stores look like underperformers because the retail industry focuses on sales outcomes. In fact, paying store managers and frontline teams based on sales outcomes is so ingrained in the retail industry that the idea of shifting to a compensation plan based on sales per visitor, or even simply including it as another variable in compensation models, will likely face resistance.

However, if retailers are serious about creating financial incentives to drive business outcomes, they need to shift to a compensation plan based on sales per visitor, or at least one that includes sales per visitor as a variable. If they don't move beyond the "sales outcome" compensation mentality, the chain may overlook top-performing talent and miss opportunities to learn and leverage ideas from the store managers and store teams that are really effective at serving shoppers and converting their store visits into sales.

Getting line of sight with your field leaders and store teams about what to focus their attention on and how you measure and incentivize performance will save money by not overcompensating store teams that don't deserve it. Furthermore, store managers that have high sales per visitor results should be promoted to work in stores with higher store traffic volume, since these managers have proven to be capable of delivering better results.

Incentivizing and creating a performance management system that recognizes the right behaviors will result in better business outcomes and more engaged and appreciated employees. This system has the potential to reduce labor cost by eliminating the additional pay and perks currently being awarded to store managers and store teams that are not doing an effective job at converting the store traffic their stores receive.

A store's overall sales don't define the store team's performance, but a store's sales per visitor does, and the only way you can truly measure it is with store traffic and conversion rates.

# 🛒 Chapter Takeaways

- Store labor is critical for conversion performance. Proper labor allocation and scheduling can boost conversion rates, whereas poor management can lead to reduced sales and higher costs.

- Treating labor as a cost to be minimized rather than a resource to optimize can result in missed sales and long-term damage to customer loyalty.

- Aligning labor schedules with store traffic data is essential. Scheduling based on sales alone often leads to inefficiencies, especially during high-traffic periods.

- Traditional metrics like sales per labor hour can be misleading. A more accurate measure is sales per visitor, reflecting how well labor converts traffic into sales.

- The traffic-to-labor ratio helps assess whether labor is allocated efficiently. Favorable ratios often lead to higher conversion rates, whereas unfavorable ratios can result in lower performance.

- Compensation models that reward sales outcomes can unfairly favor stores with high traffic. Incentivizing based on sales per visitor ensures recognition for converting traffic and improving average sale values.

- Disparities in conversion rates, even with aligned traffic-to-labor ratios, can indicate issues like poor staff deployment or inadequate training. Further investigation is needed.

- Revising compensation models to focus on sales per visitor better reflects store team performance and identifies top-performing talent.

## PRACTITIONER'S ADVICE

- Regularly compare traffic-to-labor ratios across stores to identify inefficiencies and adjust labor allocations accordingly.

- Focus on sales per visitor to better understand labor productivity and guide store performance evaluations.

- Investigate low conversion rates despite proper labor allocation to identify issues like tasking, staff motivation, or training gaps.

- Reevaluate compensation plans to reward conversion and average sale success, aligning incentives with business outcomes.

- Train management at all levels on the importance of labor in driving conversion and average sale (which when combined create sales per visitor) and how to use traffic data effectively.

## CHAPTER 4

---

# In Search of
# SUPER CONVERTING
# Stores

Focusing on conversion rates is one of the best ways to maximize sales performance in physical stores. And that's what most retailers are solving for—more sales. Always.

When you analyze store traffic and conversion rate performance for a wide array of retailers, what you come to learn is there are always some stores in every chain that have extraordinary conversion rates. We know that circumstances beyond the store team's control, like an aggressive promotion that drives buyers into the store, impact conversion rates. But some stores simply produce vastly superior conversion performance, and they do it consistently. I call these stores "Super Converters."

Every hour of every day shoppers leave stores without buying, even though they intended to make a purchase. However, these Super Converter stores are able to convert their store traffic into buyers at a significantly higher rate than the other stores do. They not only deliver better results—based on the variables they can influence, conversion rate and average sale values—but they also hold the keys to driving conversion rate performance across the entire chain.

# Benchmarking Conversion Rate Performance

The first step is to assess the conversion performance of every store in your chain. Whether you have two, two hundred, or two thousand stores, the process is the same.

This sounds simple enough, but it requires more than merely listing your highest- to lowest-converting stores. Here's why.

Conversion rates can vary dramatically across stores in the same chain for myriad reasons, and one of those reasons is the volume and nature of traffic a store gets. For example, a high-traffic store located in a mall will almost always have lower conversion rates than stores that are off-mall. Retailers that have a broad portfolio of store types, such as mall, strip plaza, freestanding, etc., will find it useful to cluster stores by store type and then compare the conversion performance across similar store types.

Regardless of how or if you cluster your stores for analysis, the important step in the process is to examine a store's conversion performance relative to the store traffic it receives. A real-world example from a chain with over three hundred stores will help illustrate.

# Store Traffic Contextualizes Conversion Rate Performance

The following chart is a scatterplot showing conversion rate on the vertical axis and average daily store traffic count on the horizontal axis. Each dot represents the conversion performance and average daily traffic for each store in the chain. In this example, the arrows that intersect the chart indicate the average results aggregated for the entire chain. Across this chain, stores receive 350 store visits per day on average and convert 40% of their store traffic into sales. The larger dot at the center of the scatterplot represents the chain average to which all the stores will be compared.

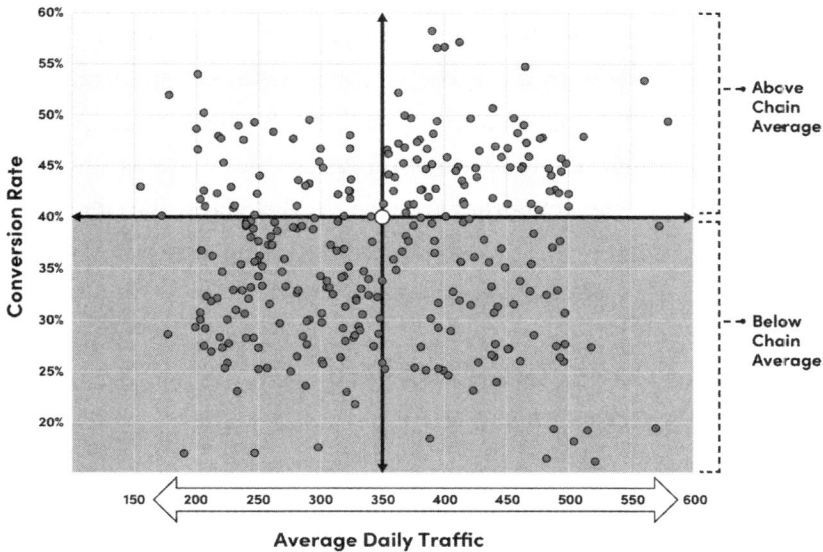

This is a useful way to analyze comparative store conversion rate performance because it enables you to immediately see how each store is performing relative to its unique traffic opportunity as well as to all other stores in the chain. Displaying results this way makes it apparent which stores are converting above or below the average conversion rate for the chain.

## Quadrant Analysis—Focusing on Sales Drivers

Conversion rates vary considerably across retail categories, but they can also vary significantly across stores within the same chain. This conversion performance variation is a result of many factors including store format (mall versus off-mall), geographical location, product mix, inventory levels, and, most importantly, store personnel who serve the shoppers. The reality is that every brick-and-mortar store is unique, and these unique characteristics need to be considered.

As the chart shows, each store is in one of four quadrants based on its average daily traffic and conversion rate performance. Each quadrant provides important insights that inform the strategies and tactics field leaders could use to optimize conversion rates and drive sales results in the stores they oversee. Additionally, the quadrants enable marketing teams to pinpoint where traffic generation efforts would be most and least productive.

## QUADRANT ONE: HIGH TRAFFIC AND HIGH CONVERSION

Stores in this quadrant are among the best performing stores in the chain. They not only receive the highest store traffic, but they are also the best at converting their traffic into sales.

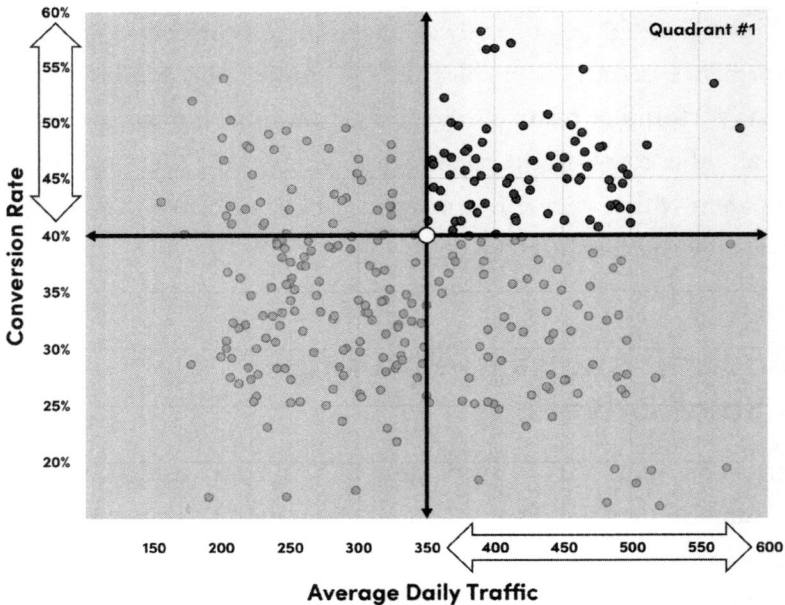

What are the store managers and store teams doing in these stores to achieve the high conversion performance they are producing?

Store traffic and conversion data can't tell you what these stores are doing differently, but the data clearly shows that these stores are producing superior conversion outcomes—and it's worth the time and effort to understand how!

Of course, some of these stores may have some unique attributes that might contribute to or explain their exceptional conversion rate performance. Or the exceptional results may be a function of how the store manager operates her store and how productive the store team is. Because these stores are producing the best outcomes, it only stands to reason that these same stores are where the best operating practices can be found.

It would behoove head office decision-makers to consult with these store managers to identify the processes and practices that can be leveraged across all stores. A good place to start would be to ask: How is store team labor being used? How do these stores manage their peak traffic hours? How are these stores managing the checkout process?

Beyond being a source of best practices that can be leveraged across the entire chain, the marketing team should target these stores for additional store traffic stimulation. As the highest converting stores, driving more traffic into these stores would result in a higher return on the marketing investment than in stores that have low conversion rate performance.

## QUADRANT TWO: LOW TRAFFIC AND HIGH CONVERSION

Stores in quadrant two receive store traffic volume below the chain average of 350 counts, and some receive among the lowest store traffic in the entire chain. Remember, store teams don't control the amount of traffic they receive, so the fact that overall sales in these stores are low doesn't change the fact that they are top-performing locations when you narrow the focus to conversion rate, which is a variable the store team can influence.

Unfortunately, the store managers and teams in quadrant two often don't get the acknowledgment or the compensation they deserve due to low sales volume. Compensation, promotions, and other benefits that retailers bestow on their best performing stores are almost always driven by store sales results, not conversion rate.

Just like the stores positioned in quadrant one, the stores in quadrant two should also be investigated to identify conversion best practices that can be applied to other stores, especially those that have similar levels of store traffic but low conversion rate performance. These stores have demonstrated their ability to convert store traffic into sales and consequently should be targeted by the marketing team to direct store traffic stimulation efforts.

## QUADRANT THREE: LOW TRAFFIC
## AND LOW CONVERSION

Stores in quadrant three are the most challenged. These stores have both low store traffic and low conversion performance. The store manager and store team can't be held accountable for having low store traffic, but they are accountable for conversion rate performance, which is lagging well behind most other stores in the chain.

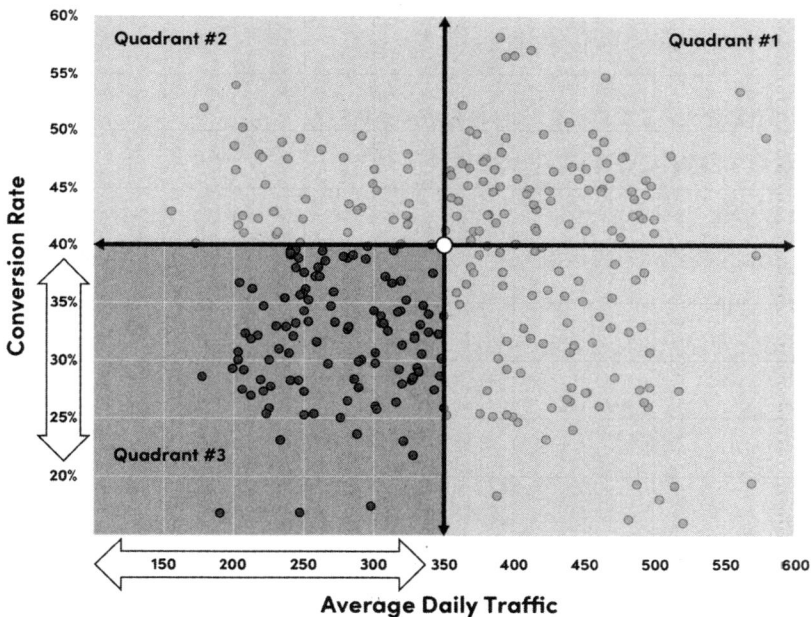

Just like stores in quadrant two, stores in quadrant three have among the lowest store traffic in the chain, but unlike stores in quadrant two, these stores are not converting the traffic they do receive. Improving conversion rate performance should be the number one priority for these stores.

Driving more store traffic to these stores would not be an efficient use of marketing budget or effort since these stores can't convert the low traffic they already receive. In fact, driving more traffic into stores that can't convert effectively could further exacerbate their poor performance and create a poor shopping experience for the shoppers who do visit.

It is possible that the low conversion performance in these stores may be caused by some unique characteristics of the store itself. However, management needs to understand what the conversion barriers are in these locations and make some changes to improve results before marketing spends another nickel on driving more traffic to these stores.

## QUADRANT FOUR: HIGH TRAFFIC AND LOW CONVERSION

Stores in quadrant four have high traffic, but low conversion. Recall, a store's traffic volume defines its sales opportunity size, so stores in this quadrant present exciting opportunities to drive sales results through improved conversion performance.

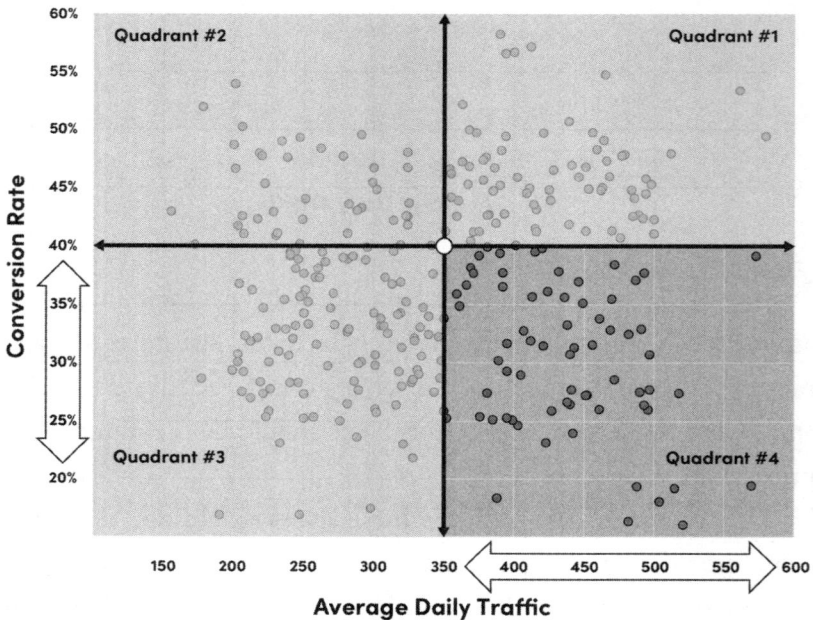

Quadrant four is where you will most likely find any mall-based stores in the chain. Mall-based stores almost always have more incidental store traffic as shoppers wander the mall. Again, store teams cannot be held accountable for the traffic they do or don't get.

It's also worth noting that store traffic and conversion rates tend to be inversely related. As store traffic volume increases, conversion rates often sag as store teams struggle to convert the traffic into sales.

Like the stores in quadrant three that struggle with conversion, the same applies here. Driving more traffic into these already high-traffic stores that have low conversion rates is counterproductive. More store traffic just might make the shopping experience and conversion rate performance even worse.

Management needs to understand what the conversion barriers are in these stores. Given the high traffic these stores receive, even modest improvements in conversion rate performance will produce a meaningful lift in sales.

Quadrant analysis provides an effective way to establish conversion performance benchmarks and inform performance improvement tactics to guide field leaders, but there's another group of stores that warrant much more examination: the **Super Converters**.

## Identifying and Leveraging SUPER CONVERTING Stores

Achieving conversion rates above the chain average is commendable, but there is a group of stores that significantly outperforms the chain average. While the benchmark for what defines a Super Converter will vary by chain, a good heuristic is the top 20% of all stores in the chain.

A good way to identify the level that defines Super Converter performance is to find the highest conversion rate that is achieved by stores across every store traffic volume. In the following example, stores converting at 45%—five percentage points above the chain average of 40%—or higher would be considered Super Converters.

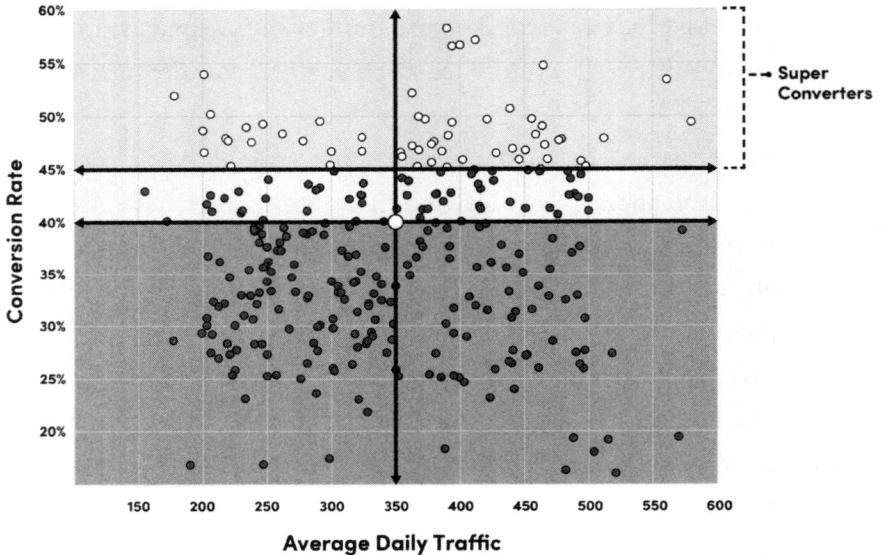

When you examine Super Converter stores more closely, you discover that they are a diverse group. These are not just low-traffic stores that have high conversion rates because they have few shoppers to serve. Stores across every traffic volume from low to even the highest traffic stores can be Super Converters.

And that's part of what makes these stores so intriguing.

Super Converters can be new stores or old stores, small stores or big stores, high sales- or even low sales-volume stores, and everything in between. Regardless of the differences, these stores all have one thing in common: They convert *significantly* more of their store traffic into sales than most stores in the chain.

Since Super Converters can be found at every store traffic volume level, it begs the question: If these stores are Super Converters, can all stores be Super Converters?

The fact is, not every store will achieve Super Converter performance, but every store can improve conversion performance. And it's well worth the effort when you consider the significant sales impact of even a modest increase in conversion rates.

In this example of a three-hundred-store chain, average daily traffic per store is 350 visits and the average conversion rate is 40%. This chain also has an average sale value of $40. We now have everything we need to assess the impact of conversion rate performance on sales.

Recall, sales are a function of store traffic, conversion rate, and average sale. For the chain in our example, the results are as follows:

[Traffic] x [Conversion Rate %] x [Average Sale $] = Sales

$$350 \times \boxed{\begin{array}{c} 40\% \\ \downarrow \\ 42\% \end{array}} \times \$40 = \begin{array}{l} \$5,600 \\ \\ \$5,880 \end{array}$$

If average daily traffic and average sale values remain constant, then a two-point increase in conversion rates, from 40% to 42%, would generate an incremental \$280 per store per day in sales. This may appear to be underwhelming at first blush, but it's not.

Small improvements in conversion rate add up. When you extrapolate these results across all three hundred stores over the course of 360 operating days, the impact is significant.

---

350 traffic counts per day x 360 operating days x 300 stores = 37.8M store visits per year

---

$$37.8M \times \boxed{\begin{array}{c} 40\% \\ \downarrow \\ 42\% \end{array}} \times \$40 = \begin{array}{l} \$604.8M \\ \\ \$635.0M \end{array}$$

A two-point conversion rate improvement across this chain would deliver over \$30M in incremental sales based on the exact same amount of store traffic. This example may appear extraordinary, but it's not. Increasing average conversion rates across an entire chain by two points (or more) is very achievable. And it's done one store at a time, every hour of every day.

Remember, improving conversion rate performance doesn't require you to invest more on promotions or marketing to generate store traffic. You just have to focus the attention of the store team on converting the shoppers they already have in their stores.

But how do you do it? That's where we turn our attention next.

## 🛒 Chapter Takeaways

- Focusing on improving conversion rates is one of the most effective ways to maximize sales in physical stores, and it is important to know how every store is performing relative to their unique store traffic opportunities. To accurately assess conversion performance, store traffic volume should be taken into consideration. This approach prevents misleading conclusions. Quadrant analysis helps categorize stores based on traffic and conversion rates:

  - Quadrant 1: High Traffic & High Conversion: Top performers to study for best practices.

  - Quadrant 2: Low Traffic & High Conversion: High performers needing more traffic.

  - Quadrant 3: Low Traffic & Low Conversion: Challenged stores where conversion improvement is critical.

  - Quadrant 4: High Traffic & Low Conversion: Stores with high potential where improving conversion can boost sales significantly.

- Even small increases in conversion rates can result in substantial sales growth across a large chain. In the example shown, a two-point improvement in conversion would generate over $30 million in incremental sales annually for the three-hundred-store chain.

## PRACTITIONER'S ADVICE

- Prioritize conversion rate improvement as a key strategy for boosting sales. Regularly analyze conversion performance to identify improvement areas.

- Use quadrant analysis to categorize stores and tailor strategies for each. Focus on improving low-converting stores and leveraging high-performing ones.

- Direct marketing efforts toward stores with high conversion rates to maximize ROI and avoid driving more traffic to low-conversion stores until performance improves.

- Identify super converting stores and study them to uncover practices that can be implemented chain wide.

- Apply best practices from Super Converters across the entire chain to elevate overall performance.

- Recognize that small, continuous improvements in conversion rates can have a massive impact when applied across multiple stores.

## CHAPTER 5

---

# Conversion Rate Optimization in Physical Stores

Conversion Rate Optimization, or CRO, is a well-established practice in the online world with literally hundreds of firms offering CRO services to help e-commerce retailers improve conversion rates for online stores.[1]

CRO is defined as a system for increasing the percentage of visitors that convert into customers. In the online world, conversion is a result of offers, site design, and navigation; in physical stores, conversion is a result of dynamics of the store experience and is greatly influenced by inventory, product mix, merchandising, and especially the store team.

Think of each physical store as a unique and very complex algorithm that ingests store traffic and produces sales. Each store's unique conversion algorithm has a multitude of variables, including the store's physical characteristics, geography, inventory levels, product mix, merchandising, and, most importantly, the store manager and her store team. The alchemy of these elements creates the shopping experience and contributes to the store's conversion algorithm and ultimately to the sales outcomes it produces.

In my experience, retailers generally don't focus on optimizing conversion rates in their physical stores; instead, they focus on sales results. Consequently, CRO is largely untapped by retailers in their physical stores, and that's why it presents such an exciting opportunity.

However, to optimize a store's conversion performance, you first need to track store traffic because you can't calculate conversion rates without it!

I never get tired of seeing the reaction of retail executives when I present an analysis of store traffic and conversion rate performance of their stores for the first time. There are almost always two shocks: First, the shock of knowing how many people actually visit their stores. And second, the shock of seeing how low their conversion rates are.

When you consider that improving conversion rate performance is one of only two ways store teams can influence sales outcomes, it behooves every retailer to focus on CRO in their physical stores.

Every retailer is unique, so how they apply CRO in their stores will vary, but the basic process of how to conduct CRO is substantially the same for any retailer, and I have a methodology for how you can do it in your stores.

Let's start by reviewing an example of how CRO is done online compared to physical stores.

## Conversion Rate Optimization— Online Versus Physical Stores

If you are an online retailer looking to optimize your conversion rates, conceptually, the process is relatively simple.[2]

This retailer may have two versions of their online store: Version A and Version B. You direct a similar amount of web traffic to each of the websites that have variations in layout, color, offerings, navigation, and other design elements. The variations are all in the service of improving conversion performance, and even subtle changes can have a meaningful impact on conversion results.

Next, you calculate conversion rates of each website, and you declare a winner. Then you repeat this process over and over. CRO is a continuous process of refining the website in pursuit of ever-higher conversion rates.

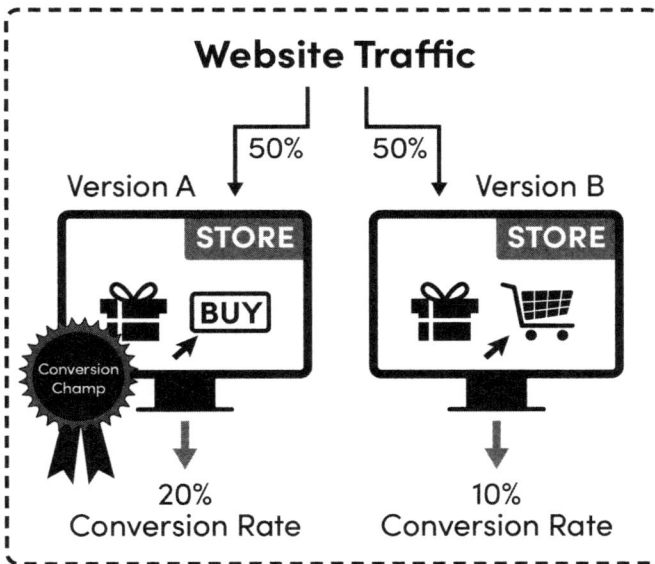

While this is a gross simplification of the CRO process, this is essentially how online conversion rate optimization works at a very fundamental level. However, as you will soon discover, it's significantly more challenging to do CRO in physical stores for several reasons.

First, websites are relatively easy to modify and launch. Since all the work is done online, changes to the look, colors, navigation, and offers can be made and pushed live quickly. The conversion rate results can be viewed almost immediately. In physical stores, it takes more time to identify and make changes and for the store teams to implement those changes.

Second, every physical store is unique. Unlike e-commerce websites where the designer can control the look, feel, and navigation, the same cannot be said for physical stores. Remember, every brick-and-mortar store has different site characteristics: square footage, number of entrances, number of checkouts, and layout. The demographics of the shoppers in the area can also vary. The competitive landscape in the store's trading area, inventory levels, product mix, and most importantly, the amount of labor and how productive the store team is are all part of the store's conversion algorithm.

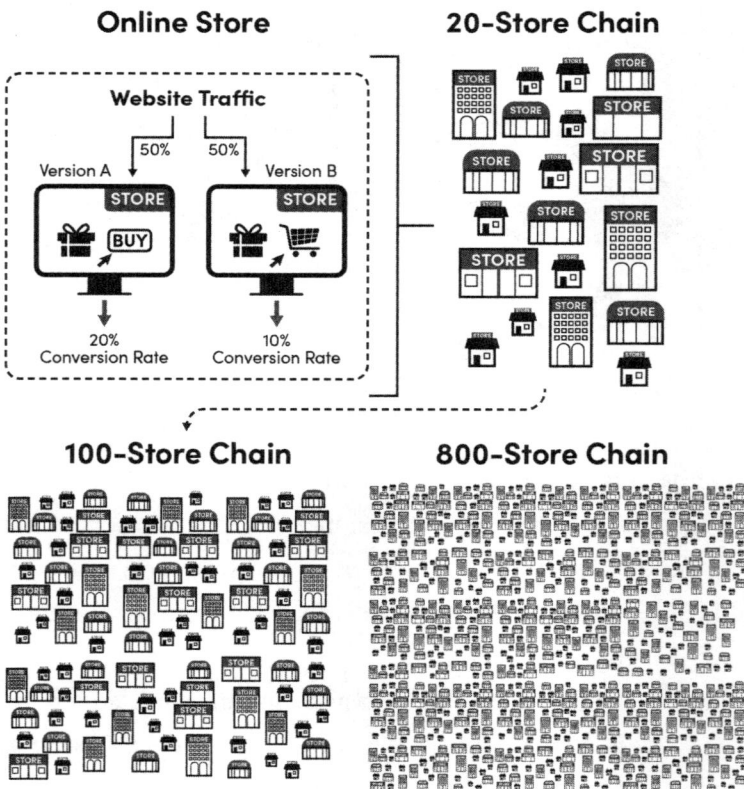

In this regard, a chain of twenty stores will require twenty different approaches to CRO to account for the unique attributes and characteristics of each store. It's not hard to imagine how much more complicated the process becomes if you have one hundred or eight hundred stores. No two stores are exactly alike.

## CRO for Physical Stores— Methodology Overview

The following graphic provides an overview of a methodology for doing CRO in physical stores. The process is the same regardless of how many stores you have.

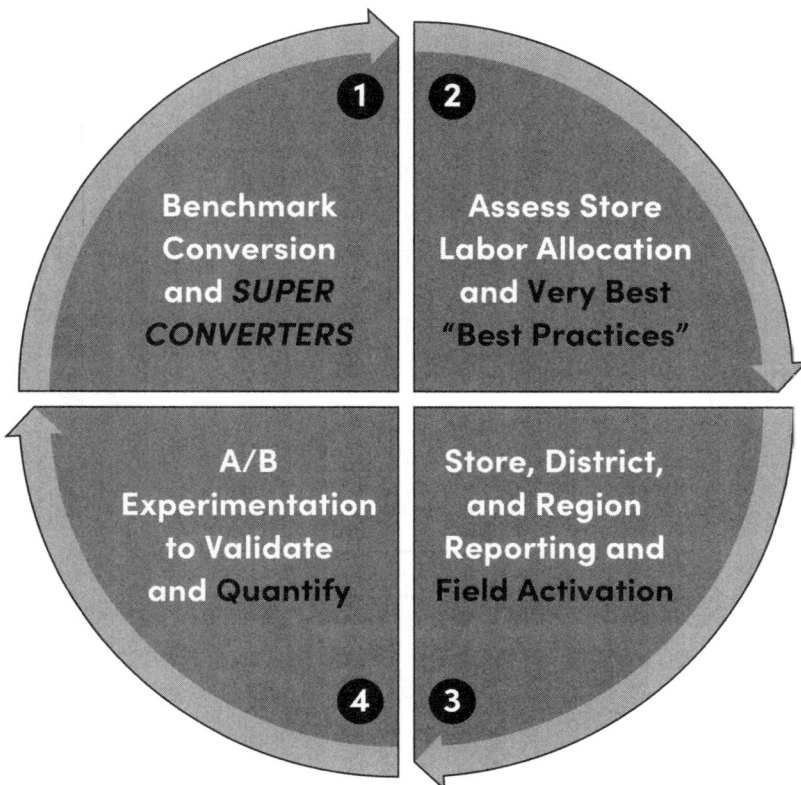

Benchmark
Conversion
and *SUPER
CONVERTERS*

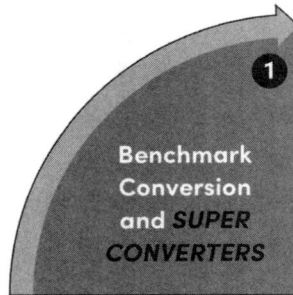

## STEP 1: BENCHMARK CONVERSION PERFORMANCE AND IDENTIFY SUPER CONVERTING STORES

To improve conversion rates, you must first know how all your stores are performing. Using the conversion rate performance mapping exercise from chapter 4 is the place to start.

Recall, conversion rate performance can be impacted by the amount of traffic a store receives, so looking at conversion performance in relation to the amount of traffic a store receives is critical. While it may be useful to categorize stores by store type, such as mall versus off-mall, stores that receive similar traffic volumes should reasonably be expected to achieve the same or similar conversion rate performance.

**Quadrant #2**

Low Traffic and
High Conversion

- High conversion performance, but low traffic volume
- Look for best practices
- Focus on driving traffic opportunities

**Quadrant #3**

Low Traffic and
Low Conversion

- Low conversion not due to traffic volume
- Investigate to identify conversion barriers

**Quadrant #1**

High Traffic and
High Conversion

- Best performing stores
- Investigate for best practices
- Continue to drive traffic opportunities

**Quadrant #4**

High Traffic and
Low Conversion

- Large traffic opportunity store
- Conversion may be related to traffic volume
- Investigate conversion barriers

By benchmarking conversion rate performance as shown previously, you can immediately see how conversion performance varies across all stores with the same or similar traffic volumes. Note how all the stores displayed in the box on the chart have similar store traffic, but significantly different conversion rate results, ranging from below 20% to a high of 50%. Understanding why is part of the CRO process.

## *LEVERAGING SUPER CONVERTERS*

Once you have benchmarked conversion performance for all your stores, you can identify the Super Converters. The next step is to understand what's driving their extraordinary conversion performance.

The objective is to identify ·pecific actions, activities, processes, or behaviors these store managers and frontline teams do. Keep in mind that some Super Converters may be achieving their outstanding results because of factors outside of their control and that are not related to their actual performance. Therefore, it's important to analyze conversion drivers and barriers to understand what's replicable in other stores and what's not.

For example, if a super converting store had a much higher allocation of labor relative to other stores with similar traffic volume, then it could be that their conversion performance is merely a function of having more store labor. In fact, since labor allocation plays such a big role in conversion rate performance, it warrants its own entire step in the process!

## *THE VERY BEST "BEST PRACTICES"*
## *COME FROM SUPER CONVERTERS*

When you speak to retailers about improving conversion rates in their stores, they often ask: What are the best practices from other retailers that we should apply to our stores?

The implication of the question is that other retailers might somehow have better answers for how to improve conversion rate performance. But because every retail business is different and has a multitude of different operating processes and chain-specific variables, beyond some high-level, generic bromides like "staff to traffic," you will not drive conversion performance in your stores by trying to copy what other retailers are doing.

When it comes to identifying the very best conversion performance improvement practices, retailers need to look no further than their own super converting stores.

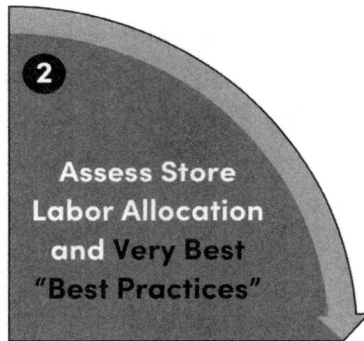

## STEP 2: ASSESS STORE LABOR ALLOCATION AND IDENTIFY CONVERSION BEST PRACTICES FROM SUPER CONVERTERS

The very best "best practices" come from your own stores, specifically your super converting stores. But before you begin to identify and implement these best practices in non–super converting stores, you must confirm that their conversion performance is not merely a result of having more labor relative to the traffic they receive compared to non–super converting stores. Calculating and comparing traffic-to-labor ratios will answer this question and help you measure how productive your labor is.

## LABOR ALLOCATION AND CONVERSION PERFORMANCE

In chapter 3, I described a simple method for allocating labor across stores and measuring the productivity of the labor in each store. This is a very important step in the CRO process for physical stores.

The store team has the greatest ability to influence conversion rates since they are closest to the shopper and facilitate the sales transaction. Therefore, the amount of labor and, even more importantly, how this labor is deployed at store level are among the most important drivers of conversion performance.

It's not realistic to expect stores that have less labor—and sometimes a lot less—to deliver conversion rates of super converting stores that may have more labor. You have to compare traffic-to-labor ratios of stores that have the same or substantially similar store traffic volume. Overlaying conversion rates will make it immediately clear if labor is being efficiently allocated across stores and provide a fair basis of comparison.

Once you identify stores that have lower labor allocations compared to your super converting stores with similar store traffic volume, the next step is to experiment with applying more labor in these stores. However, this is not an exercise in throwing more labor at stores and hoping for the best.

Adding more store labor should come with clear expectations for the store manager about the conversion rate performance they should achieve. More on this in Step 4 on A/B experimentation and quantifying the impact of changes.

## THE VERY BEST, BEST PRACTICES

When it comes to identifying the very best, best practices for conversion rate improvement, focus on your stores that are doing the best job at converting their store traffic into sales—regardless of the sales volume they generate. As noted, some super converting stores may be low-sales-volume stores that get overlooked because of their low store traffic.

It's important to focus on your own stores because they will generally have the same systemic opportunities and challenges as every other store in your chain. They should all have the same POS and other internal systems, processes for inventory management, merchandising plans, tasks, training, and exposure to the same promotions and advertising.

Furthermore, when it comes time to replicate the conversion rate performance from super converting stores, it's more convincing and far more compelling to store managers and the frontline team knowing that what they are being asked to do is being done by other stores in the chain. Having this operational credibility is important when it's time to roll out an initiative to all stores in the chain, as store managers and store teams will be much more likely to align to a new process or behavior if they know that what they are being asked to do has actually produced better results in other stores. In short, they will know that it's possible.

## IDENTIFYING VERY BEST, BEST PRACTICES

The best way to identify the very best, best practices is to conduct interviews and group discussions with your super converting store managers.

The super converting store managers should be grouped by store traffic volume so that the best practices will be most relevant to the managers of stores that have similar traffic volume. These groupings can be further refined by clustering by store type. For example, mall-based stores are compared only to other mall-based stores. Typically, this type of best practice sharing is conducted within a district or region of stores, but the problem is that not all stores in the same district fall into the same or similar store traffic volume grouping.

The sessions should be facilitated by head office personnel, most likely store operations leaders. The goal is to capture any operating processes or behaviors that these store managers and their teams do that other stores are not doing. And don't be too surprised if there are no obvious differences, since the operating procedures in these super converting stores might be only subtly different than other stores. But what you know for certain is that conversion rate performance is significantly better, so drilling into the detail is useful.

Here are some sample questions worth exploring:

- How do you balance serving shoppers versus completing tasks?

- How do you schedule your store team during peak traffic hours?

- How do you train your new store team members, and what do you focus on?

- What attributes do you look for in hiring store team members?

- How do you manage the checkout process when the store is busy?

- How do you conduct your daily store team huddles, and what do you discuss?

- How do you manage promotional periods or shopping holidays?

- As store manager, what role do you play in converting store visits into sales?

- What are the conversion barriers in your store that cause shoppers to leave without buying?

It's human nature to want to talk about ourselves and especially to share our knowledge with others. Not only will conducting these conversion best practice sessions uncover some of the very best practices that can be applied across all stores, but it will also give your super-converting store managers acknowledgment and encouragement knowing that their ideas matter.

Once these conversion best practices sessions are all completed, and the ideas captured, they should be presented to head office personnel, especially the store operations leadership and the workforce management team, to help inform training procedures, compensation and incentive programs, and store manager and store team recruitment strategies.

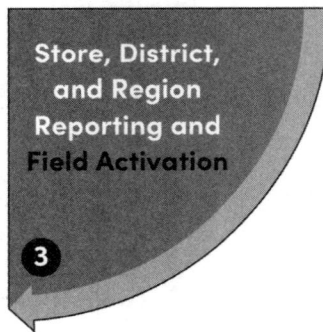

Store, District,
and Region
Reporting and
Field Activation

**3**

## STEP 3: PROVIDE EASY-TO-SPOT CONVERSION REPORTING FOR STORE TEAMS AND FIELD LEADERS

To improve conversion rate performance, store managers need to know where the opportunities are and be able to direct their store team resources accordingly.

As I described in chapter 2, providing your store managers with simple, visual reporting that clearly shows where conversion rate sags are occurring down to the hour of the day is required.

It's not good enough to provide your store managers with dense, numeric conversion rate results in a form that makes it virtually impossible to spot conversion opportunities. Access to data is not the same as providing actionable insight.

But even insightful conversion rate performance reporting alone won't deliver better conversion performance if store managers don't use the insights to alter processes or behaviors in their store to improve conversion rate performance. There should be a clear line of sight from the store-level insights to district, region, and head office. All field leaders must be able to coach and encourage their store managers using these very same insights.

If conversion performance isn't important to your district or regional managers, you shouldn't expect store managers to focus on it either. More on this in the next chapter.

## STEP 4: CONDUCT A/B EXPERIMENTATION TO VALIDATE AND QUANTIFY CONVERSION IMPROVEMENTS

Before you add more labor to stores, roll out new processes, or invest in other store programs to improve conversion performance across the chain, you should test the ideas. Not only will testing validate the impact of these efforts, but it will also help you financially quantify the potential impact and enable you to build a business case. Furthermore, quantifying the impact of conversion improvement programs will help you prioritize projects based on their expected impact and financial return.

A/B or test versus control group experimentation is a well-established methodology that can be applied to assess your conversion improvement initiatives. As you conduct these experiments, you may discover that what works in one store may not work in others.

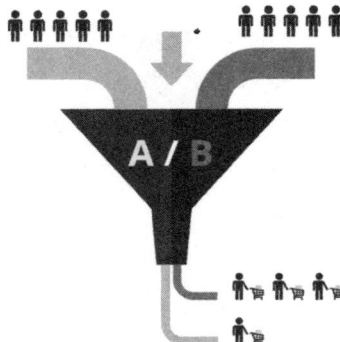

It's important to remember that outcomes of any experiment are always uncertain. So even if a conversion improvement experiment you conduct doesn't deliver the impact you expected, acquiring this insight is still valuable.

I will discuss experimentation in detail in chapter 7 and show you how any retailer can conduct A/B experiments. For now, I'll leave you with a mini case study of a real-world example that illustrates how even a small change can deliver meaningfully better outcomes.

## CRO Delivers Meaningful and Measurable Impact—Mini Case

**Background:** During an annual executive team presentation to review store traffic and conversion performance across the chain, an important insight was identified: Conversion performance during the early part of the day was consistently underperforming conversion performance in the latter part of the day. Further analysis confirmed that this early day–part conversion sag was occurring every day of the week and systematically across virtually all stores.

*continued*

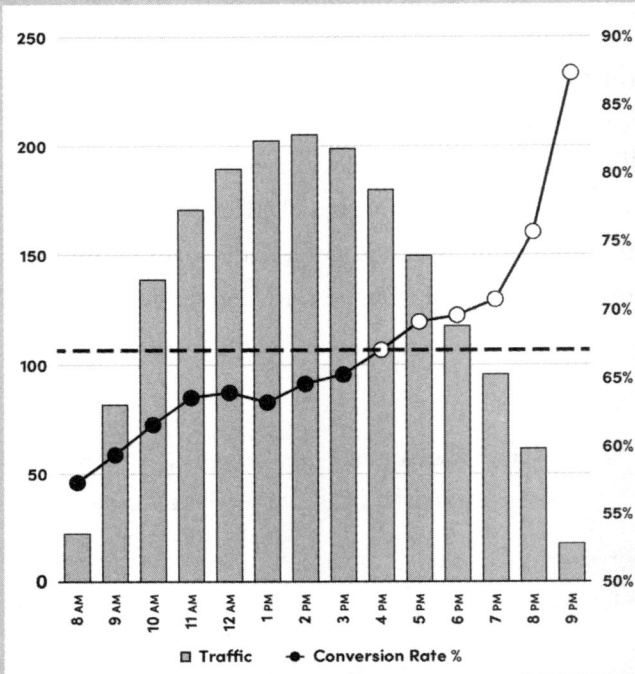

Traffic    ●— Conversion Rate %

**Insight Leads to Testable Hypotheses:** Based on this insight, management hypothesized that if the early day–part conversion sag was occurring systematically, then it was possible that conversion performance could be systematically improved across all stores. A series of follow-up meetings were conducted with the field leadership team, including the head of store operations and district managers, to identify possible theories for why it was occurring and to develop tactics to improve conversion performance.

**The Experiment:** The field leadership team identified "labor focus" as the likely cause of the systematic conversion sags.

Store teams can become very focused on tasks, especially in the early hours as they prepare the store for the day ahead, and this can take focus away from serving the shoppers. A sample of stores from each district was selected as the Test group, with the remaining stores in each district as the Control group. Test stores were required to focus their effort on serving shoppers between the hours of 9 a.m. and noon. There was no additional labor required. The experiment was conducted over a four-week period.

**The Results:** Test stores outperformed Control stores each week of the experiment, resulting in an overall conversion improvement of 80 basis points. This translated into a sales lift of approximately $42,000 over the four weeks in the small Test group with the potential to deliver over $1M across the chain. As this case makes clear, when it comes to CRO in physical stores, even modest increases can have a material impact on business results.

# Conversion Rate Optimization— Putting All the Pieces Together

Just like online retailers that continuously and relentlessly work at improving conversion rate performance on their e-commerce sites, so too should retailers in their physical stores.

## CRO-for Physical Stores

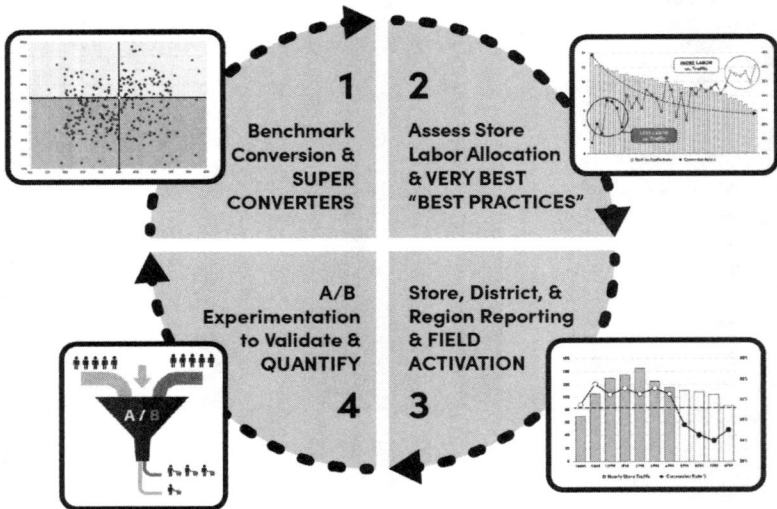

While it is more challenging to apply CRO in physical stores than it is online, I would argue that it's even more important to do so in physical stores. After all, it's in physical stores where the vast majority of sales are transacted and where the largest sales opportunity exists as measured by store traffic.

Far too many retail operators today still believe that it's a given that their stores will convert all the traffic that they could have into sales, so the conversion rate is just another metric in a world that already seems to have too many. But what these retailers fail to appreciate, and remain in denial about, is that every hour of every day shoppers visit their stores with the intention of making a purchase but leave without buying. These are lost sales that could have been made if the retailer was more mindful about conversion rates.

Here's the ironic part: Most retailers are desperate to drive sales, but instead of focusing on conversion rate, they fall back on old-fashioned, non-data-informed training, sales incentives, or other techniques that may create a modest sales lift, but often don't sustain.

Adopting a Conversion Rate Optimization mindset will ensure that the focus remains on the shopper in the store and that every store visit holds the potential to be a sale. However, as much as CRO provides a framework, there is one ingredient to improving conversion rate performance that is critical to success—getting the store team on board, which is where we turn next.

## 🛒 Chapter Takeaways

- Conversion Rate Optimization (CRO) is widely conducted on e-commerce websites but underutilized or nonexistent in physical stores. Optimizing conversion rates in physical stores presents a significant opportunity for retailers to increase sales without increasing traffic.

- Unlike online stores, every physical store is unique, with varying site characteristics, inventory, product mix, and store teams, which makes CRO more complex but equally if not more important.

- The first step is to benchmark conversion rate performance across all stores so that you can identify Super Converters that consistently achieve higher conversion rates. These stores provide valuable insights and best practices that can potentially be leveraged across all stores.

- The effective allocation and deployment of labor are crucial for optimizing conversion rates. Comparing traffic-to-labor ratios across all stores helps determine if labor is being used efficiently and effectively.

- The best conversion rate improvement practices come from stores in your own chain, and especially Super Converters. Identify and replicate the specific actions and behaviors that drive their superior performance.

- Easy-to-understand reporting is vital. Store managers need clear visual reporting on conversion rates to identify and act on missed conversion opportunities. Simple, actionable insights are key to improving store performance.

## PRACTITIONER'S ADVICE

- Implement CRO strategies. Regularly review and optimize conversion rates in physical stores just as you would on your e-commerce website. Focus on maximizing the sales potential of existing store traffic.

- Adopt a CRO mindset. Encourage a continuous focus on conversion rates as a central metric in driving sales. This shift in mindset can lead to long-term, sustainable growth by making every shopper visit count.

- Conduct A/B testing before rolling out new processes or labor changes chain-wide to validate their impact and quantify potential improvements. This helps in building a business case and prioritizing initiatives.

# CHAPTER 6

---

# Winning over the Store Team—Getting Line of Sight

H aving the right amount of labor allocated to serve the traffic a store receives is critical. A store is understaffed when it simply does not have an adequate amount of personnel to serve the store's traffic volume. The store will then underperform relative to its store traffic opportunity as shoppers leave without buying, despite intending to purchase.

But even when ample labor is allocated to a store based on its traffic opportunity, that alone does not ensure that conversion rates and sales per visitor performance will be optimal.

Store labor is only effective if it is directed to support the conversion effort. In fact, even less labor can convert more visitors into buyers if the labor is deployed effectively and is focused on facilitating conversion.

The following one-star online review from an exasperated shopper looking to buy a television is a good illustration of what happens when the store team is not focused on conversion.[1]

Wow! Went here to purchase a new television. I was advised by an employee that he'd be right over to help. Cool, I shopped for everything else I needed and then waited in the TV aisle. 10 minutes later, he still hadn't been back to help. I go up to the service counter and ask if someone can help me with TVs. The girl behind the counter said she'd page someone. Cool. I went back and waited in the TV aisle. 10 more minutes go by. Multiple employees are watching me read tags and try to understand the TV recommendations guide. Not one single person offers to help. I go back to the service counter and ask again for help. The girl's demeanor changed completely, and she said, "Look there are only so many of us here, and we have other stuff to do, so you're just going to have to wait!" I was seriously in shock. I went back to the TV aisle yet again to get my basket, and I was approached by one of the employees who was pacing the store and watching me struggle. Finally, I thought, someone is here to help. Nope! He came up to me to apologize for not being able to help stating that they had some stuff going on and it would be a few more minutes before anyone could help. At this point I decided to leave. As I'm walking out the front door the original employee who said he'd be by to help was standing at the front like a greeter and said to me, "Sorry I couldn't help you." It was the most bizarre experience ever. The store was empty. What a joke.

In this real-world example, there were no less than six opportunities for the store team to engage with this shopper and convert him into a customer. But despite the many opportunities, this shopper left without making a purchase, and then declared, "It was the most bizarre experience ever. The store was empty. What a joke."

So what happened?

It is possible that these were simply a bunch of lazy, uninspired, underperforming frontline workers. If that is true, then these workers need to be better managed and trained, then if they still don't deliver the desired outcomes, they should be replaced by workers who have the right disposition and who are willing to apply the effort required to serve customers.

But let's give the store team mentioned in the online review the benefit of the doubt. What if this wasn't a case of these workers being unmotivated to assist the shopper, but rather a case of simply not being clear about the important role they play in the conversion process, which started the moment the shopper first entered the store?

What seems to be missing from the shopping experience described in the online review is that no one on the store team took accountability for the shopper. They engaged him the moment he entered the store, but then he was left on his own to find the help he needed. And despite the shopper's efforts to get assistance—by directly asking for it and then providing visual cues showing his interest—he was unsuccessful in procuring the product he was seeking to purchase.

And this is not an isolated occurrence. A more extensive analysis of online reviews for a regional department store chain identified several causes for why shoppers were leaving without buying. The findings were an eye-opener to the retailer.[2]

☆ **Controllable factors**

In this case, we examined 929 online reviews and discovered that 57% of the reasons for non-buying were a result of something the store team could control or influence. In other words, lost sales the store could have had.

The biggest reason shoppers left this retailer without buying related to the "Service experience," which accounted for 27% of the negative reviews. The attitude and engagement of the frontline store team with shoppers is often the difference between making a sale or not. Dismissive, unfriendly, and disengaged frontline store personnel are conversion killers.

Other operational factors such as "Store cleanliness," "Long checkout lines," and "Couldn't find help" combined for another 30% of the negative reviews. These are all solvable issues.

Not every visitor who enters the store can be converted into a sale no matter how attentive and engaging the store team is. But that is entirely beside the point. Since there is no way to discern which store visitors are visiting to make a purchase versus those who are merely exploring with no intention to buy, the store team should assume that all shoppers have visited to make a purchase and serve them accordingly.

Shoppers shouldn't need to work that hard to exchange their hard-earned money for the goods the retailer has to offer. The store team's primary purpose is to facilitate the purchase and to convert as much of the store traffic into sales as they can, and they should be held accountable for accomplishing this.

## Getting Line of Sight on Conversion—and Accountability

If conversion rate performance is not important to your district or regional managers, the store operations team, or the executives, you shouldn't expect store managers or the store team to care either. Creating a "conversion culture" requires the commitment and effort of all stakeholders to not only establish its importance, but also to see that the effort sustains in the long term.

Retail businesses are complex operations—even smaller chains with only a few locations. Retailers are continually launching new initiatives and adjusting priorities, so it can be a challenge for store teams to stay focused on conversion. From the store teams' perspective, a constant stream of new initiatives can feel like the "flavor of the month" with lots of energy to start before it peters out. What may be critically important one month is never mentioned the next.

To make this even more challenging, staff turnover rates of frontline retail workers are as high as 60% by some estimates and among the highest of any industry.[3] Store managers are constantly recruiting and training new team members, which can negatively impact service levels and ultimately conversion performance.

To achieve true alignment, it's important that all stakeholders see the same information, interpret it the same way, and have a shared understanding about what actions to take to improve outcomes.

Store managers and frontline teams will remain focused on the things that are important to the district and regional managers they directly report to as well as the senior functional leaders and executives they encounter. Instead of discussions focused on store sales, the discussions should be about conversion rates and sales per visitor performance—in other words, the outcomes the store team can influence.

To get line of sight, all stakeholders must have a consistent view of the store traffic trends and conversion rate results as well as a common language and understanding for how they interpret the results. For example, if store sales are down because store traffic is down (i.e., the opportunity got smaller), but conversion rates and sales per visitor results are up, then the store is performing well compared to the traffic opportunity it receives. Anyone who looks at these results should come to the same conclusion, which ultimately creates accountability for the results.

Another aspect of getting line of sight relates to how the insights are presented. Store managers should be focused on hourly conversion results and daily trends. These managers need insights that are presented in a simple, obvious way that shows them where they are missing conversion opportunities down to the hour of the day so that they can make the necessary operational adjustments to improve conversion rate performance and track the impact of their efforts.

District and regional managers should see roll-up results of all stores under their purview. Having easy and ready access to the store-level insights will aid them in coaching their store managers to drive conversion performance and to prioritize which stores to focus their attention on.

Head office executives and functional department teams should be able to see a chain-wide view of store traffic and conversion performance, broken out by regions and districts. These stakeholders should also be able to easily drill down to view store-level results to help inform operational decisions and formulate broader, chain-wide strategies.

## Delivering the Insights— Push Reporting and Data Portals

When it comes to delivering store traffic and conversion rate insights, there are generally two ways this is done: [1] prepared reports that are generated and then automatically emailed to managers, and/or [2] online data portals that require users to log on in order to see their results.

### AUTOMATIC PUSH REPORTING

The key advantage of an automated push report is that the insights are already preformatted and presented in a consistent way. A well-designed store traffic and conversion performance push report should make the insights obvious and provide the right level of detail for each user.

As the global head of store operations for a 350-store jewelry chain put it to me, "I don't want my store managers logging on to a data portal to poke around looking for answers . . . I want to give them the insights that I know they need and that I want them to focus on in a consistent format."

For store managers, the store traffic and conversion results should be presented down to the hour of the day and to trends at the daily and weekly level. Store managers should be focused on their busiest store traffic hours and ensuring that they deploy their store team in a way that maximizes conversion and sales per visitor results based on the traffic opportunity the store receives.

These store reports should also provide a forward-looking view of results organized by day of the week, to the hour, so that store managers can plan their store staff schedules for the two weeks ahead based on the expected traffic volume and timing.

## ONLINE DATA PORTAL

The key advantage of an online data portal is that the store traffic and conversion insights can be interrogated and explored beyond the static insights contained in push reports. This is especially useful for district, regional, and head office users who need to monitor and compare performance across store groups, at aggregation levels such as districts and regions, or by store groupings and/or time frames that were not contemplated in the push reports.

Additionally, data portals are portable, making it easy for users, like district managers who are always on the go, to view results wherever they have access to the internet.

Both approaches have merit. Automatic push reporting as well as an online data portal provide the best of both worlds, and having multiple access points to this vital data will improve the probability that managers access and use the insights.[4]

## STORE MANAGERS ARE NOT DATA ANALYSTS

Because store managers and the frontline team have the greatest ability to influence conversion rate performance, you must provide them with simple, easy-to-interpret store traffic and conversion rate insights.

Before a store manager will ever undertake an action or behavior change, they need to first understand what the insights mean and have the confidence to make a change. It's important to remember that store managers are not data analysts. Their time should be spent on the sales floor, directing activities, setting priorities, and serving customers as needed. It's unrealistic to expect store managers, assistant managers, or store team leads to extract insights from data that requires too much time, effort, or data skills to analyze and spot actionable insights.

It's also worth noting that not every manager will be comfortable making data-informed decisions. Some managers are intimidated by analytics and struggle with interpreting data. As the CEO of a twenty-store specialty chain told me, "I have some managers who don't know how to turn on a computer."

## What Store Managers Should Do Every Day

Notwithstanding the lack of data analysis skills, virtually any store manager should be able to understand and act on store traffic and conversion insights—they do not need to be data scientists to use and apply them. Even the most junior or data-intimidated manager should be able to take action on these insights with a small amount of training and encouragement from their district manager.

Store managers should review their store traffic and conversion performance at the beginning of each day. And answer the following three questions:

1. What was our store traffic count and conversion rate yesterday?

2. What hours of the day did we miss conversion opportunities?

**3.** Based on today's store traffic forecast, what actions can I take to improve conversion rate performance?

Part of the challenge in improving conversion rate performance relates to adjusting behaviors based on the busyness of the store. As store traffic volume builds, it can be a challenge to manage the number of shoppers visiting, which is where the conversion sags often occur. To manage the store traffic volume, store managers need to be able to adjust behaviors and redirect store team resources as needed.

When store traffic is high, the store team should be focused on providing quick assistance with the goal of engaging as many shoppers as possible. The priority should be on the checkout line and facilitating the sales transaction.

When the store is busy, the reality is that not every shopper will get the ideal service experience that you aspire to deliver. However, shoppers will be more patient and understanding if there is an obvious attempt by the store team to serve shoppers efficiently. With that said, making the sale must remain the focus.

When store traffic is low, this is the perfect time for store teams to take breaks, focus on tasks, and luxuriate the shoppers who are in the store with extra attention, focusing on both conversion and driving up average sale values.

Managing the ebbs and flows of store traffic and maximizing conversion rate performance is the ongoing challenge every store manager must manage. Converting every shopper who visits the store into a sale is not realistic. The goal is for every store to convert more of their store traffic into sales. Arming store managers with the basic insights they need to focus their effort can go a long way to achieving conversion rate improvements, and small improvements can add up to material improvements in sales results.

## REVIEWING DISTRICT RESULTS— WHAT TO LOOK FOR?

Just as every store manager must understand their store traffic and conversion trends, the same goes for the field leaders. How does their district compare to the other districts? Regions? Total chain? Knowing if your results are in line with broader results or an outlier is an important insight that all field leaders should have. Here's what field leaders should look for when reviewing results and what they should do with them.

1. **Overall District Trends.** Field leaders should see a roll-up of the store traffic and conversion rate trends for their district. Context matters, so understanding how the district compares to other districts and overall chain results is important to understanding if their results are consistent with others or an outlier. For example, if traffic is down 5% in the district but down 8% chain-wide, then the field leader will know that her results are better than the chain, despite the decline.

2. **Results for Each Store in the District.** Field leaders must understand the results and trends for each store in their district. The objective is to identify how each store's results compare to the other stores in the district, region, and the entire chain. And while every store matters, special attention should be given to the outlier stores in the district. For example, if store traffic is down 5% across the district, but one store is seeing a 10% increase in store traffic, having this insight will enable the field leader to start formulating strategies, like adding labor to assist with the store traffic increase.

3. **The Unique Attributes of Each Store.** The store environment is dynamic. Many factors can influence results, and the field leader needs to keep this in mind as they review store-level results. For example, a store in the district may have a new, inexperienced store manager. Or perhaps a store has had a hard time filling frontline team positions, so the store is understaffed. Or maybe the store is in a mall that's undergoing a major renovation that is disrupting traffic. Whatever the issue, being mindful of the unique circumstances each store is experiencing, as well as controllable and noncontrollable conversion factors, is important when reviewing and comparing results.

4. **Prioritize Store Manager Callouts.** Field leaders should be meeting regularly with every store manager under their purview; however, some stores need more attention than others. For example, if the district manager sees that a store in the district is experiencing a significant increase in traffic, and conversion rates are dropping precipitously, they will want to prioritize engaging with this store manager to identify ways to mitigate the conversion loss, assuming the cause is controllable.

Having access to store traffic and conversion insights is essential, but field leaders must be more than merely informed; they need to be "conversion coaches" for store managers.

## Conversion Coaching—The Field Leader's Most Important Job

Improving conversion performance requires a change in behaviors or actions. However, sometimes store managers aren't sure what actions to take. Furthermore, making changes creates risk, and store managers are often reluctant to make those changes.

Field leaders should be the "conversion coaches" for the store managers. As the conversion coach, they should work with the store manager to identify potential conversion improvement tactics in her store and share best practices from Super Converter stores. Most importantly, field leaders should encourage the store manager to implement changes or undertake action to effect a change in conversion performance.

Collaboration is key to making this work. When a store manager knows that she has the support of her field leader, she will be much more likely to make changes, and this is the only way to discover conversion rate improvements.

Keeping store managers engaged and focused on improving conversion rates requires field leaders to be focused on it. And the best way to do this is to make store traffic and conversion a regular part of daily or weekly interactions.

Here are some tips for how field leaders should engage with their store managers.

1. **Schedule a Time to Review the Store Traffic and Conversion Rate Results.** Most field leaders already conduct regular calls or visits with the store managers they oversee. Part of these calls should include a review of the store traffic and conversion rate trends. Discussing this data regularly will not only help ingrain the concepts, but it will also make clear that the data is important. If field leaders never discuss store traffic and conversion, you shouldn't expect store managers to make it a priority.

2. **Start with the Positives and Maintain an Encouraging Tone.** Store managers need encouragement, especially

when the store is struggling to improve results. But even in underperforming stores, field leaders should be able to find something positive to build on. For example, identify times of the day or days of the week where the store is performing well, then focus on the areas of opportunity.

3. **Make the Dialogue Collaborative.** Store managers will be much more engaged and willing to make changes if they know that they have the support of their field leader. Field leaders should treat the discussion as a collaboration and not an interrogation. Brainstorm ideas, share best practices, and formulate conversion improvement tactics together. This will reduce the risk of the effort for store managers and lead to action.

4. **Identify Action Items and Revisit on the Next Call.** Formulating tactics to improve conversion rate performance is the first step, but unless these ideas are acted upon, results won't change. It's imperative that field leaders keep the ideas on their radar by reviewing results and outcomes on the next call. Knowing that the field leader will be reviewing action items makes it clear to the store manager that it's important. Over time, this will become a natural and normal part of the field leader/store manager engagement.

5. **Remind Store Managers to Focus on What They Can Influence.** Despite improvements in conversion rates and average sale values, a store's sales results still might not be at the level required due to declining store traffic. Field leaders must remind store managers to focus on the things they can influence—conversion rate and average sale values.

## SETTING CONVERSION RATE GOALS— THE WRONG AND RIGHT WAY

If you're trying to improve conversion rate performance—or performance of anything—having goals can be profoundly useful. Goals focus attention and provide a basis for tracking progress.

But as much as conversion rate goals are useful, it's critical to set goals the right way. Setting conversion rate goals the wrong way can have all sorts of negative consequences and ultimately be counterproductive. Setting conversion rate goals for stores is more challenging than you might expect. It's not good enough to set "global" targets across all stores. Even setting conversion rate goals by store type (e.g., mall versus off-mall) will not account for the unique characteristics of each store or provide the precision required to set achievable goals.

A real-world example will help illustrate.

To achieve overall sales targets, the leadership team of a four-hundred-store specialty retailer asked for our assistance to set conversion rate goals for their stores. Each store's historical conversion rate performance was mapped, current trends were considered, and unique conversion rate goals were set for each store. The results of the first quarter are shown in the following chart.

## Conversion Performance vs. Original Goal

Conversion Actual vs. ORIGINAL Goal by Store - Variance in BPS

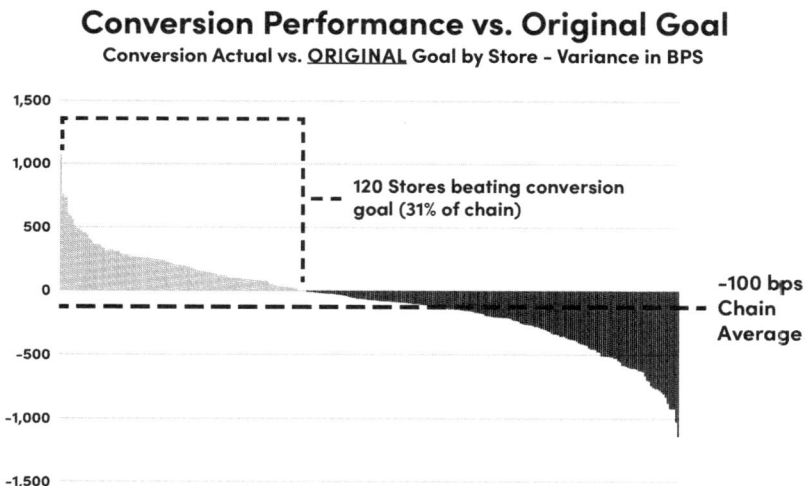

120 Stores beating conversion goal (31% of chain)

-100 bps Chain Average

As the chart shows, the chain underperformed its conversion goal by 100 basis points (bps), even though about one-third of the stores were meeting or exceeding their goal. And many of these stores exceeded their conversion goals by more than 200 basis points, or two full points of conversion.

Nonetheless, about half the stores were not hitting their goals, and the executive in charge was not pleased—and understandably so.

But there was much more to the story than the lackluster conversion rate performance. Overall sales were way off-plan, and a big part of it was store traffic. Store traffic was up 10% compared to the prior year, but it was still down from pre-pandemic levels. Conversion rates on average were 45%, which was up over 3% compared to the prior year and about flat versus pre-pandemic levels.

In an effort to drive sales performance, the executive mandated an across-the-board conversion rate target of 60% for every store. We reran the conversion rate actual performance versus this new, chain-wide conversion goal, and the results are shown in the updated chart.

## Conversion Performance vs. Updated Goal

Conversion Actual vs. UPDATED 60% Goal by Store - Variance in BPS

Only eleven stores, or about 3% of the entire chain, were meeting or exceeding the conversion rate goal. This new higher conversion rate goal was not well received by the field leaders and store managers.

Setting conversion rate goals is important, and even stretch goals are fine. However, when you set targets too high, with no consideration to how stores are performing or noncontrollable conversion factors, you set the field leaders and store managers up for failure.

## The Right Way to Set Conversion Goals

Since every store is truly unique—the physical layout, store type, the market it's in, the demographics of shoppers it serves, the local competitive landscape, and most importantly, the store manager and frontline team—then it only makes sense to set conversion goals for each store individually.

Of course, this takes more time and effort, but providing stores with conversion goals that are achievable and relative to historical conversion rate trends of each store will get better buy-in from your field leaders and store managers. Resist the temptation to set chain-wide conversion rate goals. As illustrated in the previous example of how not to set conversion goals, if you set them too high or without any consideration to the unique characteristics of each store, you can demoralize your field leaders and frontline teams, which can lead to disengagement. This not only hurts conversion performance, but it also contributes to employee turnover.

The following example illustrates a better approach to setting conversion rate goals.

This sporting goods retailer set a company-wide conversion rate improvement goal of 35%, five percentage points higher than its current average conversion rate performance of 30%. Initially, the CEO wanted every store to strive for a 35% conversion rate.

The following chart shows the actual conversion rates for a sample of stores compared to the new 35% conversion rate goal. As you can see, a 35% conversion rate would be easy to achieve for some stores, but completely unrealistic for stores like Store #10, Store #11, or Store #12.

| | Store 1 | Store 2 | Store 3 | Store 4 | Store 5 | Store 6 | Store 7 | Store 8 | Store 9 | Store 10 | Store 11 | Store 12 |
|---|---|---|---|---|---|---|---|---|---|---|---|---|
| Actual Conversion Rate | 40% | 38% | 36% | 34% | 33% | 30% | 30% | 30% | 28% | 22% | 21% | 20% |
| Target Conversion | 35% | 35% | 35% | 35% | 35% | 35% | 35% | 35% | 35% | 35% | 35% | 35% |

A far more effective way to set conversion goals is to apply a conversion rate growth target to current conversion rate performance. The current actual conversion rate performance already accounts for the unique characteristics of each store, so conversion rate goals relative to each store's past performance will be more realistic and achievable.

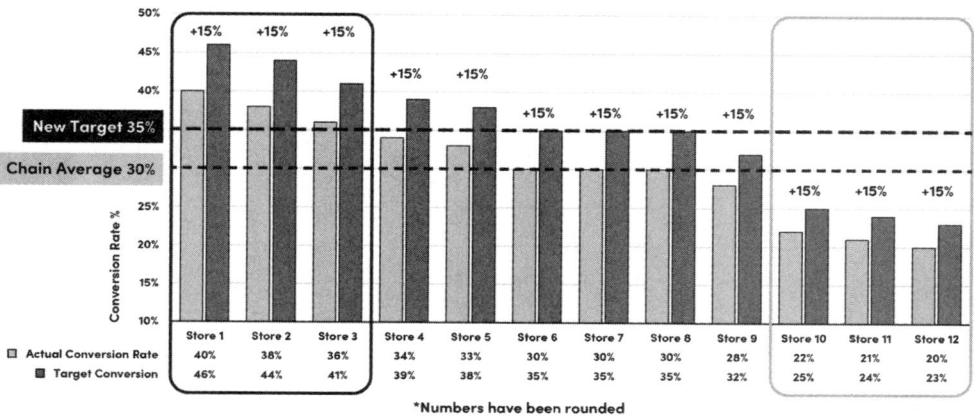

| | Store 1 | Store 2 | Store 3 | Store 4 | Store 5 | Store 6 | Store 7 | Store 8 | Store 9 | Store 10 | Store 11 | Store 12 |
|---|---|---|---|---|---|---|---|---|---|---|---|---|
| Actual Conversion Rate | 40% | 38% | 36% | 34% | 33% | 30% | 30% | 30% | 28% | 22% | 21% | 20% |
| Target Conversion | 46% | 44% | 41% | 39% | 38% | 35% | 35% | 35% | 32% | 25% | 24% | 23% |

*Numbers have been rounded

The chain-wide goal of 35% is still the goal, but instead of trying to get all stores to hit a one-size-fits-all goal, each store must contribute to achieving this by improving their share.

Getting field leaders and store managers to buy in to conversion goals is critical. Setting realistic and achievable conversion goals will enable this.

## Reality Check Conversion Goals— Sometimes They Need to Be Adjusted

Conversion rates can swing day-to-day and hour-to-hour. Hitting a conversion goal can be very rewarding and encouraging for managers and help drive performance across the chain. But conversion rate sags are inevitable. Stores can have a bad conversion day or even a bad week. The important point is that they stay focused on conversion rate improvement, and over time, results will improve.

The following chart shows the store traffic and conversion rate trend by day for one specialty store. This store was able to achieve a 14% conversion rate, but on other days (and especially on weekends), conversion rates were as low as 6%.

## Traffic and Conversion Daily Trend

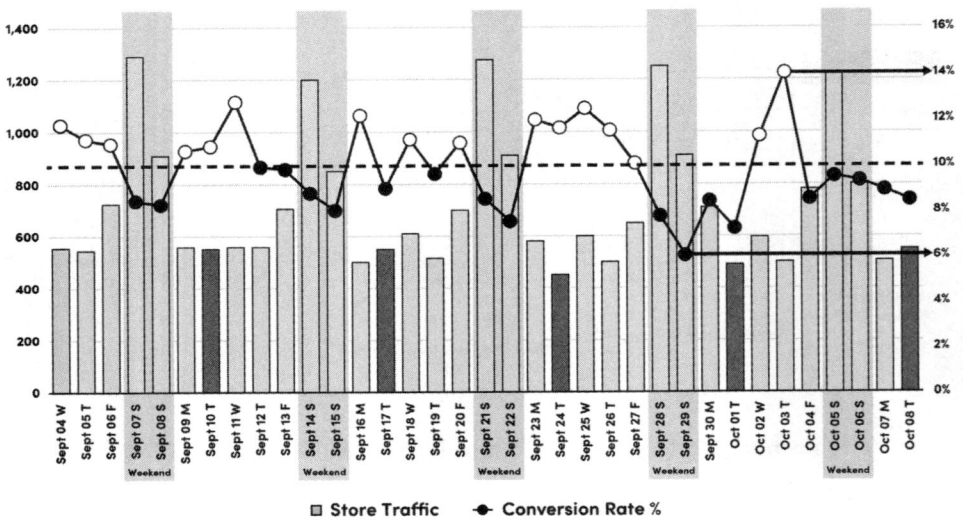

Store Traffic     Conversion Rate %

Conversion rate goals can be very effective at keeping store managers focused, but they also need to be reviewed regularly. Whoever is responsible for setting the conversion rate goals—typically someone in the store operations team at the head office—must consider the changing conditions and extenuating circumstances that can dramatically impact conversion rate trends in the stores. Then they should determine whether the goals need to be adjusted.

The idea of adjusting conversion goals might sound as though it defeats the purpose of having a goal in the first place, but there are good reasons to do it. An example will help illustrate.

To generate store traffic, a large specialty chain decided to start accepting Amazon returns after the operations team had already set conversion goals for each store. Store traffic did indeed increase, up 10% on average across the stores where it was rolled out. However, what was not fully understood was how this new service would impact conversion rate performance.

While store traffic increased, conversion rates sank since many of these Amazon returns store visitors were much harder to convert than shoppers who visited the store intentionally to shop. Conversion rates were diluted down, which caused overall conversion rates to fall, and stores systemically started to miss their conversion goals.

In this case, the retailer adjusted conversion rate goals to account for this new, harder-to-convert traffic the Amazon returns generated. This action made it clear to the store teams that head office was mindful in their goal-setting approach, which helped keep store managers and frontline teams engaged and focused.

## A Final Word About Conversion Goals

As mentioned, conversion rates can swing day-to-day and hour-to-hour. There will be days when conversion rates suck. Don't worry about it. It happens.

Whatever you do, don't make conversion rate goals punitive. Setting goals that are too high or in a way that doesn't reflect the realities in the stores is a surefire way to have store managers and field leaders disengage.

The objective is to stay focused on the shoppers in the store and to serve them in a way that results in a sale. Every hour of every day presents opportunities for new store traffic and for stores to improve conversion rate performance. And that happens best when store managers and teams are encouraged and supported by their field leaders as well as head office teams and executives.

## 🛒 Chapter Takeaways

- Store managers and frontline teams must understand their role in the conversion process and be held accountable for it. A lack of accountability can lead to missed sales opportunities.

- Establishing a clear, consistent view of store traffic and conversion performance across all levels of management—from store managers to executives—is crucial for creating line of sight for all stakeholders and a "conversion culture" mentality that sustains long-term focus.

- Field leaders, and especially district managers, play a critical role as "conversion coaches," guiding store managers in identifying and implementing conversion improvement tactics.

- Conversion rate goals should be individualized for each store, considering its unique characteristics and past performance. Unrealistic or blanket goals can demoralize teams and lead to disengagement.

- Conversion rate goals may need to be adjusted based on changing conditions or new challenges, such as increased store traffic from new initiatives like accepting Amazon returns. Goal setters need to be mindful of factors that impact conversion rate performance that the store team may not be able to control.

- Conversion improvement requires collaboration between store managers, field leaders, and head office teams. Engaging all stakeholders ensures that everyone is aligned and working toward the same goal.

## PRACTITIONER'S ADVICE

- Store managers must clearly communicate the importance of each frontline team member's role in the conversion process. Encourage accountability by providing feedback and recognizing efforts to improve.

- Provide all levels of management with access to the same store traffic and conversion rate performance results and ensure that insights are presented and interpreted consistently across the organization.

- Field leaders should regularly engage with store managers to discuss conversion trends, share best practices, and collaborate on store-level conversion improvement tactics.

## CHAPTER 7

---

# Using Store
# Traffic to Answer
# "Did It Work?" Questions

R etail is a perpetual motion machine. Every hour of every day presents new opportunities and challenges. And the retail industry is full of technological solutions to help retailers perform better—an almost mind-boggling array of solutions from the most mundane to the fantastical. This is both a blessing and a curse.

If you have ever had the opportunity to visit the National Retail Federation's annual conference in New York City, dubbed the "Big Show," you'll know what I mean.

At the 2024 show, there were some forty thousand attendees from more than ninety countries.[1] It is without compare and has rightly earned the title of the largest and most important retail industry conference in the world with over one hundred sessions, numerous keynote presentations, and expert panels covering a wide range of topics, including AI, customer experience, retail operations, and more. The Big Show provides attendees with insights and strategies to navigate the changing retail landscape.

The moment you step into the vast Javits Center where the conference has been held for more than a decade, your senses will be assaulted by a kaleidoscope of almost one thousand solution providers anxious to demonstrate their wares.

But with so many solutions and so many vendors to choose from, even deciding where to start is a challenge for many retailers, even the largest. As one senior vice president of operations for a thousand-plus store chain said to me, "We get pitched on hundreds of solutions every year, but we can only realistically test a handful." If a retail enterprise of that size can only test a handful of solutions every year, consider how challenging this must be for most other retailers, especially smaller retailers.

Even deciding which solution or solutions are most needed is a challenge. While that answer is as different as every retailer, what's most important is that there is a clear understanding of what the solution can deliver and how you can measure the impact. Or more simply, did it work?

While not every solution presented at the Big Show was specifically for physical stores—for example, some were targeted at e-commerce capabilities or warehousing solutions—most of them connected to the physical store in some way. Ostensibly, the pitch is that the solution will enable the retailer to do something better, faster, and/or more efficiently.

As compelling as these solutions sound, and the wonderful benefits vendors claim accrue to their users, it behooves every retailer to try to measure and quantify the impact themselves, and the way to do that is through experimentation. Unfortunately, initiatives are too often implemented in stores without any quantitative assessment. Instead, decisions are based on nothing but anecdotal feedback. The following real-world example illustrates the point.

At the 2023 National Retail Federation Big Show, I attended

an interesting session on the productivity impact of deploying handheld devices to store associates. The technology vendor that sold the devices to the retailer hosted the panel discussion, and three members of the retailer's senior operations team talked about their experience.

The executive vice president of store operations spoke about the productivity gains of using the new technology, which by that point had been provided to only a select number of associates in each of the hundreds of stores the retailer was testing it in. Based on the results from these test stores, the executive from the retailer said that his chain was intending to roll out the devices to many hundreds more stores and ultimately to every store associate in their 1,700 stores. Rolling out this many devices represented a significant investment, but this chain's leadership was convinced that the productivity gains made it worthwhile.

During the Q&A part of the session, I asked the executives how they were measuring the productivity gains that these handheld devices were delivering. Specifically, what quantitative measures were they using to come to their conclusions? The answer: They interviewed store associates who were using the devices, and they said the devices were helpful.

Wow. That's it? Really?

Making a case to invest millions of dollars in a solution should be based on more than merely how people feel about it. There should be some quantifiable way to measure the impact, yet this enterprise-class retailer relied on anecdotal feedback from their associates. How can you possibly build a financial case for a multimillion-dollar investment based on this? Or have any confidence that it's having an impact on store results?

A better approach would have been to select a sample of stores, provide *all* the associates in these test stores with the handheld devices, and then measure the impact on conversion rates and sales per visitor. Since these devices, in part, enabled associates to locate product faster and find product information, it would be reasonable to expect that conversion rates and/or sales per visitor results would increase in these stores compared to stores that didn't have the benefit of this terrific technology.

This is merely one example of how you can use store traffic data to answer the question, "Did it work?" There are an almost unlimited number of in-store initiatives that can be tested using store traffic data, conversion rates, and sales per visitor data.

Experimentation is not only about testing the efficacy and quantifying the outcomes of some new "shiny" technology. Any decision you make that impacts the physical store—offering new services, changing product mix, process changes, store layout, adjusting labor schedules, training programs, marketing campaigns, merchandising, virtually anything—can and should be viewed through the lens of store traffic and the impact it has on conversion rates and sales per visitor results.

In all fairness, not everything can be easily measured or even measured at all. But the fact is a lot can be, and store traffic data plays a vital role in contextualizing the outcomes, assessing and quantifying the impact, and answering the most important question: *Did it work?*

## Experimentation and Testing— Not Just for Big Retailers

It may seem like experimentation and testing are only for the largest, most sophisticated retailers, but this is not the case at all. Any retailer of any size can and should understand the impact of the major and/or important decisions they make.

The fact is that retailers are already making decisions, implementing new technologies, trying new things all the time, but what most aren't doing—or at least not consistently—is measuring the outcomes and quantifying the impact of these initiatives. And even when they do, sales outcomes are often the key measure used to assess efficacy. But as we know, sales outcomes are greatly impacted by the amount of traffic a store receives, and this can obfuscate the real impact unless you break down the results into their underlying sales drivers—store traffic, conversion rate, and average sale values.

## Deciding What to Test

Here's a simple guideline: Anything that you are looking to for a sales lift should be viewed through the lens of store traffic data to contextualize the results, and the "success signal" should be expressed in conversion rates and average sale values, or collectively, sales per visitor. Here are some examples:

- Task management
- Self-checkout
- Store layouts
- In-store merchandising displays
- Product mix
- New service offerings, such as Amazon Pickup Lockers
- Sales training programs
- Labor allocation and scheduling
- Store hour changes
- In-store process changes

Referring to our model of how retail sales are generated as I explained in chapter 1, there are two general types of experiments: [1] store traffic experiments and [2] experiments regarding activities or initiatives inside the store that impact results.

Since store traffic, conversion rate, and average sale are the only three underlying drivers to sales outcomes, it only stands to reason that results from any experiment you conduct should produce a signal in these variables.

Let's start with the most straightforward experiments, which are related to store traffic.

## STORE TRAFFIC EXPERIMENTS

Virtually every store traffic experiment that I have been involved with has to do with driving more traffic to stores. Since driving store traffic opportunities is the primary role of marketing, this just makes sense. So by definition, these experiments are all about the effectiveness marketing or promotions has in creating sales opportunities in the store.

Of course, not all marketing efforts are conducted to drive in more store traffic per se. For example, brand marketing is often intended to position the retailer in the market.

I know this might sound like heresy to marketing gurus, but if retailers' marketing budgets are not being invested in initiatives to drive prospective traffic into stores or create a predisposition to visit, then what is the point of investing money in marketing?

Marketers today have never had a greater ability to target marketing to select markets, regions, or even an individual store, and this capability is easily within the grasp of virtually any retailer. For most retailers, measuring the impact of marketing initiatives gets distilled down to one thing: Did sales go up? And obviously, for the retailers that don't track store traffic, what else can they do? But exclusively looking at sales is not only the wrong measure of marketing impact; it will also lead you to make bad decisions. The following example will illustrate why.

This retailer ran a sale event on the third Saturday of the month. Based on the sales results, this was not a successful event—the third Saturday had the lowest sales compared to the other Saturdays in the month.

## Average Sales: Saturdays

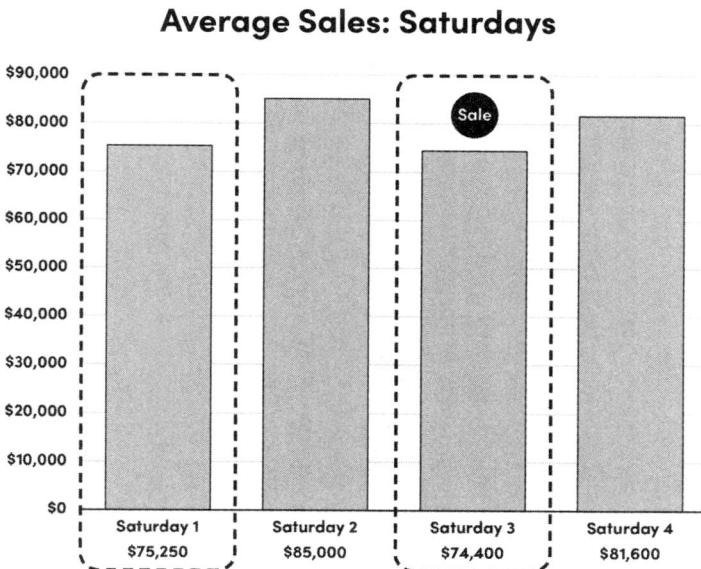

| Saturday 1 | Saturday 2 | Saturday 3 | Saturday 4 |
|------------|------------|------------|------------|
| $75,250 | $85,000 | $74,400 | $81,600 |

Without store traffic data, there would be no way to contextualize what happened on the day of the sale. When you contextualize the sales results with store traffic data, you reach a completely different conclusion—this promotion was actually very effective at driving prospects into the store, but the store was unable to convert this traffic, and consequently, sales underperformed expectations.

## Average Sales: Saturdays in Context

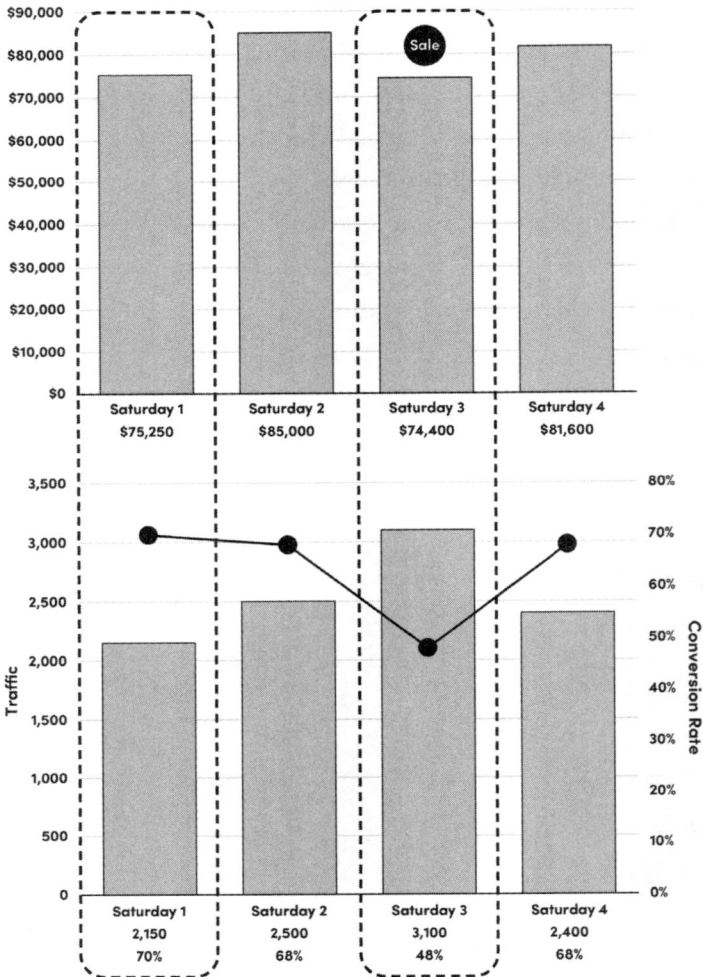

| | Saturday 1 | Saturday 2 | Saturday 3 | Saturday 4 |
|---|---|---|---|---|
| Sales | $75,250 | $85,000 | $74,400 | $81,600 |
| Traffic | 2,150 | 2,500 | 3,100 | 2,400 |
| Conversion Rate | 70% | 68% | 48% | 68% |

Sales were low on the sale day, but traffic was up significantly compared to the other Saturdays. This sale event was effective at driving store traffic—which is what marketing is supposed to do—but the store didn't or couldn't convert the traffic, and consequently, sales were low.

Based on these findings, how effective would you say the sales event was? The sales results told one story, but the store traffic data told a completely different one. Store traffic on the day of the sale was up 24% compared to the prior Saturday and up 29% compared to the following Saturday.

Without store traffic data this insight could not have been acquired, and this retailer may have decided to try something different—and potentially less effective at driving store traffic—instead of focusing on what really happened. The store team didn't convert the traffic opportunity the marketing had delivered for the sales event.

## IN-STORE INITIATIVE EXPERIMENTS

If you think of the physical store as an algorithm that ingests visitor traffic and produces sales outcomes, then anything you do inside the physical store will impact the algorithm in some way. And every store is a unique algorithm itself.

The goal of experimentation is to determine whether the initiative or change had an impact and then quantify the impact. If this sounds a lot like conducting a simple return on investment (ROI) analysis, it is, but the approach is nuanced for in-store initiatives.

In a typical ROI analysis, you make a financial investment, determine the lift in sales, and then calculate whether the cost of the initiative delivered a sufficient return on the investment. But when it comes to in-store initiatives, this approach doesn't work because of the influence store traffic can have on sales results.

Remember, store traffic is a variable that the store team can't control or influence, but it impacts sales. So to measure the impact of the in-store initiative on sales outcomes, you must neutralize the store traffic effect.

Here's an example to illustrate.

A retailer decided to test a new sales training program for sales associates with the goal of increasing sales performance. Five stores were selected as the test group, and a month after the training was completed, the sales results from the test stores were compared to a control group of five randomly selected stores from the region that did not receive the training.

The sales results before and after the training for the two groups are summarized in the following chart.

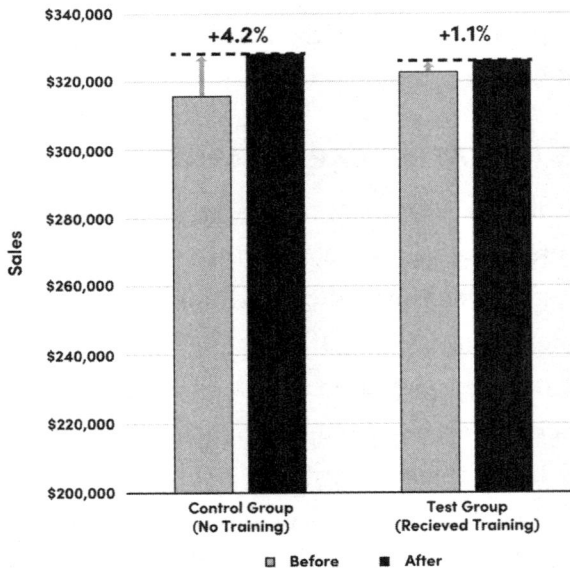

The control stores that did not get the training saw their sales increase by 4% from the previous month, while the test stores that did get training saw their sales increase by only 1.1% compared to the prior month. Based on these sales results, there is only one conclusion: The training program wasn't effective.

But what's missing from this analysis is any consideration of how store traffic may have impacted these results. Only by breaking out results into the underlying sales drivers can we truly understand what impact the training may have had.

[Store Traffic Count] x [Conversion Rate %] x [Average Sale $] = Sales

The following table includes this additional information for both groups, and now we can understand exactly what happened.

| | Control Group | | | Test Group | | |
|---|---|---|---|---|---|---|
| | Before | After | % Change | Before | After | % Change |
| Total Traffic | 33,000 | 36,000 | 9.1% | 36,000 | 29,250 | -18.8% |
| Conversion Rate | 32% | 30% | -6.3% | 30% | 35% | 16.7% |
| Average Sale | $30 | $30 | 0.0% | $30 | $32 | 6.7% |
| Sales | $316,800 | $329,400 | 4.2% | $324,000 | $327,600 | 1.1% |

The control stores had a 4.2% increase in sales, but what we now know is that store traffic was up 9.1%. Remember, store traffic defines the sales opportunity, and the opportunity got a lot larger for these stores. But what we can also see is that the conversion rate dropped by 6.3% and average sale values were flat. The net result is that sales still grew by 4.2%, even though these control stores had a decrease in conversion rate. The sales increase was entirely driven by the increase in store traffic, which is something the stores don't control.

The test group story also changes dramatically when we consider the impact of store traffic.

Store traffic in the test store group decreased by 18.8%, but conversion rates were up 16.7%, increasing from 30% to 35%, and the average sale was up 6.7%, increasing from $30 to $32. The store traffic decline stunted the sales lift and obfuscated the terrific conversion rate and average sale results that these test stores were delivering.

Another way to assess the impact is to examine the sales generated for every visitor who entered the store and compare how each group performed. The sales per visitor is calculated by dividing total sales by total traffic or by simply multiplying conversion rate by average sale. These results have now been added to the following table.

| | Control Group | | | Test Group | | |
|---|---|---|---|---|---|---|
| | Before | After | % Change | Before | After | % Change |
| Total Traffic | 33,000 | 36,000 | 9.1% | 36,000 | 29,250 | -18.8% |
| Conversion Rate | 32% | 30% | -6.3% | 30% | 35% | 16.7% |
| Average Sale | $30 | $30 | 0.0% | $30 | $32 | 6.7% |
| Total Sales | $316,800 | $329,400 | 4.2% | $324,000 | $327,600 | 1.1% |
| Sales per Visitor | $9.60 | $9.00 | -6.3% | $9.00 | $11.20 | 24.4% |

In the control group, sales per visitor declined 6.3%, going from $9.60 per visitor in the before period to $9.00 after. The control group stores got more traffic but converted less of their traffic into sales. In the test group, sales per visitor increased from $9.00 in the before period to $11.20 after the training—that's a significant 24.4% increase.

While there is no way to say with 100% certainty that the sales training drove these results, if nothing else changed between the control and test groups other than the sales training, then it's reasonable to conclude that it made the difference.

Based on this analysis, how effective would you say the sales training was?

Without store traffic data, it would have been impossible to acquire this insight. And instead of rolling out the sales training program to additional stores, this retailer may have abandoned the sales training program—a program that had a significantly positive impact on the outcomes in the test store group.

Now let's get into the nuts and bolts of setting up an experiment and the things that you should consider as you begin the process.

## Terminology: A/B or Test Versus Control?

In general terms, whether you refer to your experiment as A/B or Test Group versus Control Group doesn't matter. I don't want to get hung up on terminology, but my preference is to refer to an experiment as Test stores versus Control stores, so that's how I will refer to it. The key point is that to understand the impact of anything, you need to compare it to something.

However, unlike experiments conducted in laboratories where influences can be strictly controlled or significantly minimized and the impact precisely measured, the same cannot be said for experiments in physical stores. The physical world is messy and unpredictable. It's in a constant state of flux, and results can be impacted by outside factors that are impossible to control or even identify. But as challenging as this is, it's still worth the effort, and it doesn't take a team of statisticians to do.

Once you have decided on an initiative to test, the first step is to define the experiment with a simple description of the hypothesis, expected outcomes, and key measures.

# Structuring Your Experiment

The first step in the process is to clearly identify what you're testing and the outcomes you're expecting. To ensure that all stakeholders and decision-makers are aligned, you should write it down and communicate it so that there is no confusion.

- **Hypothesis:** This is a simple statement about what you expect the experiment to determine. Going back to the sales training example, the hypothesis is: *Stores that receive the new training program will produce better sales outcomes than stores that don't receive the training.*

- **Store Traffic Experiments—Key Measure:** For store traffic–related experiments, the most obvious measure is store traffic. But even for traffic experiments, I recommend including conversion rate, average sale, and sales per visitor results in your results tracking. Here's why.

  Even though you may be primarily interested in how traffic trends change, you should also keep an eye on the other sales drivers, namely conversion rate and average sale, so you can understand what impact any traffic changes may have had on these results.

- **In-Store Experiments—Key Measures:** For all experiments related to initiatives conducted in store, the key measures are always conversion rate, average sale value, and sales per visitor. That's it. You can certainly add other measures if you like, such as customer experience scores, but it's not required.

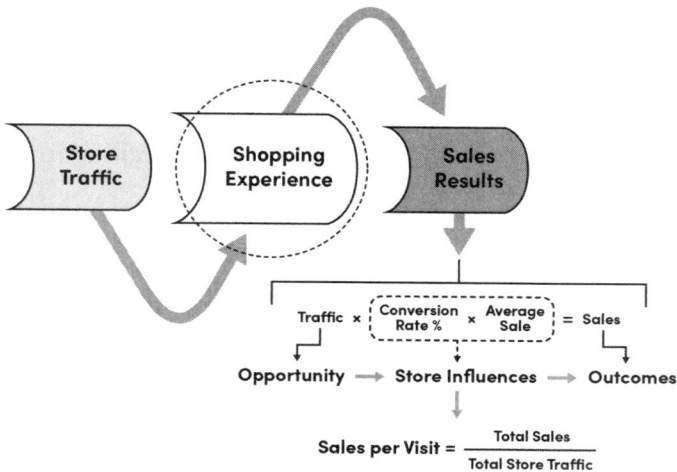

Any experiment that you conduct where you are expecting a change in sales outcomes should first produce a signal in the stores' conversion rates, average sale values and, collectively, sales per visitor results.

Since conversion rates and average sale values are the only two ways that store teams can influence sales outcomes, it only stands to reason that we should see a measurable change in either of these metrics—or both metrics—if the initiative being tested is having an impact on outcomes.

Recall, sales per visitor is simply calculated by dividing total store sales by total store traffic. It's essentially a metric that combines conversion rate and average sale values—the two variables that store teams can influence.

And while you might argue that by tracking sales per visitor, there's no need to also track conversion rate and average sale values for your experiment, I argue that you still need to track these metrics. Sales per visitor is a good measure of the overall outcome, but it's also important to know *how* you got there and the impact the initiative may have had on each of these metrics.

By breaking out the conversion rate, average sale values, and sales per visitor measures, you will be able to assess not only the overall impact the initiative had on sales outcomes relative to store traffic, but you will also know how each contributed to the overall outcomes. For example, if conversion rates are strong, but average sale values are weaker, then further refinements or program adjustments focusing on driving average sale values may be in order.

The next step is selecting your store groups.

## Selecting Test and Control Stores

I touched on the challenges of conducting experiments and measuring results in physical stores in chapter 5. Since no two physical stores are alike, it's impossible to be completely comparable, so the goal is to select stores that have similar store traffic volumes and mix of store types. For example, you don't want to include only mall stores in the test group and only off-mall stores in your control group.

Another common question that comes up is: How many stores should you include in an experiment?

From a strictly statistical standpoint, the answer will depend on how many stores you have in your chain. But what I have discovered working with many types of retailers, from large enterprises with over a thousand stores to small independent chains with less than ten stores, is that store selection often comes down to a judgment call. Statisticians would refer to it as a "convenience" sample. The truth is most retailers I have encountered don't use formal statistical modeling when conducting experiments, in part because they don't have the internal expertise.

But just because you don't apply formal statistical methodology to your experiment doesn't mean that it's not valid or that you won't produce meaningful or actionable insights. Remember, retail stores are not laboratories. The physical world is constantly changing and is impacted by myriad things that you can't control.

Furthermore, there is often a cost associated with conducting an experiment. If statistical modeling says that you should include two hundred of your one thousand stores in a sample, it may not be practical or financially feasible to do this—even for the largest retailers.

And even if we look past formal statistical methodology, it doesn't mean that you shouldn't be thoughtful about which stores you select for your experiments. You should. And one of the most obvious things you should *not* do is conduct multiple, simultaneous experiments using the same test stores.

One major chain I worked with said that they have a group of stores that they use for all experimentation. When I asked why they used the same test stores for all experiments, the answer was simply, "because that's the way we have always done it." The obvious problem with using the same stores for all experiments is that if you conduct multiple experiments in the same stores, you'll never know which experiment produced which result. You don't need to be a statistician to see how this is a problem!

The objective in store selection is to choose test and control stores that have relatively consistent performance and are free from any extenuating circumstances or issues that could compromise the results.

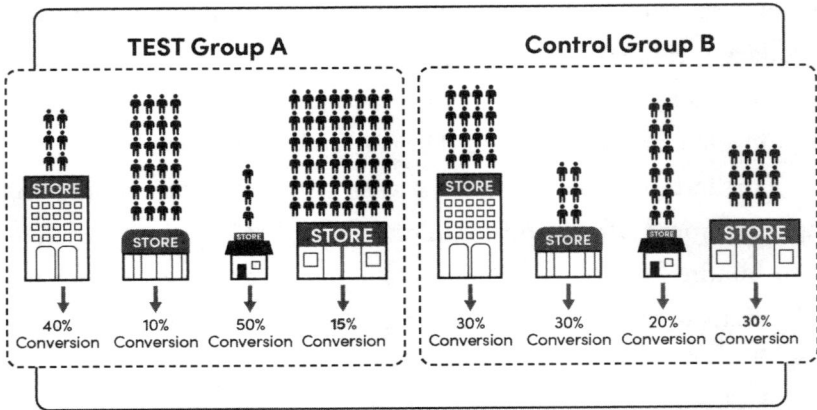

Here are some basic guidelines for selecting stores to include in your experiment:

- **Be Practical.** The number of stores and which stores you select for your experiment is your judgment call. Don't worry if you start with a small experiment and only a handful of test stores—you can always expand the experiment to additional stores as a follow-up experiment to validate your findings.

- **Match Test and Control Stores from Similar Geographic Markets if Possible.** Since store results can be impacted by events occurring in the markets the stores reside in, such as weather and localized economic dynamics, selecting both test and control stores in the same market improves comparability.

- **Include a Similar Mix of Store Types and Traffic Volumes.** Don't use mall-based stores for the test group and off-mall stores for the control group. By selecting stores with similar traffic volumes and formats, you will enhance comparability since these stores are serving a similar number of shoppers.

- **Consider Operational Factors or Other Circumstances That Could Impact Results.** There's always a lot going on in stores, so exclude stores undergoing renovations, stores with new store managers, or stores in markets that are experiencing dramatic changes. You can't control every circumstance, and circumstances can change midway through an experiment, so be prepared to eliminate stores from your experiment if circumstances warrant it.

- **Eliminate Stores with Bad or Incomplete Store Traffic Data.** One of the ways an experiment can become compromised is by using bad or incomplete data. Before a store is included in an experiment, the traffic and conversion rate data for both test and control stores should be reviewed for completeness. If data is missing, or there are wild swings in conversion rate trends, these are telltale signs that you have a data issue, and these stores should immediately be excluded. The following charts show examples of what "bad" traffic and conversion rate data looks like.

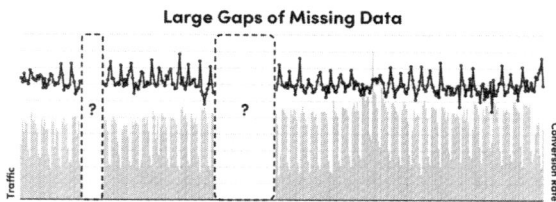

Large Gaps of Missing Data

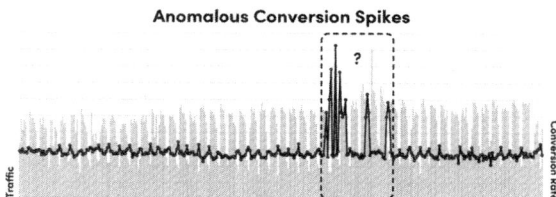

Anomalous Conversion Spikes

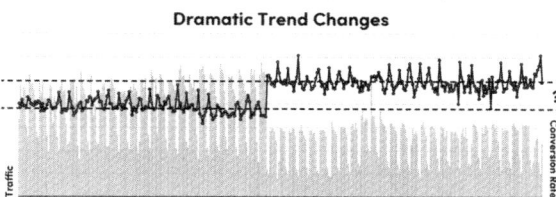

Dramatic Trend Changes

Store traffic data is vital, and it should be reviewed regularly to ensure that it remains complete and reliable. In the first chart, there were large gaps in the store traffic data. These stores should be eliminated from the experiment.

Another telltale sign that you have a data problem is when you see wild swings in conversion rate trends. If a store has been converting traffic at 20% consistently, and then the conversion rate jumps to 40%, there may be a problem with the store traffic data and/or the transaction data that is used to calculate conversion rates.

I'll discuss how you can keep your store traffic data clean and complete in chapter 11. But suffice it to say, before you begin any experiment, you are well advised to double-check the data quality and completeness to ensure that your experiment outcomes are a result of what you're trying to test instead of from bad underlying data.

Once you have selected your test and control stores, you then need to establish your experiment time frame.

## Selecting the Experiment Time Frames

When conducting an experiment, it's not good enough to merely select your test and control groups, conduct the experiment, and compare results during and at the conclusion of the experiment period. There are two time frames that need to be selected for your experiment.

**Experiment period.** The first time frame you need to decide on is the actual experiment period. This is the time period when the new initiative will be implemented and be in full effect in all the test stores. It's important to remember that new initiatives can take time to implement in stores, so it's vital to ensure that all test stores have been fully implemented by the start of the experiment period.

**Baseline period.** This is the period before the experiment initiative is implemented in your test group stores. In order to fully understand what impact a new initiative may have, you must know how the two groups were performing relative to each other before the experiment and then factor these results into your final conclusions.

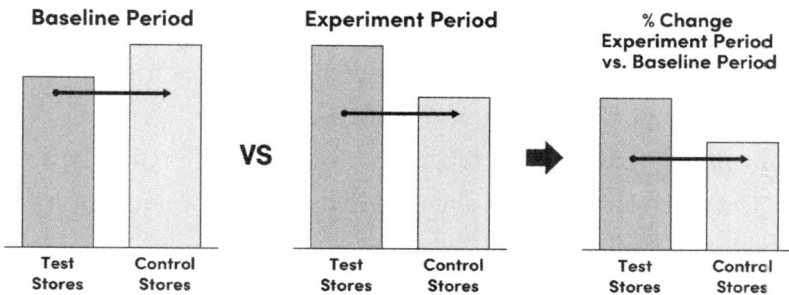

For example, if the control stores were outperforming the test stores before the experiment, it's reasonable to assume that they would have continued to outperform the test stores during the experiment period if nothing else had changed. Comparing results from test and control stores during the baseline period will enable you to include this prior performance differential in your final experiment impact assessment, giving you a more accurate view of the experiment's true impact.

## Year-over-Year or Same-Year Results?

Ideally, you want to include year-over-year (YoY) results in your experiment assessment. By including YoY results, impacts influenced by seasonality get included and provide additional precision in your findings. In the baseline period, you will calculate the YoY results for the test group and the control group. In the experiment period, you will look at YoY results for test and control groups and then calculate the change in performance.

If you don't have complete YoY data for both the test and control stores, you can still conduct your experiment using the data from the current year. Without YoY data, you will not be able to account for any seasonality impacts, but this doesn't mean that your conclusions are any less valid.

Ultimately, the experiment's objective is to measure the performance difference between the two groups of stores based on each group's own performance trend—whether you use YoY data or data from only the current year, relative performance differences between the test and control groups should still be detectable—assuming the experiment had an impact.

## How Long Should the Experiment Be?

Determining the duration of the experiment is a judgment call. The longer the experiment period, the more reliable your results will be. But again, practicality should be part of the decision. In my experience, selecting a four-to-eight-week experiment period is most typical. That said, I have seen experiments go on for many months. However, the duration, in part, will be determined based on the nature of the experiment.

Once you have established your experiment period, you then need to select your baseline period. I recommend selecting a baseline time frame that is about twice as long as the experiment period. For example, if you are running a four-week experiment, I would use the prior two months for the baseline period. Adding a second month to the baseline period helps smooth out results and minimizes any performance spikes that may have occurred during the baseline period.

Remember, physical stores are not laboratories, and you can't control every variable. What's important is that you thoughtfully select your test and control stores, ensure the underlying data is complete and accurate, and then compare the performance of the two groups.

## Launching the Experiment

In a perfect world, you would want to conduct your experiment as a "blind" experiment, where the participants—in our case, store managers and frontline teams of the test stores—do not know an experiment is being conducted. The reason for a blind experiment is because there is a risk that just by knowing an experiment is being conducted, test store teams' behaviors may change, and this can impact results. But the reality is that this can be very difficult, if not impossible, to do.

In my experience, it's fine to let the test group store managers know that you are conducting an experiment, but you shouldn't share results or discuss the findings with either test or control group managers until the experiment is done and you have your final results.

The most critical part of launching the experiment is implementing the initiative in the test group so that they all start at the same time, or as close to the same time as possible. Keep in mind that you may need to account for implementation time to get the initiative up and running.

For example, I worked on an experiment to measure the impact of a new labor scheduling solution for a large apparel chain. Before test store managers could start scheduling staff using the new solution, they needed to be trained on the system, and then there was a series of sample schedules produced running in parallel with the existing labor scheduling system. In this case, the actual experiment didn't start until all the test stores started to create and assign labor based on the new scheduling system.

Once the experiment is launched, the real fun begins—tracking the results.

## Tracking Results During the Experiment

While the goal is to determine the overall impact of the initiative at the conclusion of the experiment, you should also track results on a weekly basis. By tracking results weekly, you will be able to see how performance is trending over time. Depending on the initiative, it may take time for it to get traction and for the results to appear—if they appear at all.

In this type of experimentation, trends are very enlightening and help to contextualize what the final results ultimately reveal. A real-world example will help illustrate.

The following charts show the conversion rate performance of a test group of stores versus a control group over a four-week period. In Week #1 of the experiment, both the test and control groups saw declines in YoY conversion rate performance. This is a good example of how "better" results may mean less worse than the control group.

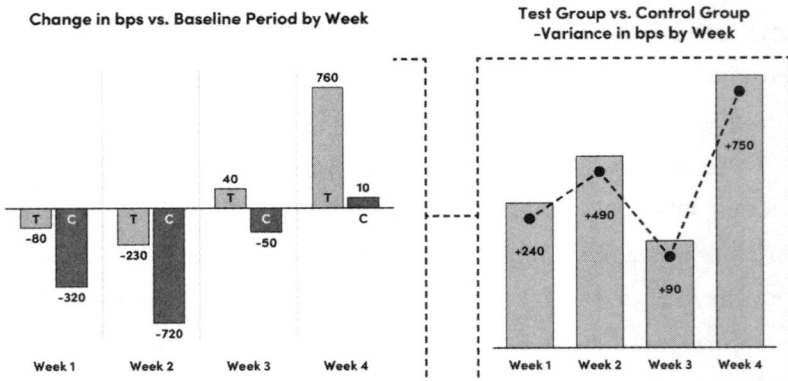

Change in bps vs. Baseline Period by Week

Test Group vs. Control Group -Variance in bps by Week

YoY conversion performance was down 80 basis points (bps) in the test group, but it was down 320 bps in the control group, so the conversion rate performance differential between the test and control groups was 240 bps as shown on the righthand side of the chart. Said more plainly, the test group outperformed the control group by 240 bps in Week #1 of the experiment.

As the experiment progressed, you can see that the performance gap was even larger in Week #2 of the experiment, despite both groups having YoY declines in conversion rates. Remember, this is not about whether conversion rates are positive or negative, but rather how conversion rates are changing in the test group versus the control group.

In Week #3, YoY conversion rates turned positive for the test group, while the control group was still down, but now only by 50 bps, so the performance differential was 90 bps. In Week #4, the final week of the experiment, conversion rates in the test group increased dramatically up 760 bps and up only 10 bps in the control group, resulting in a performance differential of 750 bps.

As impressive as these results are, and how encouraging the trend is, this does not represent the experiment's final results. The final results will be captured when we compare the test and control groups to their performance during the baseline period. Nonetheless, the trends begin to tell a story, and the apparent acceleration of conversion rate performance differential implies that the test group results are getting better over time, which is exactly what you would expect to happen as the test store managers become more familiar with the new scheduling system and the scheduling optimization starts to produce results.

Now let's put all the pieces together for the final assessment of the experiment and quantify the impact.

# Final Results and Interpretation

Once the experiment period ends, it's time to put all the results together, including the comparative performance from the baseline period. Let's start with conversion rates.

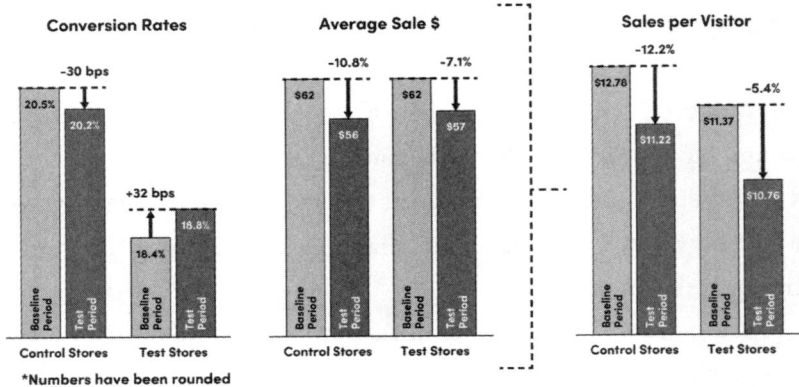

*Numbers have been rounded

In the control group, conversion rates were 20.5% on average in the baseline period, and then declined to 20.2% during the experiment period, for a net difference of 30 bps. In the test group, conversion rates were 18.4% in the baseline period and increased to 18.8% for a 32-bps improvement. Remember, we are not concerned with what the actual conversion rate is, but rather the change in conversion rate performance between the two groups.

What was interesting about this experiment was that the average sale values in both the test and control groups declined in both the baseline and experiment periods. But as you can see, average sale values were down less in the test group than they were in the control group.

When you combine the conversion rate and average sale results together in the sales per visitor results, the outcomes are clear: Both the test and control groups saw their sales per visitor numbers decline, but the decline was significantly larger in the control group compared to the test group using the new labor scheduling system.

Breaking out the conversion rate and sales per visitor results by individual test store enabled us to determine whether the overall results were driven by a handful of test stores that performed well and brought the overall average up, or whether the improved performance occurred more broadly among the test stores.

| Test Stores | Variance vs. Control Stores | |
|---|---|---|
| | Conversion | Sales per Visitor |
| Store 1 | 9.8% | 13.5% |
| Store 2 | 8.5% | 9.8% |
| Store 3 | 1.1% | 1.2% |
| Store 4 | -3.2% | -1.6% |
| Store 5 | 7.6% | 4.0% |
| Store 6 | 2.2% | 7.8% |
| Store 7 | -4.3% | 1.7% |
| Store 8 | -6.3% | 3.0% |
| Store 9 | 2.6% | 11.6% |
| Store 10 | -2.2% | 5.3% |
| Store 11 | -9.9% | -13.2% |

**Conversion
6 of 11**
Test Stores
Outperformed
Control Stores

**Sales per Visitor
9 of 11**
Test Stores
Outperformed
Control Stores

As the table shows, from a conversion rate perspective, six of the eleven test stores outperformed the control group, and nine out of eleven test stores outperformed the control group based on sales per visitor.

Any way you slice it, the results were clear: Test stores that had the new labor scheduling system outperformed the control stores.

But what was it worth financially?

## Quantifying the Financial Impact

Once you have the final results of the experiment, it's reasonable to apply the performance lift the test group delivered and extrapolate it across all stores in the chain and then calculate what the impact on top-line sales would have been. The results from the labor scheduling experiment are summarized in the following graphic.

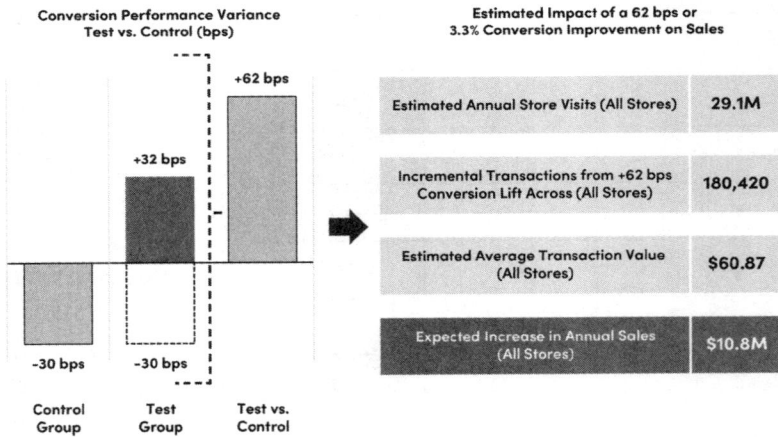

The control group saw conversion rates decline by 30 bps from the baseline period to the experiment period, while the test group saw conversion rates increase by 32 bps. When we calculate the net difference, we need to account for the decline in the control group. The test group made up the 30-bps decline that the control group saw and increased their results by an additional 32 bps, so the net difference is a 62-bps conversion rate gain in the test versus control group.

It's reasonable to assume that the 30-bps decline in the control stores is what would have happened in the test group had they not implemented the new labor scheduling solution. That's why it's called the "control" group. Since the new labor scheduling tool was the only thing that changed between the two groups, it's reasonable to conclude that the conversion rate and sales per visitor performance differential was a result of the new tool.

Now that we know the conversion rate differential, we can extrapolate the results across all three hundred stores in the chain over the course of the entire year to calculate what the estimated sales lift would be if the scheduling solution was rolled out to every store.

We start with store traffic. This chain received 29,100,000 store visits in a year across all 300 stores. If average conversion rates increased by 62 bps, then the total number of sales transactions would increase by 180,420 (29,100,000 x .0062 = 180,420) incremental sale transactions. With a $60.87 average sale value, we can determine that this conversion rate improvement would deliver an additional $10.8 million in sales over the course of a year.

Here's another example of an experiment impact assessment, but this time it includes an ROI (return on investment) assessment.

In this real-world example, the retailer wanted to understand two things: first, the impact of a new conversion rate reporting program for store managers, and second, the financial ROI of the program. This retailer had traffic count data, but the store managers were not provided with any detailed insights into their conversion rate performance.

In this experiment, the test group stores received conversion rate performance reporting daily that showed, to the hour, where they were missing conversion opportunities in their stores. At the conclusion of the eight-week experiment, the final results of the experiment were calculated, and the results are shown in the following graphic.

| Conversion Performance Variance Test vs. Control (bps) | | Financial Impact |
|---|---|---|
| | Total Traffic During Pilot - 9 Test Stores Only | 1,077,740 |
| +140 bps | Conversion Rate Improvement in Test Stores | 1.4% |
| | Gross Sales Lift in Test Stores (1.07M × 1.4% × $26.79) | $406,324 |
| | Gross Profit Lift in Test Stores (Estimated at 40%) | $162,530 |
| | Headcount Program Cost $1,200 per month at 7 months | $8,400 |
| Control Stores    Test Stores | ROI Based On Gross Profit Lift | 1,835% |

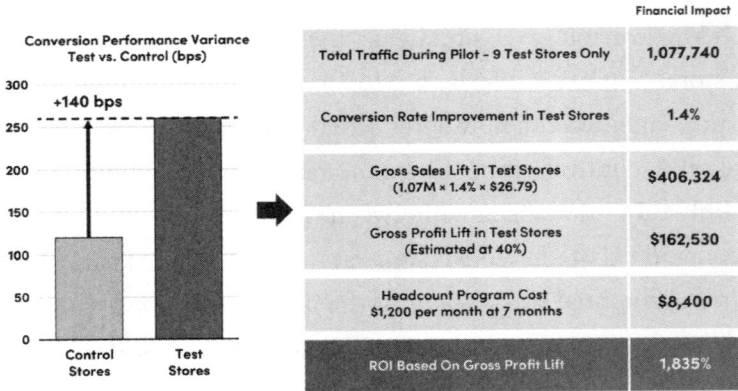

In this experiment, the test group stores had a 140-bps improvement in conversion rates compared to the control group stores. For this ROI analysis, we did not extrapolate the results chain-wide, but rather we calculated the gross sales and gross profit lifts attributed to the conversion rate reporting. Then we compared it to the cost of delivering the new reporting program. The ROI speaks for itself—the $8,400 investment in conversion reporting produced an increase in gross profit of $162,530 for an ROI of 1,835%.

## Back-Testing and Expanding Experiments

Once you have completed your experiment and reviewed the final results, the next step is to decide what you want to do next. If you're confident in the results, then roll out to all locations and move on to the next experiment. However, if the cost of the initiative is high and there's still some uncertainty about the results, then the best course of action is to rerun the experiment using a new group of test and control stores and/or to expand the experiment to additional stores.

Ultimately, this will come down to a management decision. The results from these experiments should provide sufficient insight for management to decide, even if the results are directional in nature.

Remember, physical stores are not laboratories, and it's virtually impossible to be absolutely precise. However, you will improve your chances of success by including store traffic and conversion rates in your decision-making process, instead of relying on sales outcomes that are influenced by store traffic and may have nothing to do with the initiative that you're testing.

## Final Word About Experimentation

For most retailers, there's simply not enough time nor resources to conduct a formal experiment on every initiative they launch in stores. However, I encourage every retailer to conduct experiments using this methodology on the initiatives that really matter.

Before you invest hundreds of thousands or even millions of dollars in any initiative that is hoped to deliver improved sales or in-store productivity, you should conduct an experiment to assess the potential impact. Using store traffic and conversion rate is essential.

Finally, you should think of experimentation as a continuous process. The following steps provide a road map that you can follow for any experimentation.

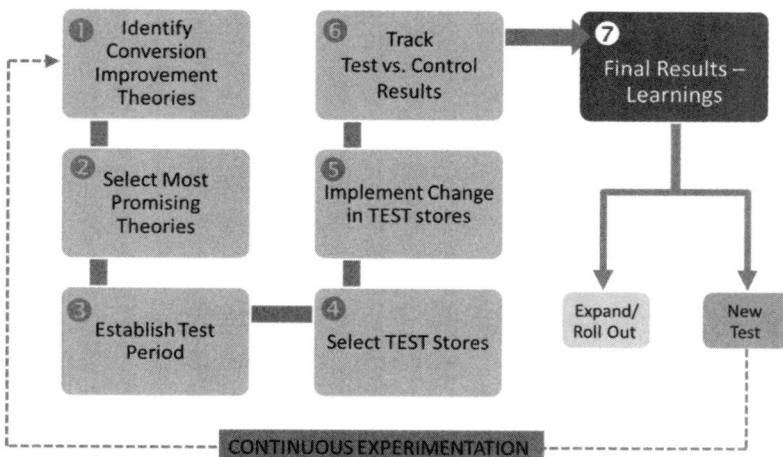

Another important area that store traffic and conversion rate insights can help with is refining store-level product mix, and that's where we turn our attention next.

## 🛒 Chapter Takeaways

- Experimentation and testing are crucial for evaluating the impact of new initiatives in retail stores. Even small retailers can benefit from measuring the outcomes of their decisions using store traffic, conversion rates, and sales per visitor data.

- Store traffic data is essential for contextualizing the results of any in-store initiative or marketing campaign. It helps retailers understand the true impact of their efforts beyond just sales outcomes.

- When conducting experiments, it's important to carefully select test and control stores that have similar traffic volumes and operational conditions to ensure comparability.

- Conversion rates, average sale values, and sales per visitor are the key metrics to track when evaluating the success of in-store initiatives. These metrics provide a clearer picture of the impact of changes than sales data alone.

- Retailers should be thoughtful about the design of their experiments, including the selection of stores, the definition of baseline and experiment periods, and the interpretation of results.

- Experimentation should be an ongoing process. Retailers should regularly test and refine their strategies to improve conversion rates and overall store performance.

## PRACTITIONER'S ADVICE

- Use store traffic data to assess marketing impact. When evaluating marketing campaigns, don't just look at sales outcomes. Use store traffic data to understand whether the campaign successfully drove more shoppers to your stores and then analyze conversion rates to see if those visits were converted into sales.

- Design thoughtful experiments. When testing new initiatives, ensure that your test and control groups are as comparable as possible. Avoid running multiple experiments in the same stores simultaneously to prevent skewed results.

- Focus on key metrics. Track conversion rates, average sale values, and sales per visitor to measure the true impact of your in-store initiatives. These metrics will give you a clearer understanding of how changes are affecting your sales.

- Consider practical constraints. While longer experiment periods can yield more reliable results, be practical about the duration and scale of your experiments. Start small if necessary and expand as you gain confidence in your findings.

- Continually test and learn. Treat experimentation as an ongoing process. Regularly test new ideas, refine your strategies based on the results, and apply your learnings across the chain to drive continuous improvement.

# CHAPTER 8

---

# Using Store Traffic and Conversion Rates to Refine Merchandise Localization

One of the key reasons people leave the store without buying is because the store doesn't carry the item they're looking for. But this is not simply about making sure you don't stock out of fast-selling items; it's also about having the right product at the right store at the right time.

A product that sells well in a store on the north side of the city may not sell as well in the store on the south side of the city. This only makes sense when you consider that the demographics of shoppers visiting one store may be quite different than shoppers who visit another store, even in the same city.

The challenge for product buyers and merchandising teams is to determine how to optimize inventory and product mix to the individual store. The pursuit of product mix localization right down to the store has become a priority for some retailers since hyper-localization should result in higher conversion rates, average sale values, and collectively, sales per visitor.

Merchandising and product buying strategies are complex and impacted by supply-chain dynamics, sourcing, availability, cost, and myriad other factors.[1] I'm not a merchandising expert, and it's not my intention to delve into the merchandising domain—there is a plethora of material on the topic from merchandising experts.

However, I am very interested in how the merchandise localization decisions are made and how store traffic and conversion insights can play an important role in refining these decisions.

## Sell-Through Drives Merchandising Decisions

Product mix decisions are largely driven by sell-through rates.[2] Merchandising teams closely monitor sell-through rates of every SKU (stock keeping unit) and base their reordering and buying decisions on those results. And while there are many other factors that buyers consider in determining what product to buy, how much to buy, and where to place it, maximizing sales and minimizing returns are the primary goals.

While it makes perfect sense to base product mix and buying decisions on sell-through rates, retailers can further refine their product mix localization decisions by contextualizing sell-through performance relative to the store traffic and conversion rates of any given store.

As I have said repeatedly throughout this book, any decision that is made based on sales results should be viewed in the context of store traffic and conversion rates, and this also applies to product mix decisions. By examining conversion rates of individual SKUs, new and different insights can be acquired that can help refine product mix decisions beyond what sell-through rates tell you.

Here's a hypothetical example to illustrate.

The sell-through rates of three different products—A, B, and C—were compared across three different stores—1, 2, and 3.

## Sell-Through Analysis by SKU by Store

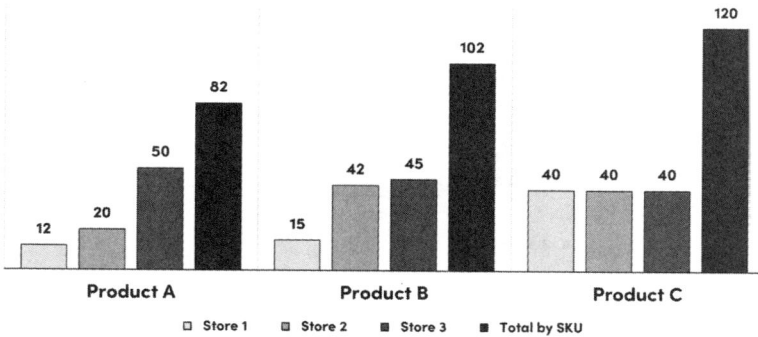

Store 1 □    Store 2 □    Store 3 ■    Total by SKU ■

From an overall sell-through perspective, Product C was the best seller—it was the clear winner. Not only did the stores collectively sell more of Product C (120 units in total), but the sell-through was strong across all three stores. Case closed.

But while these sell-through results are irrefutable, examining the conversion rate of each SKU, which considers the volume of store traffic that each store received to produce these sell-through rates, is revealing.

# SKU-Level Conversion Rates— A Different Perspective

Recall that every physical store is unique. The sell-through of any given SKU will, in part, be impacted by the amount of traffic the store receives and the ability of the store team to convert the traffic into a sale.

Let's start with Product A. Overall, Product A had the lowest total sell-through of the three products at 82 units. Store 1 sold 12 units, Store 2 sold 20 units, and Store 3 sold 50 units. In order to calculate SKU-level conversion rates, we need to divide the number of units sold by the store traffic each store received.

**Sell-Through Analysis by SKU by Store**

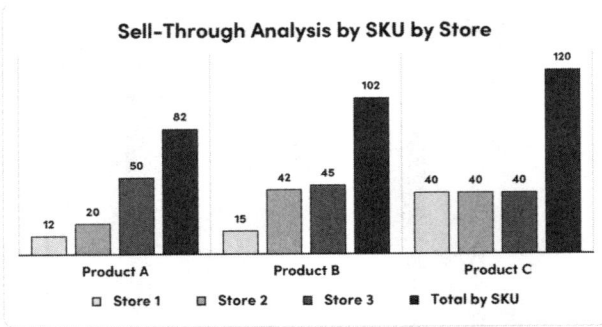

1) **Product C is the winner with the highest overall sell-through**

2) **Consistent sell-through across all stores**

**SKU-Level Conversion Analysis**

$$\frac{\text{SKU Sell-Through (Units)}}{\text{Store Traffic}}$$

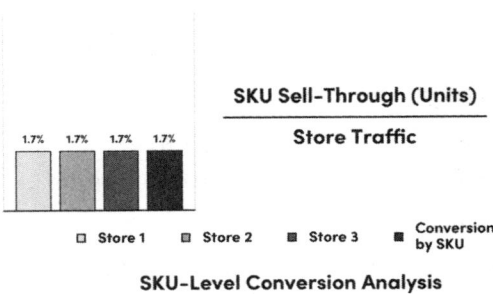

**Product A Conversion Rate**

$$\text{Store 1} = \frac{12}{700} = 1.7\% \text{ Conversion}$$

$$\text{Store 2} = \frac{20}{1,200} = 1.7\% \text{ Conversion}$$

$$\text{Store 3} = \frac{50}{3,000} = 1.7\% \text{ Conversion}$$

$$\text{Total} = \frac{82}{4,900} = 1.7\% \text{ Conversion}$$

Store 1 received 700 store visits, while Store 3 received 3,000 visits—the opportunity was much larger in Store 3, and this in part explains why they sold so many more units of Product A than the other stores did. From a pure sell-through perspective, Product A was the winner at Store 3, compared to Product B and C that sold only 45 and 40 units, respectively.

However, what the SKU conversion rate shows is that Product A had the exact same sell-through rate *relative* to the traffic each store received—1.7%. This is an important insight because it changes the conclusion and potentially the decision. Without a SKU-level conversion, the product team may have concluded that Product A was the clear winner at Store 3 and then decided to order much more of this product for Store 3, which would be a very reasonable decision based on sell-through.

**Sell-Through Analysis by SKU by Store**

Product A    Product B    Product C

□ Store 1    ▣ Store 2    ■ Store 3    ■ Total by SKU

Product A    Product B    Product C

□ Store 1    ▣ Store 2    ■ Store 3    ■ Conversion by SKU

**SKU-Level Conversion Analysis**

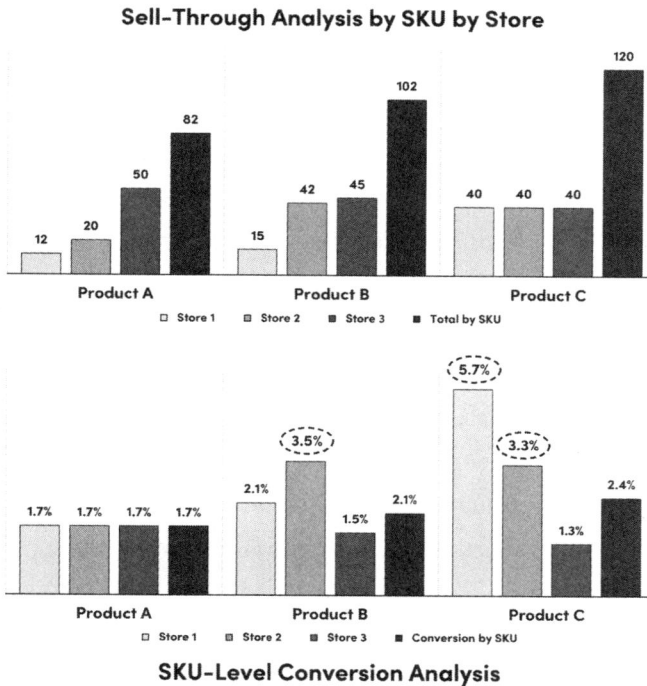

However, SKU-level conversion reveals that Product A had the same conversion rate across all three stores. The conversion rate of this SKU was no better than the other stores, but because Store 3 had so much more traffic, the sell-through made it appear to be a big winner.

Now let's examine the conversion performance of Product B across the three stores.

Overall, 102 units of Product B sold through all three stores. Compared to Product A, Product B had higher sell-through rates at Stores 1 and 2 but a slightly lower rate at Store 3.

When we calculate the conversion rates of Product B, we can see that it had higher conversion rates at Stores 1 and 2. In fact, the conversion rate at Store 2 was significantly higher—more than double Product A and significantly higher relative to the other stores. And that's the new insight that SKU-level conversion rate analysis can reveal.

Sell-through tells us that Product B sold twice as much as product A in Store 2, but the comparative conversion rates for this SKU to the other stores is where a new insight can be found.

In this case, Product B is a standout seller in Store 2 relative to its store traffic opportunity, even compared to Store 3 that sold more units—45 compared to only 42 at Store 2. In fact, Product B had the lowest conversion rate at Store 3, even though it sold more units than the other stores.

And finally, we come to Product C—the clear winner. Sell-through of this product was strongest at all three stores. You don't need conversion rates to come to this conclusion. But what the conversion rates of Product C reveal is that it didn't sell as consistently across all three stores as the sell-through rates indicate. In fact, conversion rates of Product C at Store 1 were significantly higher. Recall, Store 1 received the least traffic (i.e., had the smallest sales opportunity), so its sell-through of 40 units based on only 700 store visits makes this result extraordinary compared to the other stores.

In Store 2, Product C also had very strong performance with a 3.3% conversion rate, which was only slightly less than the conversion rate of Product B, which was 3.5%. At Store 3, Product C had a conversion rate of only 1.3%—the lowest SKU-level conversion rate of any of the products. It's still a strong-selling SKU based on units compared to the other products, but it's not a standout in this store like it is in Stores 1 and 2.

So what have we learned by calculating SKU-level conversion rates?

- Product A had the exact same conversion rate across all three stores. There was no standout performance in any of the stores, despite selling through the most units at Store 3 than any other product.

- Product B was a standout at Store 2 compared to the other stores on a conversion basis. Given the strong conversion results, this product may well be a good choice for Store 2, but not so much in Store 3 where its conversion rate was only 1.5%.

- Product C was the clear winner on a sell-through basis, but it could be a huge success based on the conversion rate performance of the SKU at Stores 1 and 2, but not so much at Store 3.

If product mix localization is all about finding signals about relative performance at the store level, then relying on sell-through alone tells only part of the story. Comparing sell-through to the store traffic opportunity contextualizes the sell-through results and reveals insights that you simply couldn't acquire from sell-through results alone.

If the goal is to find the ideal product mix for each store, then SKU-level conversion rates can help you do it. And you can't calculate SKU-level conversion without having store traffic data.

Beyond making more informed product mix localization decisions, there's another important way merchandisers and buyers can use store traffic and conversion insights, and that's to test new products.

## Mapping SKU-Level Conversion Rates Across All Stores

As the previous example illustrates, store traffic contextualizes results, and SKU-level conversion rates provide a mechanism to quantify the performance of an individual SKU or category of products in a way that removes the impact of store traffic volume on results and provides a clearer view of actual performance relative to a store's unique traffic opportunity.

Let's use another hypothetical example to see how SKU-level conversion rates could be used to measure the performance of any SKU across a large number of stores and help buying teams improve their ability to understand how any individual SKU is performing and identify opportunities to refine product mix allocations to each store. In this example, we will use a large chain with hundreds of stores.

The following scatterplot shows the conversion rate for the best-selling ocean-blue crewneck sweater in the chain. Each dot on the scatterplot represents the conversion rate of this best-selling sweater at every store in the chain. The conversion rate is on the vertical axis, and the average daily traffic of each store is shown on the horizontal axis. By visualizing the data this way, we can see how conversion rates for any given SKU vary across stores at every store traffic volume in the chain.

## SKU-Level Conversion Map—All Stores

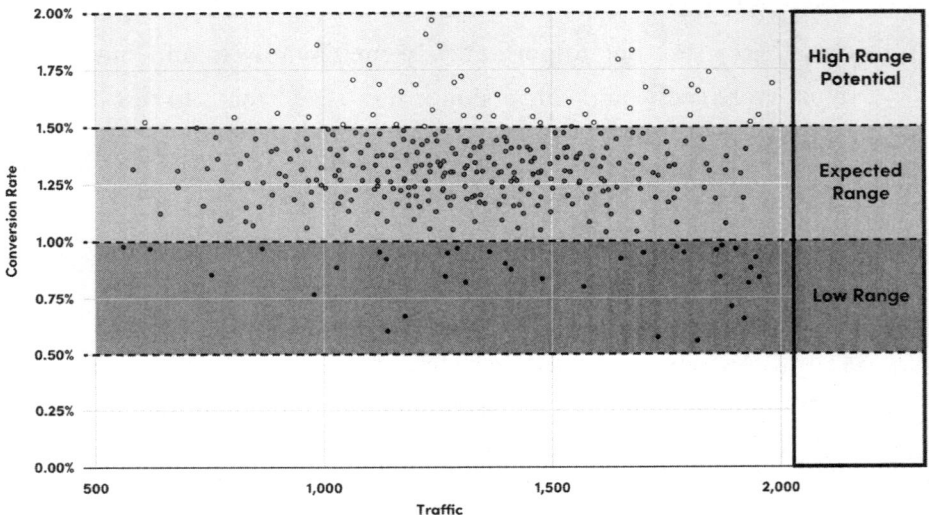

In most of the stores, conversion rates for this sweater range from 1% to 1.5%—referred to in the chart as the "expected range." As the chart shows, the conversion rate for this SKU is fairly consistent across all store traffic volumes.

Displaying the results this way enables you to not only assess the expected range of performance for a SKU, but also to see which stores are performing above and below the expected conversion rate range for any given SKU. When SKU conversion rates are in the "low range," it might be a result of the store not merchandising the product well, or it could be that this SKU is not attractive to the shoppers who visit these stores.

SKU conversion rates in the "high range" tell us that the SKU is outperforming the norm and additional allocations of this SKU may be required in these stores. And just like for SKUs in the low range, the superior conversion rate performance may be a function of exceptional merchandising treatment or selling effort in these stores, but more likely, it's a result of the SKU being more compelling to the shoppers who visit these stores.

The point of it all is that product buyers and merchandising teams now have a new perspective on SKU-level performance and new insights into what's possible in which stores.

## Using SKU-Level Conversion Rates to Assess New Product Performance

As I described in chapter 7, the only way to know if something works—or has a probability of success—is to experiment. The same applies to selecting new products to sell in stores.

Let's extend our example to now include the performance of a new SKU, a red V-neck sweater, in the same category and see how it compares to the best-selling SKU in that category. The new SKU was shipped to five test stores in the chain, and the conversion rates of the new SKU are indicated by the larger black dots on the following conversion rate performance scatterplot.

## SKU-Level Conversion Map—All Stores

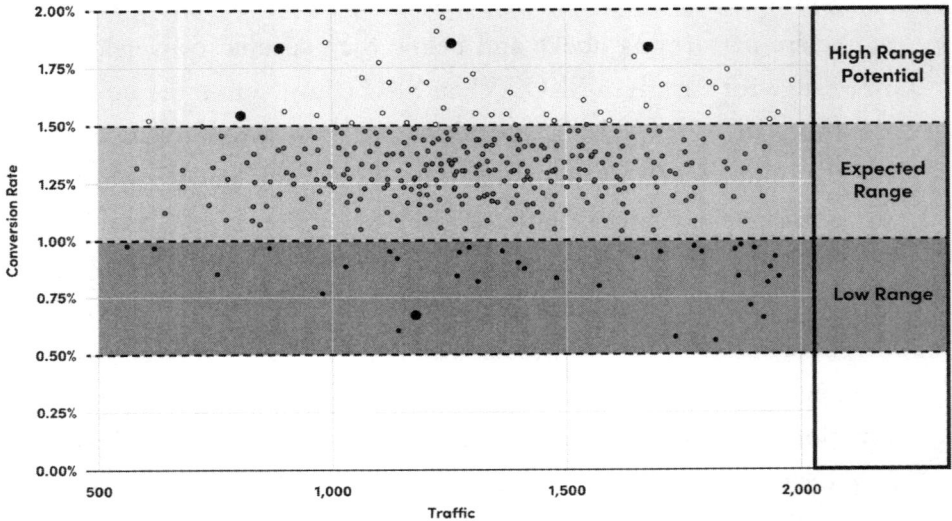

From a conversion rate perspective, the new SKU performed in the high range in four out of five test stores with conversion rates that rival the best-selling SKU in the category. In one store, the new SKU had a conversion rate in the low range.

While no one can say with certainty if a new SKU will be successful or not, by analyzing SKU-level conversion rates, product buyers will get different—and I believe better—signals of a SKU's performance relative to the store traffic opportunity that it is exposed to.

# SKU-Level Conversion
# Rate Analysis—Challenges

If you know the conversion rate of every SKU in every store and compare these conversion rates across stores, you will have a much deeper understanding of how any given SKU performs and be able to identify opportunities right down to the individual stores.

The goal of product mix localization is to have the right product at the right store, and by doing so, conversion rates and/or average sale values (collectively, sales per visitor) should increase—and that's the whole idea behind localization. Historically, a big part of the reason why this was challenging was due to the amount of data and limitations in tools to analyze it. But those days are long gone, and retailers have had the data and analytic tools to do SKU-level conversion rate analysis for years.

While many retailers I have encountered have been interested in exploring SKU and category conversion rates, the reality was that the amount of data that would need to be analyzed was simply too large and/or too difficult to compile. When you consider the number of SKUs a retailer might carry across every store, the numbers for large chains become astronomical. For example, a typical Walmart store carries around 120,000 SKUs. If you wanted to measure the SKU-level conversion rates of every one of these SKUs across their 4,700 stores, you would need to analyze 564M data points—that's a lot of data.

But while the constraints of big data may have been problematic in the past, access to powerful computer systems and data visualization tools for analyzing large data sets like this are now widely available. This is a use-case ideally suited to the strengths of artificial intelligence (AI).

Anytime you look to sell-through and sales outcomes to inform a decision, you should first examine the store traffic and conversion results to contextualize the results. Without the context store traffic data provides, you can't discern if the sell-through is high or low because it will depend upon how many shoppers were exposed to the product in the store. You should be able to answer the question: How did the SKU sell through versus the store traffic it was exposed to?

You might be wondering why the examples I've used in this chapter are hypothetical. In my twenty-one years as a traffic and conversion analytics practitioner, I have not encountered any retailer who consistently and strategically analyzes SKU-level conversion rates as I have in these hypothetical examples. This is not to say that there aren't some retailers who do this, but I haven't encountered them, and given the extensive experience I have working with retailers, I can only conclude that most retailers are simply not doing it.

Let's now move on from the hypothetical and delve into the real world of driving store traffic—which should be every retail marketer's goal—and measuring marketing impact.

## 🛒 Chapter Takeaways

- The effectiveness of product localization—tailoring merchandise to specific stores—can be enhanced by considering store traffic and conversion rates, not just sell-through data.

- Calculating SKU-level conversion rates offers a more nuanced understanding of product performance across different stores. It provides insights into how well a specific product converts into sales based on the store's unique traffic opportunity. These insights can inform better, more precise product mix and assortment decisions.

- Historically, analyzing SKU-level conversion rates across large retail chains was challenging due to the volume of data. However, advancements in technology and data analytics tools now make it feasible for retailers to leverage this data to optimize their merchandise localization strategies.

### PRACTITIONER'S ADVICE

- Go beyond sell-through rates and incorporate SKU-level conversion rates when making product mix decisions. This will give you a clearer understanding of which products resonate with the unique traffic at each store.

- Always contextualize product sell-through with store traffic data. A product might appear to perform well in one store simply because that store has more traffic, not because the product is a strong seller.

- Use available data analytics tools to manage and analyze large data sets, like SKU-level conversion rates, to refine your product localization strategies across stores.

- Analyze the SKU-level conversion rates across a sample of stores when introducing new products to gauge potential success before rolling them out chain-wide.

## CHAPTER 9

---

# Driving Store Traffic— The Retail Marketer's Goal

t's estimated that retailers in the United States collectively invest hundreds of billions in marketing and promotional spending annually.[1] Marketing remains one of the largest discretionary expenses for many retailers, and the overarching goal is to drive shopper traffic to their physical stores and websites.

Online visits play a critical role in driving traffic into physical stores since shoppers today frequently visit the retailer's website prior to visiting the physical store. By some estimates, 60% of shoppers visited online channels before completing their purchase in physical stores.[2]

Of course, marketing includes a wide array of activities, but for our discussion, I'll lump together all activities that retailers invest in to drive traffic to their stores, including traditional advertising, promotions, public relations, direct marketing, events, and numerous online activities, including social media. Given that driving traffic is the goal, it only stands to reason that measuring traffic—both in store and online—is the key measure of marketing effectiveness.

So how do retailers measure their marketing impact if they don't track store traffic? The answer is they can't—not reliably. A brief walk down memory lane for how I stumbled upon the importance of store traffic as the key measure of marketing will help illustrate.

## How I Discovered Store Traffic Is the Ultimate Marketing Measure

In 1993, I was the marketing manager for a large, single-location independent retail store that sold computers, software, and accessories. We were a successful business, with more than fifty employees and generating tens of millions of dollars in sales annually.

I began my career with the company as a sales associate, assisting customers in selecting the best personal computers for their needs as well as associated software and accessories. I worked in the store during the day and attended classes at university to complete my business degree in the evenings. Eventually, I took on the role of marketing manager and was in charge of creating marketing campaigns and promotions to help drive sales, and it was as the marketing manager that I had my store traffic "a-ha" moment.

We had just kicked off a major promotion, which was supported by newspaper ads, local TV commercials, and on-site radio remotes, where a radio deejay broadcasted live from our store and encouraged shoppers to visit. As the day progressed, the promotion appeared to be a surefire winner. The store was jam-packed with shoppers. But as the day went on, I couldn't help but notice that the sales associates weren't keeping up. They were simply not able to engage with every shopper, and I watched as many of these prospective buyers simply walked out without being served.

At the end of the day, the store owner (my boss) tallied up the sales, and remarked, "Well, that's disappointing . . . sales are OK, but I expected them to be a lot higher. I guess the promotion wasn't all that successful."

That irked me.

I didn't blame the owner for being disappointed by the lackluster sales, but it didn't seem correct to conclude that the promotion wasn't successful since the store was full of shoppers. The problem was that we didn't convert the traffic into sales.

It was at this very moment that I realized that if I wanted to truly understand the impact of the marketing investments and promotional effort, then the best measure would be store traffic counts and not sales outcomes—which were a function of how well our associates converted the shopper traffic into sales and had nothing to do with the promotion.

To my mind, the promotion did what it was supposed to do—drive prospective buyers into the store. However, if we were unable to convert the traffic because we didn't have enough sales associates, or if we ran out of product, or whatever the reason, it wasn't because the promotion didn't attract prospects. I decided that I needed to find a way to quantify the number of store visits we were receiving and then compare the visits to sales outcomes.

My boss back then believed—and too many retailers to this day believe—that driving sales is a function of driving store traffic without regard to what happens when the shopper visits the store and whether the visitor gets converted into a sale. Many retailers wrongly assume that improving sales is all about driving more traffic into the store and that everyone who can make a purchase will do so. This is a false assumption.

I was so convinced that counting store traffic was important that I set out to purchase a traffic counter for our store. After searching for some time, I finally found a company that offered a simple people-counting system. It was very basic—a couple of infrared beam sensors you attach to each side of the store entrance door frame. Every time a person enters the store, the beam sensor is tripped and logs a count.

It was exactly what I was looking for, and the $2,500 cost for the people counter seemed like a bargain compared to the $250,000 per year we were spending on marketing. If I could better evaluate our marketing efforts, then $2,500 would be a small price to pay. At least, that's what I thought.

When I pitched the idea to my boss, he was unconvinced. He said, "$2,500 is a lot to spend on this traffic counting gadget . . . we could do another radio remote for that sum!" I was shocked and disappointed by his response.

As the saying goes, necessity is the mother of invention. And what I discovered as a young retail marketer is that I needed to understand my store traffic. I was so convinced that store traffic data would be important to our business that I wasn't going to let my boss's reaction deter me. So I went to a couple of engineering students who also worked in the store part-time as they completed their studies, and asked if they could build me a people counter. Their answer: "Sure, no problem."

With $300 in components from a local RadioShack store—which I paid for out of my own pocket—and help from my engineering buddies, I built my own electronic people counter. We installed our traffic counter in the store with permission from my boss and started to collect store traffic counts. The insights were even more powerful than I had expected.

Not only did store traffic help us understand the impact of marketing, but we were also able to calculate our conversion rates by comparing store traffic and sales transaction counts. These insights helped us more effectively schedule staff to traffic, refine store operating hours, and inform a host of other decisions. Ultimately, store traffic data became a key input into virtually every major decision we made and how we operated our store.

It was about one year into this store traffic journey when I concluded that other retailers might also be interested in store traffic insights. With permission from my boss, I formally set up my company, HeadCount, as a side hustle, and I was in the traffic counting business. In my limited spare time, I started to approach local retailers and try to sell them my store traffic counters, but I was surprised to receive the same kind of objection that my boss initially gave me when I first pitched the idea.

I share my personal experience with store traffic counting as an example of how challenging it has been to encourage retailers to track their store traffic. And while store traffic counting and retailers' use of this data have advanced significantly over the past two decades, plenty of retailers still do not track store traffic, despite the obvious benefits of doing so.

## Marketing Impact on Traffic and Conversion

Let's return to our framework from chapter 1 illustrating how retail sales are generated.

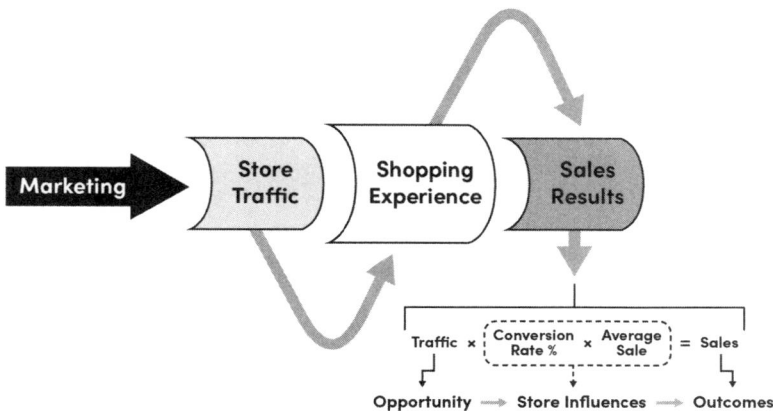

Effective marketing should drive traffic to stores, and if you track store traffic, you should see a signal in the traffic data. But as my experience as a marketing manager showed, too often retailers who don't have traffic data instead rely on sales outcomes as the measure of marketing effectiveness. This can send the wrong signal and misguide subsequent marketing efforts.

A marketing initiative may be very effective at driving store traffic, but if the traffic doesn't get converted into a sale, then you won't see the results in the sales outcomes. Or you may see a sales lift, but it might understate the traffic lift because of lower in-store conversion rates and/or average sale values.

Let's revisit the example from chapter 7 of the retailer who ran a one-day sale on the third Saturday of the month. The sales results for all four Saturdays of the month are shown in the upper half of the following chart. Based on sales alone, this wasn't a very effective promotion. Sales on the Saturday of the sale were the lowest of the entire month. This result seems completely improbable until we examine the store traffic and conversion results.

As it turns out, the promotion was very effective at driving traffic to the store. On the Saturday of the sale, store traffic soared to 3,100 visits—up from 2,500 the week prior and 2,400 visits the following week. Clearly, this promotion was a traffic success, so why are sales down?

The answer lies in the conversion rate, which was down dramatically. This store typically has a 68%–70% conversion rate, but on the day of the sale, it was down to only 48%.

## Average Sales: Saturday in Context

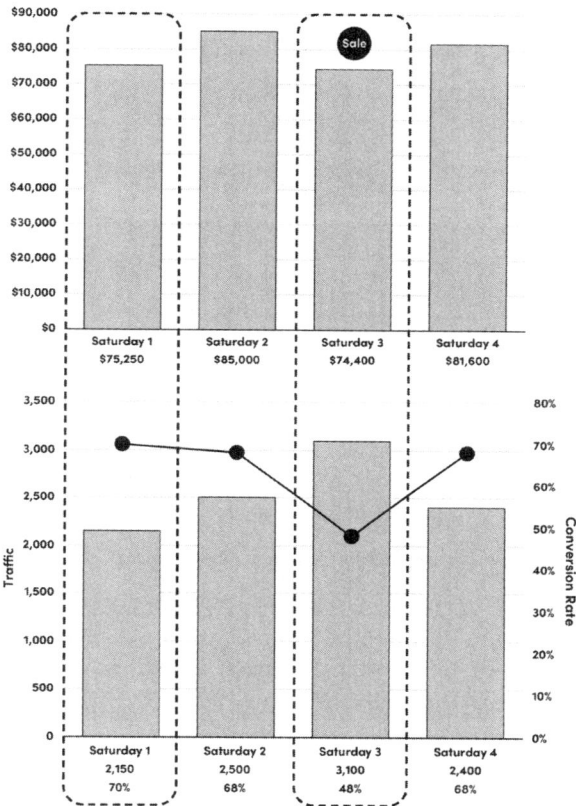

|  | Saturday 1 | Saturday 2 | Saturday 3 | Saturday 4 |
|--|-----------|-----------|-----------|-----------|
| Sales | $75,250 | $85,000 | $74,400 | $81,600 |
| Traffic | 2,150 | 2,500 | 3,100 | 2,400 |
| Conversion Rate | 70% | 68% | 48% | 68% |

Those retailers who believe that sales transaction counts are a close enough proxy for traffic would be equally mistaken. The following table shows the traffic, transaction count, and conversion rate for all four Saturdays.

|  | Saturday #1 | Saturday #2 | Saturday #3 SALE | Saturday #4 |
|--|------------|------------|------------------|------------|
| **Traffic Count** | 2,150 | 2,500 | 3,100 | 2,400 |
| **Transaction Count** | 1,505 | 1,700 | 1,488 | 1,632 |
| **Conversion Rate** | 70% | 68% | 48% | 68% |

Without traffic data, the true impact of the promotion could not be understood. Based on sales outcomes and transaction counts alone, this retailer may have concluded that the promotion was ineffective and decided to try something different next time.

In this case, the drop in conversion rate made this promotion look bad when it was actually very effective at driving store traffic. Knowing this, management can focus their attention on why conversion rates dropped so significantly during the promotion instead of looking for a new marketing program.

The primary job of retail marketing is to drive store traffic opportunities, but it can also impact conversion rates, which is why it's important to look at both metrics.

## Comparing Promotional Impact with Traffic and Conversion Rates

Some retailers run the same promotions every year, so we use store traffic and conversion rate results to help understand the year-over-year (YoY) performance of each promotion. The following real-world example will illustrate.

A 250-store specialty retailer was interested in understanding the relative performance of five major promotions that they conduct every year, so we analyzed the YoY percentage change in store traffic and conversion rates for each of the promotions, as illustrated in the following chart.

## YoY Traffic and Conversion Rate by Promotion

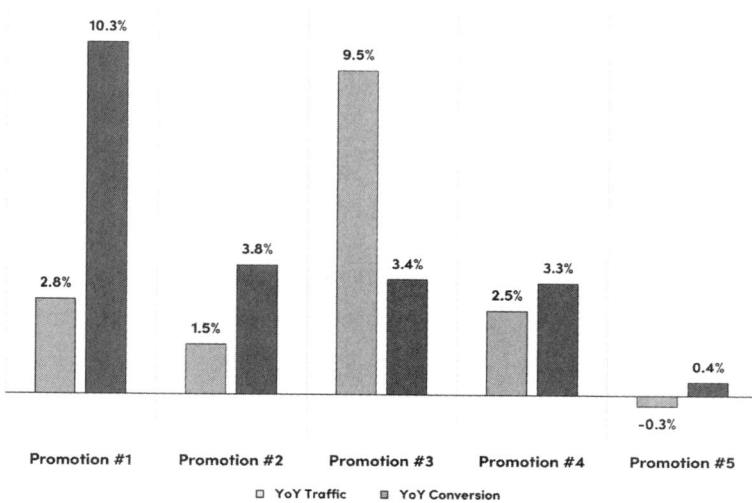

While the primary objective is to drive store traffic, promotional activity can also impact conversion rates. For example, an effective promotion that is targeted to the right audience may not deliver a significant traffic increase, but conversion rates may increase by virtue of attracting more "qualified" prospects to the store who are more inclined to purchase.

For example, Promotion #1 had a traffic increase of only 2.8% versus the prior year; however, conversion rates soared, up 10.3% compared to the prior year. For this promotion, aggressive price points on popular items were the likely cause of the conversion rate increase, even though store traffic was up only 2.8%.

By contrast, Promotion #3 saw a significant increase in YoY traffic—this promotion was obviously very effective at driving store traffic. But it wasn't just more traffic. Here, conversion rates were also up 3.4% versus the prior year—higher traffic and higher conversion rates combined to deliver exceptional sales outcomes.

Both promotions had a material impact but in different ways, and that's why examining both traffic and conversion is important.

What about Promotion #5? Traffic was slightly down from the prior year, and conversion rates hardly budged. This promotion wasn't effective, and these results make that clear.

## Promotional Impact by Store— Every Store Is Different

While the roll-up results across the entire chain provide a view of overall impact, in order to really understand the impact and to make the most of the sales opportunities the promotion provides, you need to examine each store in the chain. Every store is unique, and how impactful a promotion is can vary significantly by store.

The following chart shows the YoY change in traffic and conversion rates by store for a sample of stores during one of the promotional periods. The results are displayed from highest traffic response to lowest with corresponding conversion rates.

### YoY Traffic and Conversion Rate by Store

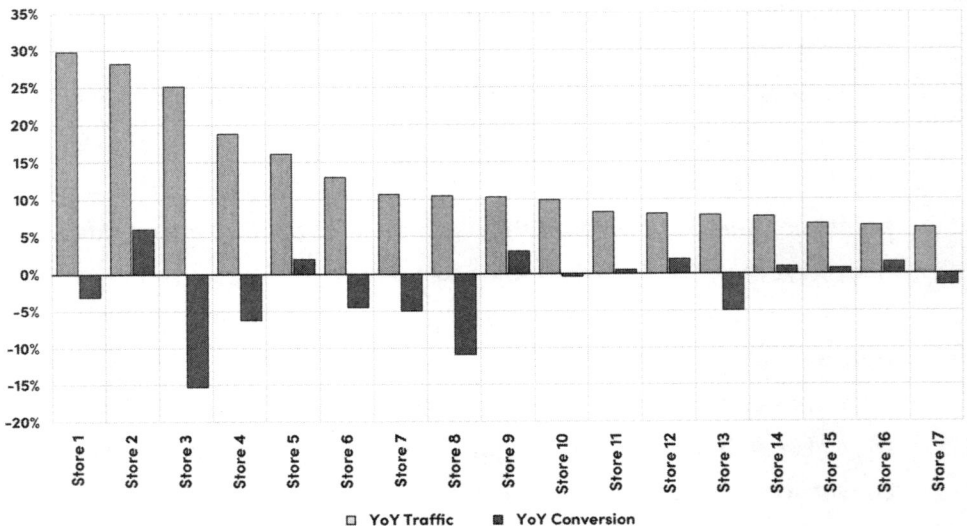

Some stores saw a significant increase in traffic while others had more modest increases in traffic. But what's also noteworthy is that conversion rates in some stores were also down.

Traffic and conversion rates tend to be inversely related, especially in assisted sales environments where interaction with a sales associate is required, as was the case with this chain. When the store gets too busy, the store team can struggle to convert all the new sales opportunities that visit the store—just like I experienced as the marketing manager of a computer store.

## Precision Targeting Promotional Traffic to the Right Stores

As the previous example illustrates, the impact of promotions on store traffic and conversion rates varies by store. Some stores might see a significant increase in traffic while others will see hardly any. Understanding the results by store will enable the marketing team to better target their promotional efforts and refine promotional messages and other campaign elements to maximize results across all stores.

But even if the promotion drives more traffic into the store, it's not a given that the traffic will be converted into a sale. If a store is understaffed, the store team is undertrained, or the store has insufficient inventory levels, the cost and effort of driving traffic to these locations is inefficient at best and could actually hurt future sales. For example, if underserved shoppers have a poor store experience, they may tell their friends or, worse, post a negative review on social media to tell the entire world about it.

In chapter 4, I presented an approach to mapping traffic and conversion performance across all stores in a chain with hundreds of stores. Recall, stores located in quadrant three were stores that had low store traffic and low conversion rates relative to the chain average.

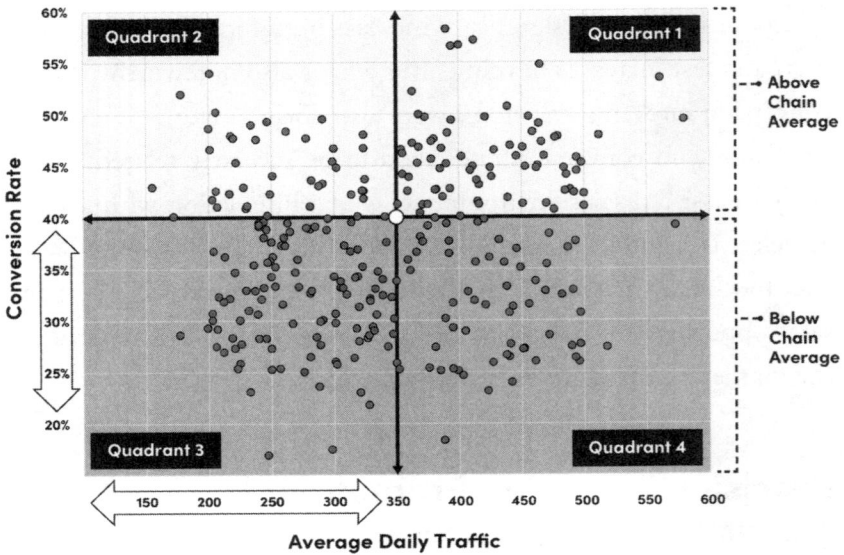

This same analysis can aid marketers in precision-targeting their promotional spend to the stores that have the best ability to convert the traffic they receive. Stores in quadrants one and two have conversion rates above the chain average, and directing more traffic to these stores will likely produce the best sales outcomes.

Moreover, before you drive more promotional traffic to stores in quadrants with low conversion rates, and especially stores in quadrant three that have low traffic and low conversion, the store operations teams first need to focus on improving conversion performance in these locations—before they get more traffic.

## Isolating Marketing Activities— What Drove What?

The prior example nicely fits into discrete, tidy promotional efforts that are easy to isolate and measure. But as we well know, it's not always so simple. The following chart shows the actual promotional activities for a general merchandise retailer over the course of one month.

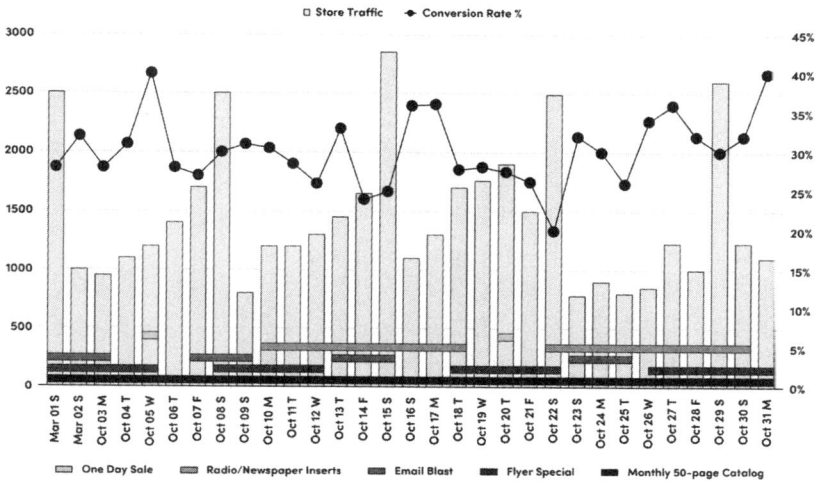

Obviously, there's a lot going on here. There's not just one flyer or one promotion, there's a whole bunch of them, and they overlap. Throw weather into the mix and you start to wonder exactly what, if anything, you can discern from the results. With so much going on, even with the benefit of store traffic and conversion analysis, it's difficult to get a handle on what's driving what. And some retailers use this complexity as an excuse for not measuring, reasoning, "It's unmeasurable, so why bother?"

Unquestionably, a promotional plan like the one shown here presents measurement challenges, even with traffic and conversion insights. But it doesn't mean you shouldn't try. While traffic and conversion analysis will not magically make it any easier to precisely measure every aspect of a complex promotional schedule like this example, it will provide additional context and insights that you could not have had otherwise.

When retailers aggressively promote by layering campaign on campaign for a solid fifty-two weeks of the year, they need to ask: What would happen if you took something away? What if you ran one less flyer, reduced the size of some of your print ads, or discontinued one flight of radio?

When your only measure is sales, the risk seems high. What if sales go down? Without context, it's a guess, and it seems risky. However, with traffic and conversion data, you have the context you need to confidently experiment. Experimentation is the only way to discover new, potentially more effective approaches that can help you make the most of every marketing dollar you invest.

## What's Your Store Traffic Worth?

If store traffic is valuable, then we should be able to assign a value to it. Knowing how much each store visit is worth can enable retail marketers to assess the return on investment (ROI) for any promotion or advertising campaign.

So what is your store traffic worth, and how can you assess its value? A look at how it's done online will give you a good place to start.

The cost to market online is driven by two primary metrics: [1] cost-per-thousand impressions (CPM) and [2] cost-per-click (CPC).

CPM is the number of impressions the ad receives online, and media platforms typically charge a fee for every one thousand impressions they deliver. The more targeted the impressions, the higher the CPM cost. CPC refers not to the number of people who see your ad, but rather to the number who actually click on it to acquire more information or take some action.[3] With CPC, advertisers pay a fee every time someone clicks on their ad, so they are only paying for visitors who have expressed intention, and this is reflected in the higher fees that CPC commands.

Google Ads is the gorilla of the online marketing world, with Meta Ads (formally known as Facebook Ads) not far behind. What makes these media platforms so valuable is the massive volume of online traffic they can access and their ability to target ads to people with the characteristics that are most likely to make them interested in what you're selling.

The CPM and CPC vary by industry, campaign type, and numerous other factors such as the use of video. As of late 2024, Google charges between $6 and $30 CPM and a CPC of $4 to $5. Meta has a CPM of about $10 and a CPC of around $0.55.[4] Google can charge more than Meta because ads displayed when someone does a Google search are thought to be more qualified, and the same rationale explains why their CPC is so much higher compared to Meta's, where ads on Facebook are more likely viewed during casual browsing versus intentional shopping.

What are the "impressions" and "click" equivalents for physical stores? The answer is store traffic. If we use Google Ad rates for CPM and CPC and apply these rates to the store traffic, we can assign a value to the store traffic. But let's first explore the question: Is a store visit an "impression" or a "click"?

I strongly argue that a store visit is much more than an impression. An impression is more akin to a person driving by the store. I would even argue that a store visit is more valuable than a click. Here's why. How much effort does it take to click on an ad? Hardly any. You can click on an ad in a second or two, and then you can click on something else seconds later. A store visit requires significantly more effort and time, and therefore when a shopper enters a store, their intention is significantly higher than a click. This explains why conversion rates in physical stores are so much higher than they are online.

But even if we use the Google CPC rate of $5 and apply it to store visits, the dollar value of these visits would be beyond belief for most retailers. In my experience, retailers don't often consider the value of their store traffic—but they should.

| | 1,000-Store Chain | 100-Store Chain | 10-Store Chain |
|---|---|---|---|
| **Annual Store Traffic** | 543,000,000 | 28,800,000 | 360,000 |

| | 1,000-Store Chain | 100-Store Chain | 10-Store Chain |
|---|---|---|---|
| **Google CPM= $10** | $5,430,000 | $288,000 | $3,600 |

| | 1,000-Store Chain | 100-Store Chain | 10-Store Chain |
|---|---|---|---|
| **Google CPC= $5** | $2,715,000,000 | $144,000,000 | $1,800,000 |

In the one-thousand-store general merchandise chain, stores on average received 1,500 visits per day, and stores were open 362 days per year (closed only for Easter Sunday, Thanksgiving Day, and Christmas Day). If the store traffic counts seem extraordinarily high, here's how it adds up: 1,500 visits per day x 1,000 stores x 362 operating days = 543M annual visits. If these 543M store visits were valued at $5 each, they would be worth a whopping $2.715 billion—yes, billion.

But even in a small specialty chain with only ten stores, at an average of 100 store visits per day, per store, over 360 operating days (this chain was closed on more days), the total annual visits are 360,000, and the CPC value at $5 per visit would be worth $1.8 million.

Calculating the value of store traffic using CPC makes for an interesting exercise that should captivate retail marketers. For most retailers, their traffic is worth more than Google's $5 CPC—a lot more.

In fact, there is a way to precisely calculate the value of a store visit, and that is by calculating sales per visitor.

# Sales per Visitor—What's Your Store Traffic Actually Worth?

There are only two ways the store team can drive sales outcomes, and that's by converting store visitors into buyers and by increasing the amount that each buyer purchases. But whether a store drives sales by increasing conversion rates or average sale, and ideally both, the goal is the same—to produce sales.

Comparing the total store traffic to the total sales the store produces enables you to calculate the value that each traffic count represented in sales. You can calculate the sales per visitor by simply dividing sales by store traffic or by multiplying the conversion rate by the average sale value.

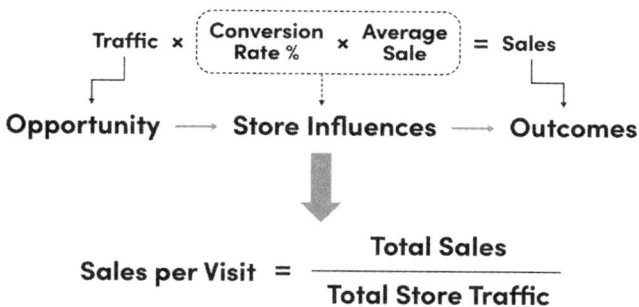

$$\text{Traffic} \times \left( \text{Conversion Rate \%} \times \text{Average Sale} \right) = \text{Sales}$$

Opportunity $\longrightarrow$ Store Influences $\longrightarrow$ Outcomes

$$\text{Sales per Visit} = \frac{\text{Total Sales}}{\text{Total Store Traffic}}$$

Understanding how much in sales stores are producing per visitor enables marketers to financially quantify the sales value equivalent of a store visit. A real-world example will help illustrate.

The following chart shows the sales per visitor results for a 138-store chain of discount department stores. The most productive store was generating $39 in sales for every visitor who entered the store, while the lowest was generating only $9 for every store visit it received. The average across the entire chain was $29 in sales per visitor. For this chain, generating $29 per visitor is almost six times higher than the CPC of $5 per visit that Google charges.

## Sales per Visitor by Store—March 2024

*Based on 138 Stores

Knowing that the stores produce $29 in sales for every visitor is an important insight for the marketing team as they plan marketing efforts and consider payback on these investments. But before we get to calculating a return on marketing investment using sales per visitor results, we need to examine how the results vary by store.

## Sales per Visitor by Store— Every Store Is Different

While the roll-up results across the entire chain reveal that average sales per visitor is $29, what becomes clear when you compare the results by store is that some stores are simply way more productive than others.

## Sales per Visitor by Store—March 2024

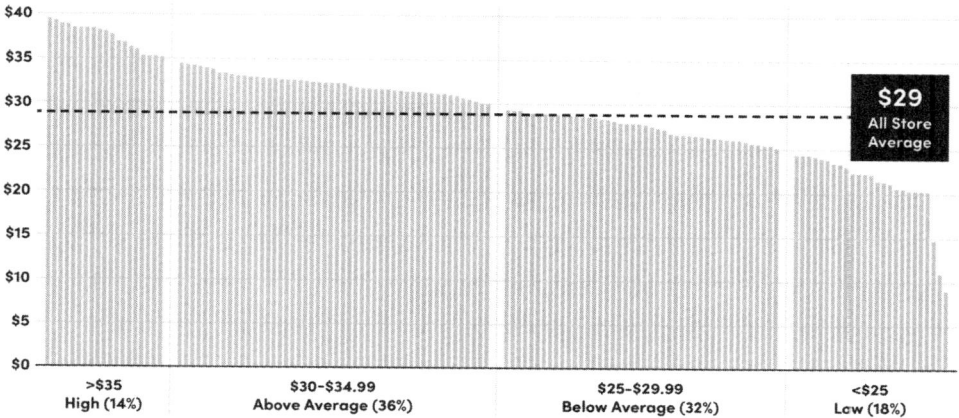

In this chain, almost half the stores were producing sales per visitor of $30–$39. Since marketing efforts can be targeted to specific regions, geographies, and even individual stores, marketers can further improve the ROI on their marketing investments by allocating more marketing efforts to the stores with higher sales per visitor results.

Having sales per visitor results for each store will enable marketers to pinpoint exactly which stores should produce the best results and where the promotional traffic should be directed.

## Using Sales per Visitor to Calculate Marketing Campaign ROI

Let's walk through a quick, hypothetical example to illustrate how this is done.

A chain with 138 stores averaged 700 visits per day per store in September of the prior year. Across all 138 stores, this amounted to approximately 2.9M store visits that month (i.e., 138 stores x 700 daily visits x 30 operating days = 2.9M).

The objective for the fall marketing campaign was to increase September store traffic by 10% versus the prior year. A 10% increase in store traffic would produce almost 290,000 incremental visits. If each of these visits generates $29 in sales and the campaign meets its traffic goal, then it should generate approximately $8.4 million in incremental sales and about $2.5 million in gross profit based on the chain's 30% average gross profit margin.

If the cost of the marketing campaign is $1 million, then the ROI on the campaign is as follows:

$$\text{ROI} = \left( \frac{\text{Gross Profit - Total Campaign Cost}}{\text{Total Campaign Cost}} \right) \times 100$$

$$\text{ROI} = \left( \frac{\$2.5M - \$1.0M}{\$1.0M} \right) \times 100 = 150\%$$

Based on this calculation, every dollar the chain invests in the fall marketing campaign should deliver $1.50 of incremental gross profit, resulting in a 150% return on the $1 million marketing investment.

Since this ROI calculation is based only on incremental store traffic generated, it is likely understating the full impact of the marketing campaign since some existing shoppers who would have visited the store anyway may choose to buy more because of the fall campaign, so sales per visitor results may also increase.

The point of all of this is that store traffic does have a value, and that value can be expressed in expected sales per visitor.

The marketing team could have simply stated that their campaign goal was to generate an incremental $8.4 million in gross sales and $2.5 million in gross profit. But remember, marketing doesn't produce sales—the store team does by converting the store traffic into sales and by increasing average sale values, which when combined define sales per visitor.

Therefore, the primary goal of marketing should be to drive sales opportunities to stores. The store team's job is to convert those traffic opportunities into sales. With store traffic data, marketers can make better decisions that produce better sales outcomes and better ROI on the marketing investments they make. And it's all made possible with store traffic data.

## Monetizing Store Traffic— In-Store Retail Media Networks

According to many retail industry experts, brick-and-mortar stores will become one of the most important media platforms for some retailers.[5] That's right, the physical store as a medium for engaging customers, creating experiences, and selling product.

I agree. In fact, I'd argue that the physical store is already among the most important media platforms for retailers to connect brands they carry with the shoppers who visit their stores.

The value of traditional media is, in part, established by the exposure to prospective buyers it can deliver. For example, in 2023 the total print circulation of the *New York Times* was approximately 330,000 per day on weekdays and 850,000 on weekends.[6] Store traffic counts represent the exposure a retailer can offer any brand.

Store traffic counts are analogous to circulation counts of a newspaper. By having store traffic data, retailers can build a case to brands for what they should expect to get in exposure for in-store marketing activities such as endcaps, digital displays, shelf-talkers, and other physical advertising opportunities within the store. The retailers can then generate incremental revenue from these activities by charging brands for the exposure.

But store traffic data isn't only useful for the retailers that are large enough to warrant a formal in-store retail media network, like Walmart, for example, which currently has the largest in-store retail media network in the United States across their massive 4,700-store base.

In fact, when I was the marketing manager of a single-location computer store, I used to solicit marketing development funds (also referred to as "co-op marketing") from the brands of products we sold in the store to help support our marketing efforts, and I used store traffic data to justify the rates I would charge these brands. My brand representatives regularly told me that no other retailers they worked with provided store traffic counts to support their funding requests, which made my requests more compelling.

Any retailer of any size can do this if they have store traffic data at their disposal.

Driving more store traffic is the goal, and store traffic and conversion rate data can help measure the impact and efficacy of these investments. Moreover, the nature and intention of store visits is changing, and it's being driven in part by the new services shoppers expect to get in-store; and that's what we will explore in the next chapter.

# 🛒 Chapter Takeaways

- Retail marketing's primary objective is to drive traffic to physical stores and online platforms, and tracking store traffic is essential for accurately measuring marketing effectiveness—just like retailers do on their e-commerce websites.

- Store traffic is a crucial metric that allows retailers to evaluate marketing effectiveness beyond sales outcomes, which are also influenced by conversion rates and operational factors that have nothing to do with marketing efforts.

- A promotion that successfully drives traffic may not always result in high sales if conversion rates are low, making it important to assess both traffic and conversion rates. Retailers often mistakenly equate sales outcomes solely with marketing effectiveness, ignoring the critical role of store conversion rates.

- Store visits can be monetized similarly to online metrics like CPM (cost-per-thousand impressions) and CPC (cost-per-click), and retailers should assess the value of their store traffic in financial terms like sales per visitor to optimize marketing ROI.

- With store traffic data, marketers can calculate the sales per visitor and then use this data to calculate the ROI of their investments.

- The physical store is evolving into an essential media platform where retailers can connect brands with consumers, and store traffic data is analogous to newspaper circulation figures, which can be used to monetize in-store advertising opportunities.

- By understanding and leveraging store traffic data, retailers of all sizes can enhance their marketing effectiveness, improve conversion rates, and generate additional revenue through in-store retail media networks or by accessing marketing support from the brands of the products they carry.

## PRACTITIONER'S ADVICE

- Target marketing efforts precisely by using traffic and conversion data to allocate resources to stores that will yield the highest ROI based on their conversion rate, average sales, and collectively, sales per visitor results.

- Recognize that traffic response to a promotion or marketing activity will vary across stores—some stores will have a higher traffic response rate than others. Marketers can better understand the impact by analyzing store-level results and comparing them across stores.

- Understand how each store's field leaders oversee response to marketing activity and ensure that store teams are equipped to handle increased traffic effectively.

- Measure conversion rates. This is important because a marketing activity may attract more qualified buyers, resulting in higher conversion rates even if overall traffic does not increase much.

# CHAPTER 10

---

# The Impact of Shopper Services on Store Traffic, Conversion, and the Amazon Effect

For many years, retailers have been expanding in-store services to create a better, more streamlined experience for shoppers. A big reason for this is to simplify and better coordinate the online and in-store experiences, which is vital when you consider that sales in physical stores are greatly influenced by shoppers' online activity.

To provide a more seamless experience from online to in-store, retailers have implemented services like buy online, pick up in store (BOPIS); buy online, return in store (BORIS); and curbside pickup. And while retailers were offering these services well before the pandemic of 2020, the pandemic accelerated demand for these services, which have now become essential for many shoppers.[1]

It's hard to deny that the implementation of these new services was good for shoppers and retailers—notwithstanding the execution challenges some retailers experienced. What was less understood was the impact these new services would have on store traffic and conversion trends.

## BOPIS, BORIS, and Curbside Pickup— Impact on Store Traffic and Conversion

Anything that changes or impacts shoppers' behaviors has the potential to affect the store traffic and conversion results. Let's walk through some examples of how these services impact store traffic and conversion, starting with one of the most popular and pervasive services, BOPIS, with almost a third of shoppers saying that they used it in 2024.[2]

### BUY ONLINE, PICK UP IN STORE (BOPIS)— IMPACT ON TRAFFIC AND CONVERSION

Today, BOPIS is widely available, especially among the largest retailers. Thoughtful retailers offer services customers want, and BOPIS is certainly one of the most popular—it's not hard to understand why. Customers get the convenience of buying online and avoid the delivery hassles and cost by simply visiting the store that's most convenient for them and picking up the order there. This saves shipping fees and gives the customer a reason to visit the store location, where they might make an additional purchase.

Retailers have been refining their processes and procedures for managing BOPIS orders for years, and some have become very adept at delivering an efficient and reliable BOPIS experience—so much so that today many shoppers expect a seamless experience regardless of how they engage with a retailer.

Services like BOPIS have become table stakes in the battle for customers, so offering this service is not only a "nice to have," but also it is increasingly a "must have."

However, a store visit generated by a BOPIS order creates a different kind of store visit intention compared to a shopper who visits with the intention to make a purchase. The BOPIS customer is there to retrieve their online order and may or may not be interested in browsing for other items or have any interest in making an additional purchase. This can have a material impact on store traffic patterns and conversion rates that retailers should be mindful of. Here's a simple hypothetical example to illustrate.

Before there was a BOPIS program, the store depicted in the following illustration had ten traffic counts and five in-store transactions for a 50% conversion rate. After the retailer launched a BOPIS program, their store traffic went up from ten counts to twelve. There were five in-store sales transactions, not including the BOPIS activity.

Three of the twelve traffic counts generated were "pre-converted" since they purchased online before the customer came to the store to pick up. In this case, these BOPIS customers didn't generate a new sales transaction because the transaction was conducted online. However, when the shopper entered the store to pick up their online purchase, they generated a traffic count.

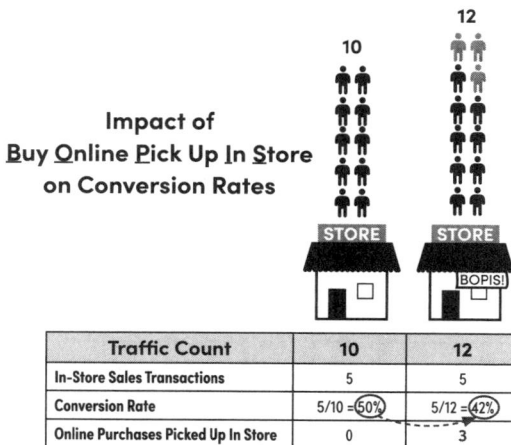

Impact of
Buy Online Pick Up In Store
on Conversion Rates

| Traffic Count | 10 | 12 |
|---|---|---|
| In-Store Sales Transactions | 5 | 5 |
| Conversion Rate | 5/10 = 50% | 5/12 = 42% |
| Online Purchases Picked Up In Store | 0 | 3 |

If you don't track the BOPIS transactions and factor them into your conversion rates, then the only thing that you can conclude from the data is that your store traffic is up and conversion rates have dropped from 50% to 42% in this example.

If you are incentivizing the store team on conversion rate performance in any way, realize that the BOPIS dynamic will likely negatively impact conversion rates, unless you account for them in some way.

In order to get a more accurate assessment of in-store conversion rate (i.e., sales made by shoppers visiting the store to shop), one approach is to remove the BOPIS visitor counts (as measured by the number of BOPIS orders filled in the store) from the traffic count used to calculate the store's conversion rate and then recalculate conversion based on this adjusted store traffic number.

By deducting the store visits generated by the BOPIS customers, the store's conversion rate in this example would increase from 42% to 56% since the five in-store sales transactions would now be compared against only nine store visits, excluding the BOPIS customers.

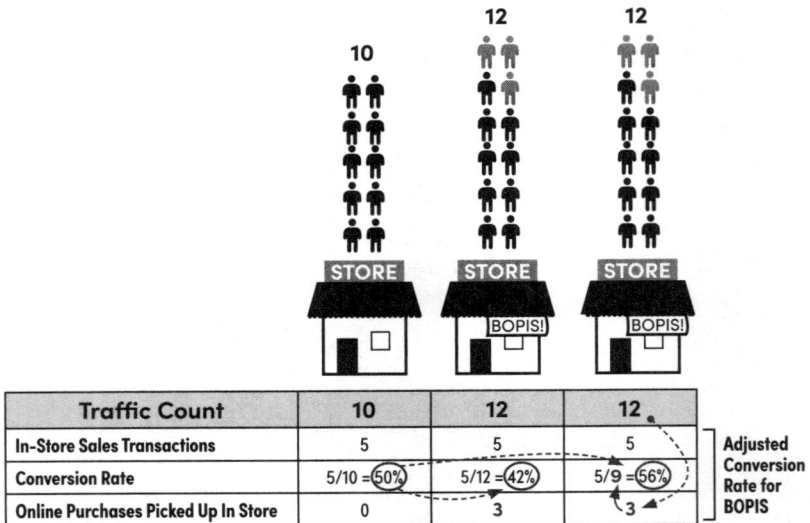

| Traffic Count | 10 | 12 | 12 | |
|---|---|---|---|---|
| In-Store Sales Transactions | 5 | 5 | 5 | Adjusted Conversion Rate for BOPIS |
| Conversion Rate | 5/10 = 50% | 5/12 = 42% | 5/9 = 56% | |
| Online Purchases Picked Up In Store | 0 | 3 | 3 | |

This approach is not perfect since some of the BOPIS customers may have also made an in-store purchase in addition to picking up their online order. If this occurs, then conversion rates will be overstated since we removed the BOPIS visit from the store traffic counts but did log a new sales transaction, which factors into the conversion rate calculation.

While I'm not a fan of adjusting store traffic numbers because any form of data manipulation can introduce errors, it's important to ensure that the store team is clear about what's driving conversion rates and how they can influence the results. When store teams are focused on driving conversion performance and then they see a drop in results because of a new service that changes store traffic intention or patterns, I would err on the side of slightly overstating conversion, which will be more encouraging for the store team.

But it's not just picking up online purchases in store that impacts results. Any store visit that gets counted but wasn't intentionally made to make a purchase will influence results, such as product returns.

## BUY ONLINE, RETURN IN STORE (BORIS)— IMPACT ON TRAFFIC AND CONVERSION

In this case, the shopper purchased online, and the product was shipped to their home, but the customer decided to return the item to the physical store. This is a smart service for retailers to offer since it gives the customer a reason to visit the store as well as an opportunity for the store team to sell the customer something else. It can also reduce the cost of processing and managing returns for the retailer.

But just like with BOPIS, these BORIS store visitors get counted by the traffic counter, and if they do not make a new purchase, then their visit will also have downward pressure on in-store conversion rates.

With BOPIS and BORIS, the customer enters the store and generates a traffic count but may or may not generate a new sales transaction. By carefully tracking the BOPIS and BORIS activity, retailers can choose to adjust their store traffic and/or their expectations about in-store conversion rate targets as they see fit. Every retailer should decide the best approach for their business, and there is no one right way to do it.

But not all services create incidental store traffic. In fact, there is another popular service that reduces store traffic—curbside pickup.

## CURBSIDE PICKUP—IMPACT ON TRAFFIC AND CONVERSION

The idea of offering a service that eliminates the need for shoppers to visit the store seems like a bad idea. Why wouldn't retailers want customers to enter the store?

The fact is, there are many reasons why this is a valuable service for shoppers, and when executed well by the retailer, it can enhance shopper satisfaction and build loyalty.[3]

During the pandemic of 2020, many retailers were required to enforce strict occupancy limits that restricted in-store traffic, and curbside helped reduce some in-store traffic. For retailers deemed "nonessential" and who were forced to close their stores, curbside pickup was virtually the only way they could generate sales.

In post-pandemic times, curbside pickup remains a value-add service that many customers still want since it can be a real time saver and is more convenient than entering the store. For example, consider a mom with a couple of young children. Instead of the hassle of transferring the children from car seats to a shopping cart and then navigating the store with the distraction that small children can create, this mom simply drives up at her predetermined time, and the goods are brought outside to her car.

Curbside pickup impacts store traffic and conversion trends in several ways. If the retailer's curbside pickup location is positioned near the store's main entrance, then extraneous traffic counts will get logged when store team members leave and re-enter the store after delivering the order to the curbside customer. Modern traffic counters won't log a count when the employee leaves the store, but a count will be logged when they re-enter the store. In this regard, the traffic count logged by the store employee acts as a proxy for the visit the curbside pickup customer would have generated if they had entered the store, so the traffic counts won't be significantly impacted. But just like with BOPIS, the best approach is to be consistent. If the transaction is included in the store's results, you should count the traffic; if the transaction is excluded from the store's results, you should exclude the traffic count.

The impact on conversion rates is more nuanced. If the curbside order generated a new sales transaction for the store and is therefore included in the conversion rate calculation, then no adjustments are required. The traffic count generated by the employee as proxy for the customer visit is counted in the conversion calculation for the store, so the results will be the same as if the customer actually entered the store and made the purchase.

However, if the curbside pickup transaction is captured through a different system (e.g., online order system that treats these transactions as separate from store-generated sales transactions), then just like BOPIS and BORIS, in-store conversion rates will be suppressed since traffic counts are being generated with no associated sales transaction.

So much of how a retailer should account for the impact of these services on their store traffic and conversion results depends on how they implement them. But regardless of what services are being offered or considered, retailers need to be mindful about how these initiatives will impact store traffic and conversion rates. A good way to do that is by comparing the activity levels of the services to the traffic a store receives.

A hypothetical example will help illustrate.

The average daily store traffic counts for three stores in a chain were compared to their respective BOPIS, BORIS, and curbside pickup activity, and the results are shown in the following table.

| | Average Daily Store Traffic | BOPIS Orders | % of Traffic | BORIS Returns | % of Traffic | Curbside Pickup Orders | % of Traffic | Total Service Transac- tions | % of Traffic |
|---|---|---|---|---|---|---|---|---|---|
| **Store A** | 500 | 5 | 1.0% | 3 | 0.6% | 5 | 1.0% | 13 | 2.6% |
| **Store B** | 600 | 30 | 5.0% | 25 | 4.2% | 22 | 3.7% | 77 | 12.8% |
| **Store C** | 1,000 | 25 | 2.5% | 20 | 2.0% | 20 | 2.0% | 65 | 6.5% |

Most retailers track the number of service transactions their stores complete, so the activity level created by these services is generally understood by most retailers that offer them. But merely counting the number of service transactions doesn't tell the whole story. The real insights come when you compare the number of service transactions to the amount of traffic a store receives.

For example, Store B processes 30 BOPIS orders on average per day, and Store C does 25. If we only compared these transaction counts, we would conclude that Stores B and C were comparable in their BOPIS activity. However, when you compare the BOPIS transactions to store traffic and then calculate the percentage of

BOPIS activity relative to traffic, you get a different and more actionable insight.

As a percentage of total store traffic, Store B has twice as much BOPIS activity as Store C does—5.0% versus 2.5%. And when we add up all the service transactions and compare them as a percentage of traffic that each store receives, Store B has almost double the activity as Store C and five times as much activity as Store A. As the saying goes, forewarned is forearmed. With these new insights, the retailer can adjust store-level operations in the stores to account for the demand for these services and deliver a better experience for customers.

It's worth repeating: There is no one right answer. Every retailer will approach this differently based on their specific objectives and capabilities to deliver. The important point is that you need to pick an approach and apply it consistently across stores. Retailers must also carefully consider how these new services will impact the store team and their ability to serve shoppers, as this too can impact conversion rates.

## Store Labor and New Services— Proceed with Caution

Offering services that provide a seamless experience between online and physical stores has become an expectation for many shoppers, and the most successful retailers are investing to deliver these services for their customers. However, any retailer who wants to offer new services in their physical stores should understand the impact that these services will have on the in-store experience, store traffic, conversion results, and frontline store personnel who are responsible for providing the services.

By examining store traffic and conversion trends and comparing them to the service activity, retailers will be able to quantify the impact these services are having relative to total traffic and be in a better position to make operational adjustments. Without store traffic counts, this wouldn't be possible.

Don't forget about the impact these services may have on compensation for store teams. For example, if you use conversion rate performance as part of your compensation plan, bonuses, or any form of acknowledgment, you must understand how offering new services may change or modify the store traffic and conversion trends.

As the previous examples show, BOPIS and BORIS visits can have downward pressure on conversion rates, and if these transactions aren't properly accounted for, then the store team may take a conversion rate performance hit that they rightly should not have because of the new services being offered.

The unfortunate reality is that while new services are being added along with new tasks for the store team to manage, the amount of labor a store gets and/or how the labor hours are scheduled have not necessarily changed, and this can cause the store team to lose focus on selling, which can cause conversion rates and customer service levels to decline.

It's wrong for decision-makers to heap more work on the store team without providing more labor to accomplish the work effectively. Many retailers are already understaffing stores to reduce costs and improve financial results, but to the detriment of conversion.[4]

Inevitably, when store teams have no choice, they will do whatever they feel is most important, while other activities get deferred or ignored completely. But with store traffic and conversion insights, decision-makers are in a better position to take action to maximize the sales opportunities and deliver a better in-store experience for shoppers.

## SELF-CHECKOUT (SCO)—
## IMPACT ON CONVERSION RATES

Self-checkout (SCO) has been around retailing since the early 1990s, when American inventor Howard Schneider developed the first self-checkout system designed to enable shoppers to scan, bag, and pay for their goods without the assistance of a cashier.[5] At that time, the goal of SCO was to improve efficiency and reduce labor costs all while providing a better shopping experience for customers.

The key benefits of, and the reasons why, retailers deploy SCO haven't changed much since its inception. The pandemic caused an urgency to deploy more SCO because it supported social distancing and enabled customers to complete transactions without engaging with cashiers.

If slow-moving checkout lines can cause shoppers to leave without buying and create sags in conversion rates, then self-checkout should surely relieve some of this pressure. There's little doubt that it does to some extent . . . but does the implementation of SCO produce higher conversion rates? That's the million-dollar question.

So what impact has self-checkout had on conversion rates? One might assume that anything that can remove a friction point in the shopping journey should result in an improvement in conversion rates. This seems like a reasonable assumption, but do store traffic and conversion results support this belief?

In all fairness, retailers don't implement SCO merely to improve conversion rates. They are also interested in reducing checkout time and providing shoppers with an alternative to lining up for a cashier, which falls under the generalized aspiration of providing a better shopping experience. However, part of the return on investment (ROI) promise of SCO is that retailers could process as many or more shoppers with fewer cashiers, and so the labor savings are also a big part of the allure for retailers.

While there is no way to say for certain that without SCO some number of shoppers may have left without purchasing, what we can say for certain is that conversion rates did not materially increase from their historical trends in the stores we examined. In those stores, SCO provided another checkout option but didn't appear to change overall conversion rates. That's not to say that it doesn't, only that we could not see the impact in conversion rates in the retailer we studied.

The following real-world example will help illustrate.

Self-checkout was rolled out to a sample of stores at this general merchandise retailer to reduce bottlenecks at checkout and deliver a better store experience. To better understand the connection between SCO and conversion rates, I spent the better part of a day observing the checkout behavior of customers in one of the stores outfitted with SCO and then compared those observations to the hourly store traffic and conversion rate results to see if I could identify a connection.

What I found curious was that despite the lineup at the cashier and availability of four self-checkout stations, customers still lined up for the cashier. This observation is a good reminder that just because a retailer makes SCO available, it doesn't mean customers will necessarily use it.

The following chart shows the hourly store traffic and conversion rates for the store I observed between noon and 1 p.m. As you can see, conversion rates sagged during this hour and between the store's busiest traffic hours of 1 p.m. to 4 p.m.

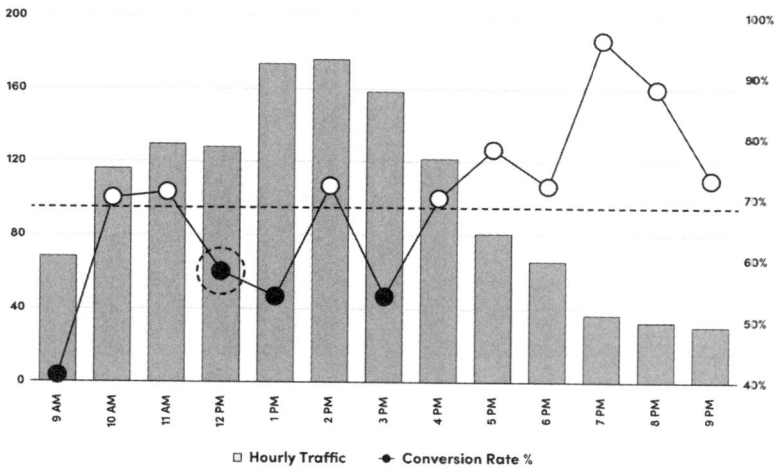

Hourly Traffic     Conversion Rate %

With store traffic data, we can compare the percentage of sales transactions that are completed using SCO compared to store traffic, and we can trend these results over time, like in the following chart.

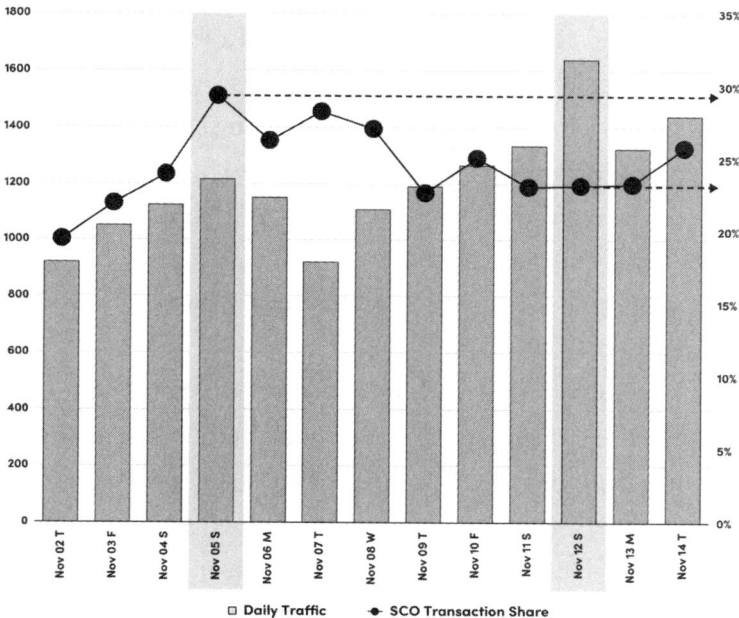

Daily Traffic     SCO Transaction Share

It is curious that on days where store traffic was especially high, the percentage share of SCO transactions was lower than it was on days where the store traffic was lower. This seems counterintuitive. If the store is busy, you would expect cashier lines to be longer and SCO activity higher. But that's not what this data showed.

| | Saturday, Nov. 5 | Saturday, Nov. 12 | % Difference |
|---|---|---|---|
| Store Traffic | 1,215 | 1,640 | 35% |
| SCO Transaction Count | 348 | 368 | 6% |
| SCO Transaction Share as % of Traffic | 29% | 23% | -21% |

For example, on Saturday, November 5, store traffic was 1,215, and the share of SCO transactions was 29%. However, on Saturday, November 12, store traffic was over 1,640 visits—the store was 35% busier—but the percentage of transactions completed via SCO was much lower at just over 23% of store traffic.

Of course, these results could be impacted by a number of other factors, including the number of cashiers available on each day, the number of SCO terminals that were up and properly functioning, and the preferences of using SCO by the shoppers who visited on each day.

The key point is that with store traffic counts to contextualize the results, the store operator has a much better understanding of how much and when SCO is being used and how the trends are changing over time.

Even if SCO doesn't directly improve conversion rates, comparing SCO activity to store traffic will enable retailers to establish chain-wide SCO performance benchmarks and help refine procedures so that they and their shoppers can make the most of SCO.

## Final Thoughts on Self-Checkout and Conversion

Does SCO improve in-store conversion rates? I was not able to answer that question conclusively and quantitatively based on the sample of stores I examined; however, that's not to say that it doesn't. I was recently traveling through LaGuardia Airport in New York City and observed several airport convenience stores with newly installed SCO terminals that were all being fully used by travelers. I suspect that in this case SCO positively impacted conversion rates.

Beyond improved conversion rates, there are other benefits to offering self-checkout, and every retailer considering implementing it should set clear expectations for the outcomes they expect.

From a labor savings perspective, again, the promise of SCO is that fewer cashiers will be required. However, instead of cashiers, retailers who have implemented SCO at scale are discovering that SCO still requires staff support to help customers navigate any technical issues (which commonly occur) and to act as theft deterrents, since it is widely believed by some retailers and the loss prevention industry that SCO has contributed to what is being described in the media as "a theft epidemic" in 2024.[6]

Despite these challenges, SCO is widely available and especially in categories like grocery. And some retailers, like Walmart, for example, have experimented with SCO-only stores. However, the tide may be turning on self-checkout. In 2024, Walmart converted these self-checkout-only stores back into traditional cashier checkouts, and many other retailers are scaling back on SCO. The primary reasons cited for this include increased theft and customer dissatisfaction.[7]

Notwithstanding the growing use of SCO, the fact is there are many retail categories where SCO just doesn't make sense. For example, furniture and jewelry stores where staff assistance is required to complete the transaction, or stores that simply don't have the transaction volume or physical space to offer SCO.

Any retailer considering implementing SCO in their stores should conduct a pilot test to understand the actual impact. Using store traffic and conversion rate insights can help assess the impact and enable retailers to make truly data-informed decisions.

## Amazon's Impact on Physical Retail

Amazon has had a profound impact on the retail industry. While this may be an extraordinary statement of the obvious, it's worth exploring how Amazon's influence has impacted store traffic and conversion in physical stores.

Jeff Bezos and the company he founded, Amazon.com, became public enemy number one to brick-and-mortar retailers once it started to gain traction in 1995.[8] Amazon's meteoric rise since then helped fuel the "retail apocalypse" narrative that was commonly reported on in the media between 2015 and 2019, when store closures and retailer bankruptcies were believed to be a direct result of the general trend of shoppers buying more online than in physical stores.[9]

The fact is that the retail apocalypse was nothing more than a clickbait headline that got trotted out by the media whenever any major retailer failed or delivered poor operating results.

Let's begin by putting Amazon's retail sales results into context. First, we need to examine online sales versus those conducted in physical stores. According to the United States Department of Commerce's second quarter 2024 report, e-commerce sales only represent 15.2% of total retail sales, which means that physical stores accounted for almost 85% of sales.[10] The vast majority of sales transactions are completed in physical stores, and that's why it's critical that retailers work on improving their in-store conversion rates.

Second, Amazon is the undisputed e-commerce champion, representing about 40% of total e-commerce sales in the United States. This is a huge share of e-commerce sales, but online sales represent a much smaller piece of the total retail sales pie. So, using the most recent estimates, Amazon's online retail sales represent about 8% of total retail sales in the United States. That's significant, but it's still modest when you consider total retail sales.[11]

And while it is true that Amazon has had a more significant impact on some retail categories and, consequently, physical retailers in these categories, such as books and electronics, Amazon is not killing retail. In fact, in recent times it's acting as more of a partner than a competitor.

## Amazon Lockers and Returns— Retailers' Faustian Bargain

Faustian Bargain: a pact whereby a person trades something of supreme moral or spiritual importance, such as personal values or the soul, for some worldly or material benefit, such as knowledge, power, or riches.

In retailing terms, the Faustian bargain is that physical retailers are willing to install Amazon Hub Lockers and/or accept Amazon returns, and some retailers even sell select Amazon products in their stores, in exchange for the incremental store traffic generated by these Amazon customers.

This is clearly a win for Amazon, which now has tens of thousands of physical locations where products can be picked up via Amazon Hub Lockers, kiosks, or where returns can be processed.[12]

But what about the retailers?

The questions retailers should be asking are: First, how much more store traffic will Amazon generate, and second, is the store traffic increase worth the time, effort, and distraction for the store teams? I worked with several retailers from various categories, including specialty, apparel, and general merchandisers, that offer Amazon pickup and/or returns, and here's one real-world example of how it impacted store traffic and conversion rates.

This apparel chain was looking to drive traffic, so they installed Amazon Hub Lockers in a sample of their stores. We compared store traffic counts to the Amazon Locker activity and determined that the Amazon-generated traffic ranged from a 1.6% to 3.0% increase across ten sample stores, with an overall average traffic increase of about 2.0%.

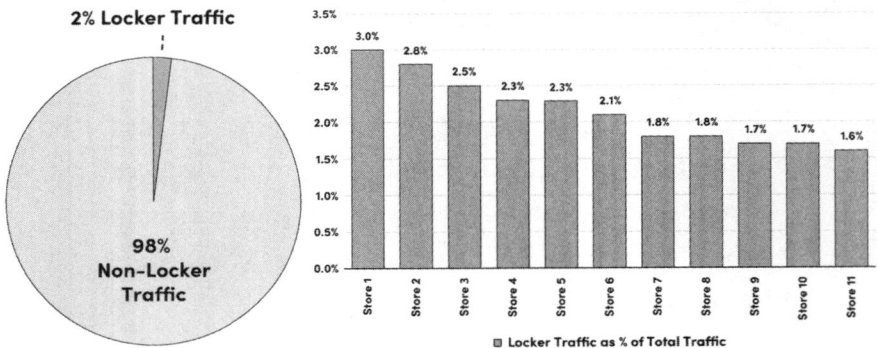

**2% Locker Traffic**

**98% Non-Locker Traffic**

Locker Traffic as % of Total Traffic

You might argue that 2% more store traffic is better than nothing, but I question whether that is true when you consider the cost to the retailer. Amazon ships, installs, and services their lockers at no charge to the retailer; however, there is an annual service fee per locker, which Amazon says is "offset by the increase in foot traffic and potential sales the retailer will get from Amazon customers picking up their packages."[13]

## The Flaw in the Amazon Traffic Proposition—Conversion Rates

I find it ironic that many retailers are willing to do virtually anything to drive more traffic into their stores, but they pay hardly any attention to what it will take to convert this Amazon traffic into sales. I suspect that Amazon chose their words carefully in their pitch selling lockers to physical retailers when they use the phrase "*potential* sales from Amazon customers picking up their packages."

Many of these retailers assume—or more aptly, hope—that more traffic will lead to higher sales. But as we know, and as the traffic and conversion rate data make clear, this is not always the case. In fact, it may be even worse if intentional store shoppers are not served because store teams are preoccupied processing Amazon returns, then leave without buying or decide to not return to the store at all in the future.

Herein lies the Faustian bargain retailers are making in exchange for more store traffic. They are trading off the time, attention, and effort that their store teams could be applying to serving and converting more of the intentional shoppers who visit their stores.

The following chart shows the store traffic and conversion rate trend for a major specialty retailer that started accepting Amazon returns in their stores.

## Weekly Traffic and Conversion Trend for All Stores Over the Last 52 Weeks

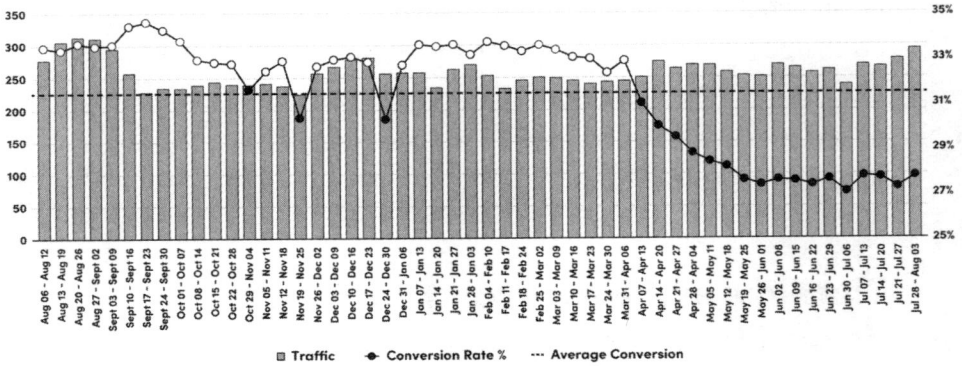

Traffic     Conversion Rate %     Average Conversion

For this retailer, Amazon returns had a materially positive impact on store traffic, which was up more than 10% versus the prior year—and that is significant for this chain. However, the more notable feature is the conversion rate trend; conversion rates are significantly down. In this case, conversion rates dropped from around 33% on average to just over 28%, and overall gross sales declined.

As retailers are discovering, it can be extremely difficult—if not impossible—to convert an Amazon store visitor into a new sale, even with incentives such as coupons for additional savings if they make a purchase. The reality is that these Amazon visitors can be very challenging to convert into a sale regardless of what incentives are offered. Forget "if they come, they will buy"—this doesn't hold up under the lens of traffic and conversion analysis.

While I appreciate the great effort retailers will go to drive store traffic, intentionality matters when it comes to conversion.

Incidental store visits generated by people who only want to drop off an Amazon return or access any other noncore service offering are likely to dilute conversion rates. But even worse, they could hurt sales by distracting the store team. These factors should be very carefully considered by any retailer considering offering Amazon returns in their stores.

## How Can Retailers Decide Whether They Should Offer Amazon or Not?

The answer is simple—conduct experiments or pilot tests and then analyze the impact on store traffic and conversion rates.

The apparel retailer I worked with did just that. They installed Amazon Hub Lockers in twenty stores and then analyzed the store traffic and conversion rate changes in those test stores compared to a control sample of stores.

Beyond analyzing overall store traffic and conversion, retailers should conduct additional experiments around incentives designed to encourage conversion of the Amazon visitors and see what sales outcomes they produce.

Beyond testing, retailers considering implementing Amazon Hub Lockers or returns processing in their stores should also be very mindful of the impact Amazon store visitors may have on the store team. Anything that distracts the store team from serving shoppers who enter the store with the intent to purchase can have a negative impact on conversion rates, and that's why it's vital for retailers to go into this with their eyes open.

I am not suggesting that retailers shouldn't consider implementing Amazon pickups or returns in their stores, but I am urging any retailer to consider it with caution. Do not assume that more store traffic will directly translate into more sales.

Furthermore, don't assume that the incremental store traffic can be served with only existing staff. Over the past decade, driven in part by the pandemic, store teams are being asked to take on many more tasks than before, and often without any additional labor hours to support it. Not only does this play a role in the retailer's ability to convert the Amazon traffic, but it also likely distracts the store team from converting the intentional shoppers who actually visited the store to buy something.

The retailer I worked with that implemented Amazon Hub Lockers in those twenty stores determined that the floor space and distraction to the store team from the Amazon visits wasn't worth it. And so far, in my experience, I have not seen a single retailer produce the sales outcomes they thought they would by implementing Amazon services in their stores.

## Self-Checkout, Just Walk Out, and "Frictionless" Transactions

If you follow the retail trade or business media featuring topics related to retailing, you will find a plethora that discuss the virtues and challenges of creating a "frictionless" shopping experience.

The idea seems sensible enough. Reduce or eliminate any barriers to shoppers being able to purchase what they want and make it convenient for them to do so. The logic follows that if you can reduce "friction," then you should be able to serve more customers and ultimately generate more sales. Not to be too cynical about it, but it's not just about making it more convenient, it is about producing more sales.

Self-checkout and its new SCO-on-steroids variant, referred to as Just Walk Out, are two ways retailers are trying to reduce friction.

### JUST WALK OUT—HYPE VERSUS REALITY

Imagine if you could walk into a retail store, grab products off the shelf, and then just walk out. Wouldn't that make for a truly remarkable and utterly frictionless shopping experience? That's exactly the aspiration Amazon had when they pioneered the technology and launched it in 2018 when they opened their first Amazon GO store in Seattle, Washington.[14]

Masters of public relations (PR) hype, Amazon's launch of their Amazon GO store did not disappoint. Curious shoppers flocked to the new store concept in Seattle, which offered what you might describe as premium convenience store food products, including sandwiches, salads, snacks, and beverages. I thought it was ironic that while the Just Walk Out technology enabled customers to leave without lining up for a cashier, they were instead lined up just to get in!

The idea of a Just Walk Out shopping experience is that customers, using a smartphone app, scan an electronic turnstile that lets them enter the store. Once in, customers can grab whatever they like and simply walk out. The shopper would then receive a sales receipt for the goods that they took and be on their way. Pretty remarkable, right?

Despite the hype, there were many skeptics, and I was one of them. As I wrote in an op-ed, "Why Amazon Go Is a 'No-Go' for Most Retailers," published by *Loss Prevention Magazine* on February 27, 2018, there are a multitude of reasons why this sort of technology is not only wildly impractical to implement and maintain, but why it also creates new barriers to the shopping experience. And at the top of the list of why Amazon's Just Walk Out is a no-go for most retailers is cost.

According to news reports when Amazon opened their first Amazon GO store, to enable Just Walk Out, the store had to be outfitted with hundreds of cameras, sensors, and scanners to accurately detect which products the shopper took.[15]

Just think about the cost of the cameras, sensors, and scanners needed to do this, along with the cabling and computing horsepower required. The Amazon GO store is essentially a supercomputer disguised as a convenience store!

And as anyone who has ever implemented any technology in a physical retail store well knows, the upfront capital cost is only the start of it. Technology needs to be constantly maintained and updated. What do you think that might cost?

Implementing Just Walk Out technology in a test store or two is one thing, but I would argue that implementing it at scale across a large number of stores would be cost-prohibitive for most retailers—and perhaps even for Amazon. As of 2024, the rollout of Amazon GO stores seems to have stalled due to disappointing sales and high operating costs.[16]

But what about the benefits? Wouldn't a frictionless check-out experience lead to higher sales and lower labor costs since you wouldn't need cashiers? Well, that's the promise, but I don't think the financial benefit would ever justify the financial investment. Here's why.

To use Just Walk Out, shoppers would need to use an app to scan at the turnstile just to get into the store. If you don't have the app, you can't get in. So some number of shoppers who might have wanted to visit the store may not be able to even get in if they don't have an app. What about those lost sales?

And the argument that Just Walk Out will enable retailers to reduce labor expense by not having cashiers is weak since these stores still require some on-site personnel to stock shelves and serve shoppers.

And finally, by their own admission, shrink (inventory loss) due to mis-scanned items occurs because it can be a challenge for the cameras and sensors to pick up on every item. When Amazon was pilot testing their Amazon GO store, they realized that some items weren't getting scanned, but they weren't too concerned with this shrink. Well, most retailers are very concerned about shrink, so that's another reason why the technology lost traction.

While I do admire Amazon's attempt to eliminate shopper

friction with Just Walk Out technology and their determination and ingenuity to develop it (not to mention the financial investment that is estimated at up to a billion dollars), it's just utterly impractical and too expensive for most retailers, and the shopper experience would be radically different than what most shoppers today probably want.

Now let's turn our attention to the one topic that is critical to the success of every other topic in this book—collecting and maintaining accurate and reliable store traffic data. Without it, nothing is possible.

## 🛒 Chapter Takeaways

- Services like BOPIS, BORIS, and curbside pickup can alter store traffic patterns and conversion rates. BOPIS and BORIS increase traffic but may lower conversion rates if these visits aren't accurately accounted for.

- Removing service-based visits from traffic counts can help in calculating more accurate in-store conversion rates, but this method isn't without challenges.

- Despite its widespread adoption, self-checkout doesn't always lead to higher conversion rates, as many customers still prefer traditional checkout methods.

- While Amazon Hub Lockers and returns can drive traffic, they may negatively impact conversion rates and store operations if not carefully managed.

- Amazon's Just Walk Out technology offers a frictionless shopping experience but is cost-prohibitive and operationally challenging for most retailers to implement and maintain at scale.

**PRACTITIONER'S ADVICE**

- Regularly assess how new services affect your store's traffic and conversion rates to make data-informed adjustments.

- Adjust performance incentives to reflect the changes in traffic and conversion trends caused by new services in order to maintain fairness and motivation among store teams.

- Run pilot tests to measure their impact on both traffic and conversion rates before fully implementing new technologies like self-checkout or Amazon partnerships.

- Ensure that any new services added to your store do not overburden staff or detract from their ability to serve core shoppers effectively.

- Weigh the financial and operational costs of implementing advanced technologies like Just Walk Out against their potential benefits in order to ensure a positive ROI.

# CHAPTER 11

---

# The Most Important Store Traffic—Yours!

I f store traffic is a gift, then it makes sense that we dig into it in detail. Conceptually, the idea of counting store visits is about as straightforward as it gets. But as you will discover in this chapter, there are many dimensions to traffic counting, and it shouldn't be taken for granted since it is the foundation for all the insights I describe in this book.

Store traffic is a gift because it represents the sales opportunities for the store. And it should be treated as a precious, nonrenewable resource. Every time a shopper enters the store, they create a sales opportunity, and knowing exactly when and how many opportunities are being created is vitally important.

But an opportunity is only valuable if it's converted into a sale, and store teams should never assume the sale is a certainty or that the shopper will be back if they don't make a purchase. Today—and more than ever in our history—shoppers simply have too many other choices of where to spend their money. It's imperative to convert every visitor that can be converted into a sale, and knowing when shoppers are visiting to the hour of the day can greatly improve the odds.

I can't fathom how any retailer can operate their business without knowing their store traffic counts. But the sad fact is, many retailers today do not track store traffic, and they are doing themselves a great disservice by not acquiring and maintaining this vital data.

Let's begin by looking at who is and who isn't tracking store traffic, and how store traffic counting technology has evolved.

## Who's Counting Store Traffic Today?

Wander through any major mall in North America, and as you pass by the stores, I encourage you to peer in and look up above the entrance. Often, you'll see an electronic traffic counter.

In fact, it may even appear as though every retailer is counting traffic, but that's not what I discovered doing a series of mall audits where I literally visited every store in a sample of malls and recorded how many and which retailers had traffic counters installed.

I conducted these mall visits in late 2023 and early 2024 and found that store traffic counter penetration rates ranged from 49% to 59%. This means almost half the retailers did not apparently have traffic counters installed. The results from a sample of these mall audits are shown next.[1]

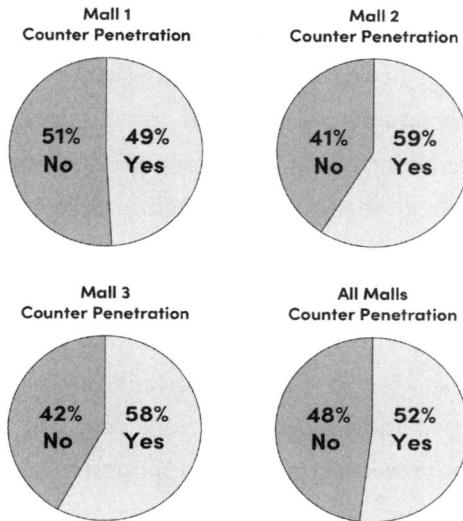

Mall 1
Counter Penetration

51% No / 49% Yes

Mall 2
Counter Penetration

41% No / 59% Yes

Mall 3
Counter Penetration

42% No / 58% Yes

All Malls
Counter Penetration

48% No / 52% Yes

My mall audit findings can hardly be considered a proper market penetration survey, and I'm not suggesting that they are. But what I do believe is that the results are directionally accurate and provide a glimpse into who is and isn't counting. Here are some other observations:

- **The largest and most successful retail brands have traffic counters.** Not surprisingly, most of the largest chains and major retail brands had traffic counters installed in their stores. It was mostly the smaller regional or local retailers that did not have traffic counters.

  This finding seems to support the notion that large chains are more sophisticated and data-minded than small and/or independent retailers, and that in part explains the difference in penetration rates of large versus small retailers. To the retailers not tracking store traffic, I urge them to reflect on why the "big players" are tracking. Perhaps they know something that you don't?

- **Some categories were more penetrated than others.** This is a function of the mix of tenants located in malls, which of course is largely composed of apparel and specialty stores. Apparel retailers, by far, had the highest traffic counter penetration rates of any mall-based category observed. The lowest-penetrated category observed was jewelry stores.

  This is curious given that in high-involvement or assisted-sales environments like jewelry stores, aligning frontline labor to store visits is especially important since average sale values are high, and the sales leverage that can be achieved by improving conversion rates even modestly is significant. And yet this category had the lowest penetration of traffic counters, even at large chain jewelers.

- **There is a lot of older, antiquated traffic counting equipment installed.** Traffic counter technology has evolved considerably over many decades. While many retailers I encountered did have modern traffic counters installed, I was surprised by how many retailers still had very old technology.

  From personal experience, I can tell you that old technology traffic counters are not as accurate as new technology, and without constant monitoring and proper maintenance, traffic counting devices and the accuracy of the traffic data can become compromised. While electronic traffic counters can function well for five or even ten years in the field before needing to be replaced, the preponderance of old equipment suggests that retailers are not keeping their traffic counting technology updated and suggests that perhaps it's fallen out of use altogether.

Visiting malls and identifying which retailers had store traffic counters installed was telling, but it was limited for several reasons: First, my observations were of mall-based stores only. Clearly, many retailers have stores in non-mall locations. Second, there was no way for me to know if the retailer was using the store traffic insights even if they had a counter installed. And third, I was only looking for traditional retail traffic counting devices.

The fact is that the people-counting market is far larger and more diverse than most people realize.

## The World Is Full of People Counters

In 2018, I was approached by I & G Systems, a UK-based consulting firm that was preparing a worldwide study on the people-counting market. Entitled, "People Movement & Location Analytics in the Retail Sector," it was and remains the most comprehensive study of the domain that I have encountered.

Contained in the voluminous study was an industry map of leading players by specialization, size, and years in the people-counting industry. With permission from the authors, I've included the graphic here.[2]

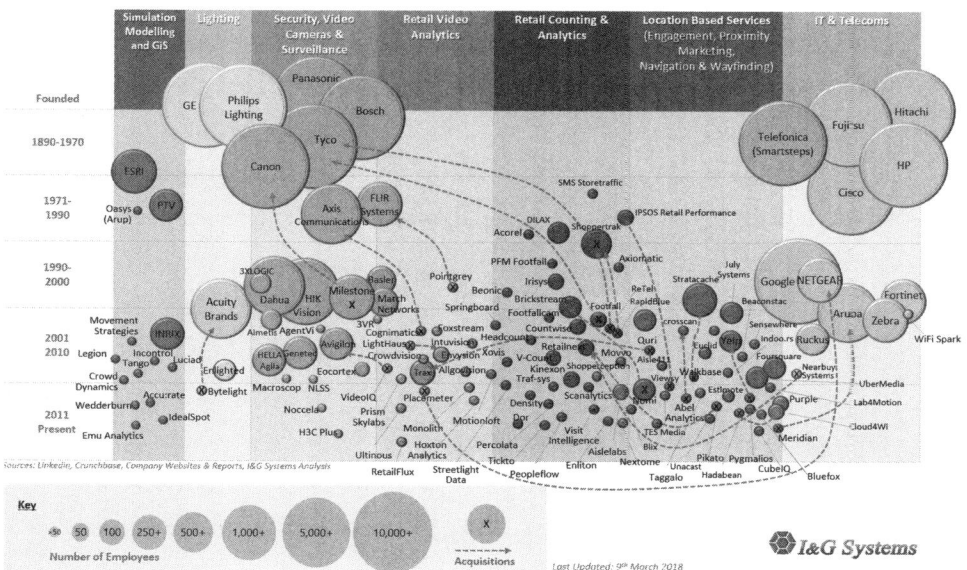

By their own admission, the report's authors acknowledge that their study is not exhaustive and that the industry continues to evolve because of new companies entering the domain, existing companies being acquired, and firms exiting the industry altogether as a result of business failure or strategic pivots.

Notwithstanding the study's limitations, what's striking about this graphic is the large number of competitors and the diversity of people-counting technologies and approaches available. If you're interested in the detail of the different people-counting players and market segments, I encourage you to get a copy of the I & G Systems study.

I will not review every traffic counting approach illustrated on the industry map, but there is one approach to acquiring store traffic data that is worth discussing in more detail, and that's loss prevention surveillance systems.

## Traffic Counting with Your Loss Prevention Surveillance System

One approach to capturing store traffic data is by using your existing loss prevention surveillance system. In fact, the loss prevention industry has been musing about this for many years, and on its surface, it makes practical sense. Why invest money in dedicated traffic counters when you can get counts from your loss prevention system?

Good question—and one that I explored in an article I wrote, "Using Loss Prevention Technology to Support Traffic Counting and Conversion," that was published in the November 23, 2015, edition of *Loss Prevention Magazine*.

Conceptually, using your loss prevention (LP) cameras to count store traffic makes sense, but I discovered several accuracy issues when working with traffic count data generated from these systems.

LP cameras are designed to be used in a certain way, and when you adjust them to be optimized for people counting, they tend to not work as well for the intended purpose—spotting shoplifters and recording security events.

One major retailer I worked with decided to use their LP provider to track store traffic, and it was, in their words, "a disaster." The accuracy of the traffic counts was constantly being questioned by the store teams, and the head office team overseeing the traffic data found itself having to spend an inordinate amount of time creating estimates for incomplete—and what appeared to be erroneous—counts. Furthermore, the analytic and reporting capabilities provided by this LP firm were also lacking.

I encountered another retailer, this time a major department store chain, that was using the traffic counts captured from sensors embedded in their security gates. Again, count accuracy was a problem, and the person in charge of the data confided in me that it took two years to get the accuracy levels up to acceptable levels and that it was still a work in progress.

While I believe the loss prevention industry has made meaningful progress in improving the traffic counting capabilities of their LP systems, in my experience it has still not gained the traction it might in the future. If LP providers want to get into the traffic analytics business, I urge them to work on getting their accuracy levels up to par with what dedicated traffic counting solutions can achieve today, and improving their reporting and analytics capabilities wouldn't hurt either.

Moving beyond LP systems, let's focus on the most common types of traffic counting technologies that I have encountered as a practitioner.

# The Most Common Store Traffic Counting Systems

There's no doubt that retailers have been tracking store visits from the earliest days of retailing. But the first electronic people-counting systems didn't arrive until the 1970s.[3]

Today, there are three general types of traffic counters most used by retailers:

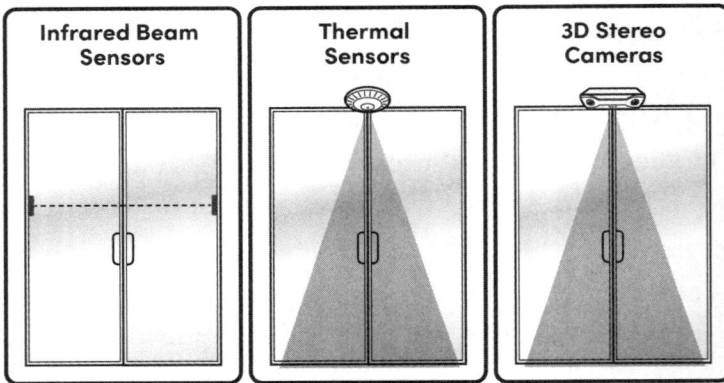

| Infrared Beam Sensors | Thermal Sensors | 3D Stereo Cameras |

- **Infrared Beam Sensors**: These traffic counters, also called "break-beam" counters, were the most-used devices in the early days of retail traffic counting. These devices were inexpensive and worked reasonably well. To capture counts, small infrared sensors were affixed to each side of the entrance door, and every time a person entered the store, their body interrupted or "broke" the infrared beam and a count was logged.

  In practice, this type of traffic counter proved to be challenging to work with and suboptimal for several reasons. For example, if the retailer positioned merchandise at the front door, the sensors would get blocked, and no counts would get registered. Also, these early devices could not detect directionality, so whether the shopper walked into the store or out of the store, a count was logged, and so to estimate incoming visits, total counts would need to be divided by two. This count manipulation compromised accuracy and made these systems problematic to work with.

- **Thermal Sensors**: Thermal sensor–based traffic counters trigger counts by detecting a temperature change from the person walking through the door. These traffic counters proved to be much more accurate than infrared beam counters, in part because the software that worked with the sensor could detect directionality. That is, it only counted the number of people entering the store, so you didn't need to manipulate the data.

  However, these devices were not foolproof. In fact, they were technically finicky and required a lot of maintenance to keep counts accurate, which was often a real challenge. For example, in some stores that had vestibules that opened to the outside of the building, the change in temperature that triggered the count could become compromised by different weather and temperature changes as customers entered the store. Additionally, these counters were not able to eliminate counts generated by children under a certain height, since counts were logged based on body heat.

  You still see thermal traffic counters installed in retail stores, but this approach to traffic counting has largely been taken over by camera-based traffic counters, which are by far the most used today.

- **Camera Sensors**: The most common traffic counters on the market today are camera-based, and more specifically, stereoscopic or dual lens devices. These are highly accurate traffic counters that can achieve count accuracy rates in the 95%+ range. These devices are like mini supercomputers attached above the front entrance of the store and use sophisticated software to set precise count zones to control what gets counted.

The people-counting camera is positioned above the entrance or sometimes on a drop-pole inside the store, and importantly it can only see a top-down view. It does not capture shoppers' faces or any other identifiable attributes, which means that privacy is maintained. When a person enters the store, the sophisticated software used to control the camera locks onto the incoming shopper and only logs a count if the person enters from the right direction and crosses the count zone threshold. Anyone who is already in the store and then walks out will not be counted because the camera detects that the direction was from inside the store.

Furthermore, if a shopper is already in the store and then wanders through the count zone, they won't be counted either, since the path through the count zone originated from inside the store. This functionality minimizes extraneous counts or the need to manipulate or adjust the counts like with beam counters.

There are some other features that make this type of traffic counter a top choice for retailers, including count elimination based on height and count audit capabilities.

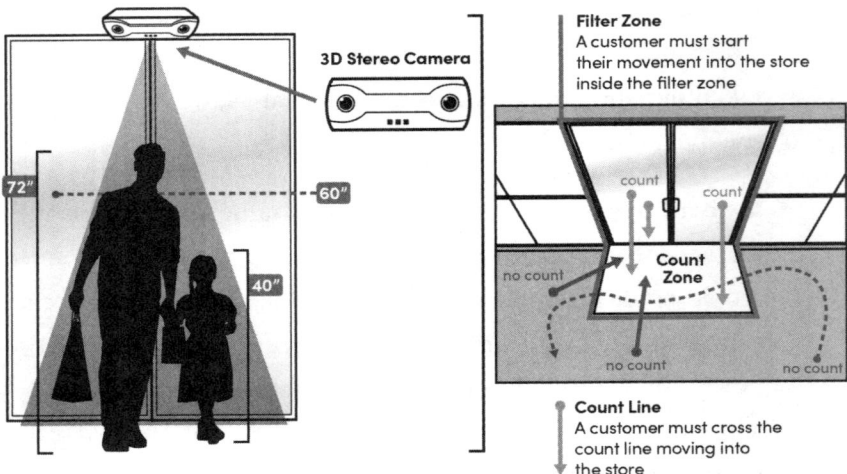

3D Stereo Camera

72" 60" 40"

**Filter Zone**
A customer must start their movement into the store inside the filter zone

count count

no count

**Count Zone**

no count no count

**Count Line**
A customer must cross the count line moving into the store

With a two-camera lens, the counter can perceive depth, which means that counts generated by people entering under a certain height are not counted. The height threshold is set using the software controls. This also eliminates counts from baby strollers and shopping carts.

But one of the most compelling features of this type of traffic counter is the ability to audit traffic counts. To conduct a count audit, technicians can record a sample of video footage of people entering the store and then compare the visual count to the counts logged by the device. If needed, the count lines can be adjusted to enhance accuracy. This is a very important functionality because it's vital that store managers, field leaders, and other stakeholders believe the counts are accurate, and having the ability to audit the traffic counts helps build confidence in the data.

## What Gets Counted?

As much as traffic counters have evolved technologically, along with count accuracy rates, no traffic counting system is 100% perfect. And it's not necessarily because the counter isn't accurate. The challenge in store traffic counting is related more to what gets counted and not how.

Today even the most sophisticated traffic counters can't reliably eliminate counts generated by delivery people, non-shoppers, store staff, or people shopping together as a group, despite good effort on the part of some device manufacturers to try to solve this.

Let's start with staff elimination. Ideally, counts generated by staff should be removed from store traffic counts since these counts do not represent actual shoppers. This can be especially problematic in low-traffic retail environments like high-end jewelry or other specialty stores that receive only twenty or thirty store visits per day. Even a few staff counts will impact conversion rates.

Retailers will often ask if there is a way to eliminate counts generated by staff, and the short answer is yes, but it's not completely accurate and comes with a cost. For something to not get counted, the camera needs a signal. This can be done visually with a specially designed name tag that the camera can see or through an RFID (radio frequency identification) tag worn by the staff member. The RFID tag sends a signal that the traffic counter can pick up and eliminate the count.

In my experience, the accuracy of staff elimination is not great. In our testing, we found that staff counts were only eliminated 75%–85% of the time. When you consider the additional cost of providing all staff with RFID tags, as well as the ongoing costs of replacing lost tags, the pursuit of count accuracy becomes questionable. And the visual name tag approach has its own challenges. If staff forget to wear the special name tag, then obviously the staff elimination functionality is lost.

While I have no doubt that eventually there will be a technological solution that will consistently and accurately eliminate counts generated by staff, today the added cost and complications of enforcing a new RFID tag or name tag policies aren't worth it for most retailers.

Beyond staff elimination, the next-most-common question I get from retailers has to do with buying groups. A simple example will help illustrate.

If I visit a store and make a purchase, and I am the only shopper for the day, then I will generate one traffic count. Because I made a purchase, I generated one transaction count, so the conversion rate for the day would be 100% (i.e., 1 transaction count/1 traffic count = 100%). But if I visit the store with my wife and two adult children, we'll generate four traffic counts. Even if we all buy something, there's a good chance we'll put everything into a single basket, which will generate only one transaction count. Four traffic counts and one transaction count would mean a conversion rate of only 25% (1 transaction count/4 traffic counts = .25 or 25% conversion rate).

| Buying Group | Traffic Count | Transaction | Conversion Rate |
|:---:|:---:|:---:|:---:|
| 👤 | 1 | 1 | 100% |
| 👥 | 2 | 1 | 50% |
| 👥👥 | 4 | 1 | 25% |

Like staff elimination, some device manufacturers have tried to solve the buying group challenge by creating algorithms that assess the size and proximity of the people entering the store. When the camera sees a group enter the store, it assesses whether the visitors should be counted as a single buying group or as individual shoppers based on their proximity to each other.

Buying-group filtering is imperfect since sometimes shoppers walk into the store in close proximity even though they are not shopping together as a group. So like staff elimination, my recommendation to retailers is to not get too hung up on buying groups. Furthermore, sometimes friends shop together and may look like a single buying group, but they are in fact individual shoppers.

On any given day, there will be some "noise" in the traffic count data regardless of how sophisticated the traffic counter technology is. These are naturally occurring counts that are difficult to consistently identify and eliminate, so the best approach is to merely focus on the trends and know that there will be some extraneous counts included.

## Keeping Your Store Traffic Data Complete and Reliable

Whenever I start working with a retailer who has store traffic data, the first thing I do is have it reviewed to make sure the data is complete and that there are no suspicious trends that might indicate that there are quality problems with the data.

Having no store traffic data to make decisions and contextualize results is bad; having unreliable, incomplete, or inaccurate store traffic data is worse because it can lead you to unwittingly draw the wrong conclusions and make suboptimal decisions, even though you believe you're making sound, data-informed ones.

Here's an example to illustrate. I started working with a specialty retailer with 293 stores that already had traffic counters installed in all their stores. They were interested in how we could help them improve their conversion rates. Before we began our work of assessing their stores' performance and looking for conversion improvement opportunities, we conducted a traffic data quality review.

| | |
|---|---|
| Number of stores in data file: | 293 |
| Stores with bad, missing, or questionable data: | 181 |
| Final number of stores included in analysis: | 112 |
| Stores with year-over-year data: | 84 |

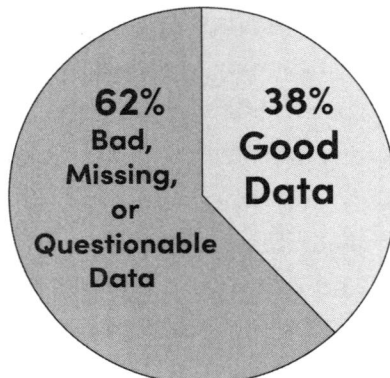

Of the 293 stores, we discovered 181 stores with questionable data including gaps or missing data and dramatic trend changes in traffic and/or conversion rates, which suggest that the data is unreliable.

This retailer was surprised—perhaps shocked is the better word—to learn that 62% of their stores had traffic data that was unreliable or problematic in some way. In this case, the retailer had traffic counters installed in their stores and just assumed that the traffic counts being generated were accurate.

Imagine if this retailer's point-of-sale data was this inaccurate? They wouldn't be in business very long.

The only way to assess the quality of store traffic data is to look at it, and the best way to do that is to examine daily traffic and conversion rates over time. Two years of data is a good sample size as it allows you to see the year-over-year (YoY) trends.

The following charts are some of the actual examples I used to illustrate why we believed that this retailer had data issues. Each chart shows the daily traffic count in the tiny bars and the line overlay represents the conversion rate for the day.

## Store #1: Missing Data and Dramatic Trend Changes

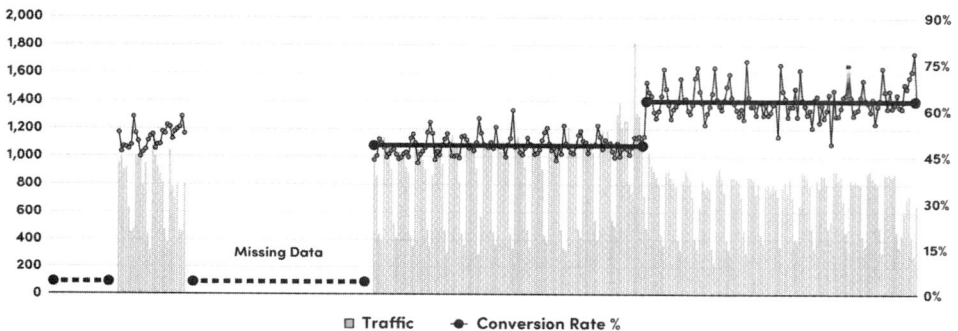

At Store #1, there was a significant amount of missing data, which is obvious to anyone who looks at the data. But in this case, it wasn't just the missing data. Notice how store traffic and conversion rate trends dramatically change on the right half of the chart. Store traffic drops significantly, and conversion rates jump from an average of 45%–50% up to over 60%.

Is it possible the dramatic trend change is simply the actual trend? It is possible, but unlikely. Given the amount of missing data in the past and armed with the knowledge that unless there was some major change in or around this store (which there wasn't), the dramatic swing in store traffic and conversion rate appears to be a data issue. I wouldn't trust this trend enough to base important decisions on it, and this retailer shouldn't either.

In the next example at Store #2, the data was all complete, but just because the data is complete doesn't mean that it is accurate.

## Store #2: Dramatic Trend Changes

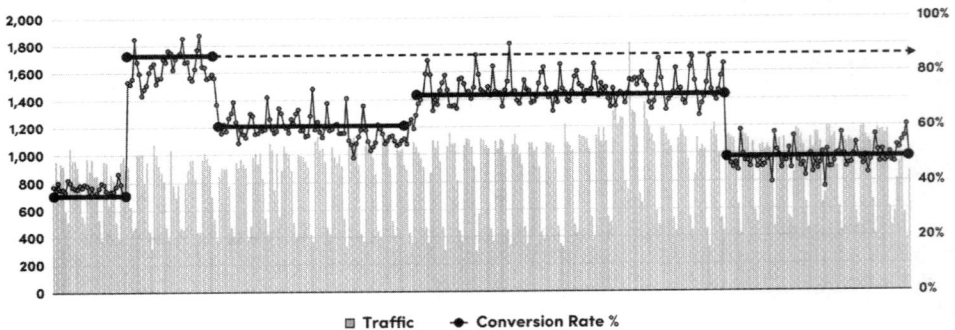

Traffic    ◆ Conversion Rate %

In this case, store traffic and conversion rates were shifting up and down for weeks and months at a time. For some periods, this store had conversion rates 80% or higher, and other periods where it was 60% or lower.

Again, is it possible these were merely the actual results for a store where the trends were shifting in a dramatic way? Yes, it is possible, but just not very likely when you come to understand how store traffic and conversion rate trends tend to move over time.

Very rarely will you ever see such dramatic movements unless some kind of profound change has occurred in a store. For example, a major store renovation might cause the trends to change significantly, but these kinds of changes are well understood.

In the next example at Store #3's location, store traffic data is intermittently missing every few days, and conversion rates spike and drop dramatically. This data appears to stabilize over the last few months, but much of the historical data appears unusable.

## Store #3: Missing and Sporatic Data

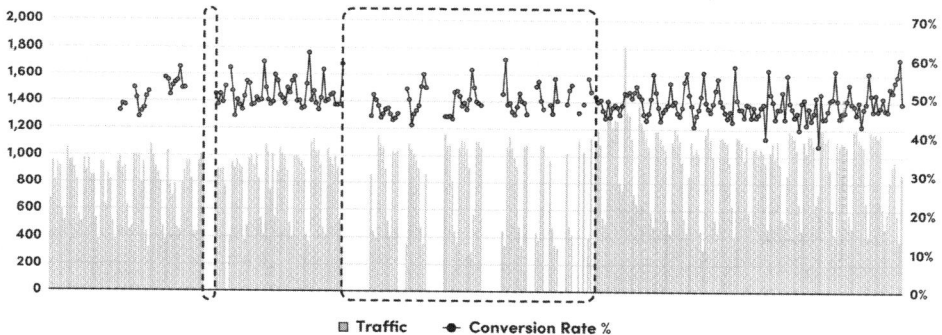

In this final example, at Store #4, the data is all complete, but it's the YoY trend that appears suspicious. Last year, this store had much lower traffic and much higher conversion rates compared to this year, where you can clearly see that the daily store traffic has increased to over 2,000 counts per day, compared to around 800 per day in the prior year. Conversion rates dropped precipitously this year as traffic spiked.

## Store #4: Dramatic Conversion Trend Change

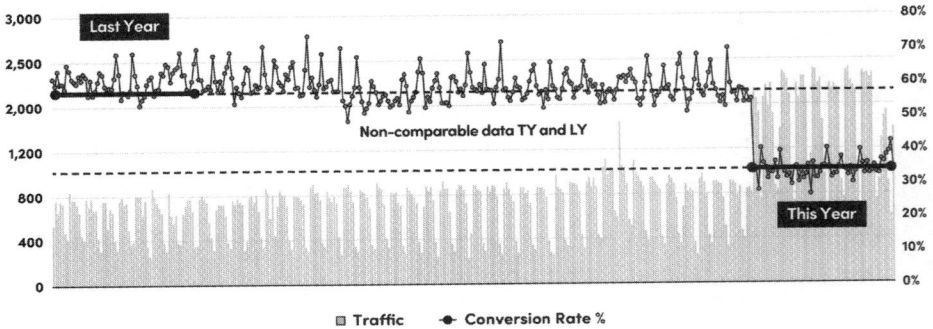

In this case, this year's results may be accurate, but because the YoY trend change is so dramatic, the safest approach is to assume that there is a problem with the data somewhere unless there is a reasonable explanation for why this might have occurred. This might be an issue with last year's or this year's data, but something just doesn't look right, and further investigation is needed.

# Why Store Traffic Data Goes Bad

Just like any electronic device, store traffic counters can fail. Even the very best traffic counters on the market today that can work perfectly for up to a decade or more without a single issue can go wonky and fail, and that's why you need to keep monitoring the data.

Here are some of the most common failure profiles of traffic counters.

- **Traffic Counter Device Fails**: These are the most obvious and easiest to spot. When a traffic counting device fails, the traffic count data simply stops. When this occurs, it's important to have a replacement device installed as soon as possible to minimize the amount of estimating you'll need to do to fill in for the data that was lost.

- **Traffic Data Becomes Compromised During Transmission:** Sometimes, the traffic counter is counting accurately, but the data becomes compromised during the transmission process. These data issues can be much harder to spot. For example, if a store has two traffic counters installed and one of the devices fails.

- **Traffic Counters Get Unplugged or Disconnected:** Most modern traffic counting devices can store days, weeks, or months of traffic count data even when power is lost, by using its onboard battery-powered memory. But if the traffic counter isn't reconnected, eventually data loss will occur.

- **Traffic Data Tampering:** This is less of an issue with modern camera-based traffic counters, but it was a more frequent occurrence with beam sensor devices. If the beam gets blocked, then traffic counts don't get logged. In one case, we discovered that a store manager was periodically placing a small sticky note over the beam sensor, which caused counts to not be logged.

What happens when you reduce traffic counts? If you reduce traffic, then conversion rates increase, and that's what we discovered was the motivation for this store manager who was engaging in this behavior. In my experience, data tampering like this is rare, but when it does occur, it can be very difficult to spot. In this case, it was only discovered after we dispatched a service technician to do an on-site visit, and the sensor-blocking behavior was identified.

When senior management was informed of what had happened, they immediately issued a new store operations policy to all three hundred of their stores. Anyone caught tampering with their traffic counters would be terminated. For this retailer, store traffic data provides vital insights that they rely on to make important decisions—tampering with traffic data is no less serious than tampering with point-of-sale data.

It's also worth mentioning that sometimes the store traffic data is perfectly complete and accurate, but the problem is with the sales transaction data that needs to be combined with traffic data in order to calculate conversion rates. This can occur if the wrong transaction data gets pulled and applied to the wrong store or if the transaction counts get duplicated. These types of issues are all just part of working with data, and one of the very best ways to keep your data clean and reliable is to constantly monitor it.

## Imputing Missing Data with Estimated Data

If for whatever reason you have missing traffic data, you should impute the missing counts with estimated traffic counts in order to preserve trends and comparability of results across stores. The estimates should be based on both historical trends as well as on current trends for the store.

In my practice, we have taken the position that if we need to create estimates for missing data, then we identify this data as "estimated." By doing so, users can understand that the results presented were imputed and should be interpreted accordingly—imprecise but very likely directionally correct.

Without constant vigilance, data imputation can also get out of control.[4] Here's an example to illustrate.

An industry colleague of mine was visiting his new client's stores, a chain of mobile phone stores. When he entered the store, he noticed there was no traffic counter installed. When he asked the store manager about his missing traffic counter, the store manager reached below the sales desk and pulled out the missing traffic counter. The store manager informed my colleague that the traffic counter had been taken down a couple of months ago, but for some reason, he was still receiving his store traffic reports.

My colleague was stunned. How could that be possible? There is only one answer—even though the traffic counter was taken down, traffic data was still getting reported because the current service provider responsible for the traffic counter was automatically imputing the missing traffic counts, and this had been going on for months!

There is no perfect way to estimate data, but it's still important to do it. An estimate is only an estimate and not the reality of what happened in the store, but the downside of not imputing the data is having data gaps, and these gaps will throw off roll-up results and store comparisons.

There's a much bigger downside in allowing your data quality to lapse, and that has to do with why you're collecting the data in the first place—to make better decisions and improve your results. As the manager of customer experience for a large specialty chain once said to me, "If you see huge swings in the data, instead of asking questions, store managers will disengage. I knew if that happened, I would lose buy-in from my store managers, and the entire store traffic and conversion program would lose traction."

So then, how do you keep your store traffic data complete and reliable?

## The Best Ways to Keep Your Traffic Data Reliable

Bad data is worse than no data. With no data, at least you know that you are guessing, and you won't be tempted to make decisions on insights informed by incorrect data, which can lead to completely wrong and costly decisions. For example, overstaffing a store because the traffic counter is overstating the visit counts.

In my experience, here are the most important things you can do to keep your store traffic data complete and reliable.

1.  **Vigilance, Constant Monitoring, and Daily Use:** There is no better way to keep your traffic data reliable than by simply looking at it daily, right down to the individual store. Retailers who look at their store traffic data daily will spot data issues when they occur. This will enable service providers to initiate technical reviews and dispatch on-site technicians if required to get the matter resolved as quickly as possible to minimize data loss and restore confidence in using the data by the store manager and other stakeholders.

2.  **Periodic Traffic Count Auditing:** Store managers are the canary in the coal mine when it comes to store traffic data. If a store manager raises concerns about the accuracy of their store traffic, a traffic audit should be conducted to validate the count accuracy. With camera-based traffic counters, the audit procedure is conducted by a trained technician who acquires a sample of video footage from the traffic-counting camera and then literally counts the number of people seen walking into the store in the video compared to the counts that the electronic system is logging. This type of visual count auditing is time consuming, but it's one of the most reliable ways to validate the accuracy of the traffic counts and to restore confidence with the store manager and stakeholders.

3.  **Replacing Antiquated Traffic Counters:** Today's modern traffic counters can operate trouble-free for many years. In fact, it's not unusual to see traffic counters work perfectly fine for five or even ten years. However, sometimes retailers can procrastinate when it comes to replacing old equipment,

and when old equipment is allowed to remain in the field, it will eventually fail completely or require so much imputation that overall averages and trends become compromised. Retailers need to treat their investment in traffic counters just as they would any vital system in their business and act quickly and proactively if there is an issue.

## 🛒 Chapter Takeaways

- Store traffic represents sales opportunities and should be treated as a critical resource. Accurate traffic counts are the foundation for valuable insights and better decision-making.

- While many large retailers track store traffic, smaller and independent retailers often do not. Surprisingly, even some large chains in categories like jewelry show low penetration of traffic counters.

- The most common types of store traffic counters include:

    ◦ **Infrared Beam Sensors:** Old technology, which is less accurate and prone to accuracy issues.

    ◦ **Thermal Sensors:** More accurate but still maintenance intensive.

    ◦ **Camera Sensors:** Most accurate and common today, offering over 95% accuracy and useful features like count auditing capability and height-based exclusions.

- Reliably collecting store traffic data in the physical world is challenging. No system is perfect. There will always be some amount of noise in the traffic count data resulting from visits by non-shoppers, staff, and people shopping together as a group.

- Data Reliability: Incomplete or inaccurate data can lead to poor decisions. Vigilance and regular data audits are crucial for maintaining data integrity.

## PRACTITIONER'S ADVICE

- Regularly review store traffic data down to individual stores to spot any issues early and maintain confidence in the data.

- Periodically audit traffic counts, especially if concerns about accuracy arise, to ensure continued reliability.

- Proactively replace aging traffic counters to prevent data quality issues and minimize the need for data imputation.

- When necessary, impute missing data with caution, ensuring transparency by labeling it as *estimated*.

# CHAPTER 12

# Retail Traffic Indexes, and How Does Google Know My Store Traffic?

There is one question that virtually every retailer I encounter asks about their store traffic: How does my traffic compare to my competitors'?

It's a good question, but it's also one that has historically been virtually impossible to answer with any degree of confidence. Either the data does not exist because the retailer doesn't track store traffic, or the retailer has the data but does not share it publicly.

## Retail Traffic Indexes—Why You Should Take Them with a Grain of Salt

A few years ago, I received a call from an economist at the Atlanta branch of the United States Federal Reserve. He theorized that brick-and-mortar store traffic would be an important leading indicator to contextualize the retail sales data the government regularly monitors and reports on. I told him I wholeheartedly agreed that store traffic data would provide important context and a meaningful indicator of industry health.

When I explained that a definitive brick-and-mortar store traffic index didn't exist, he was incredulous. How can that be possible!?

The broad confusion—both inside and outside of the retail industry—about the existence of a definitive retail traffic index (or lack thereof) is completely understandable. Because as it turns out, there's a wide—and growing—array of analytics companies that claim to measure industry-wide store traffic trends. Many of these firms happily present their results in a way that implies they are representative of the retail industry—down to the decimal point, no less.

Many of these firms publish their so-called store traffic indexes on social media, their own website, and/or issue press releases, which get picked up by and blindly reported in the media, which are desperate for sources with quantifiable data. The media coverage acts as a form of validation, and before you know it, people *think* they know what's happening with retail store traffic.

Over the course of the last decade, I have taken numerous calls from the media in reference to brick-and-mortar store traffic trends. Almost without fail, the reporter's very first question is: "Is store traffic up or down?" It's the right question to ask, but unfortunately, it has historically been unanswerable.

What's worse, when I explain the reality of retail traffic indexes and why one doesn't exist, the reporter's interest evaporates. Undeterred, and as good reporters are trained to do, they keep going until they find the source they need. And there's no shortage of analytics firms that are happy to provide them what they need, regardless of how accurate or representative they are of true market conditions. The veracity and reliability of the store traffic data portrayed as an "index" seems to be a secondary concern to some media outlets.

In some ways, I do understand the media's collective skepticism and the Federal Reserve economist's incredulity about my assertion that a reliable store traffic index didn't exist. After all, there are plenty of sources for this data, and results are being widely reported in reputable publications. I suspect that the media personnel who had reached out to me simply concluded that I was wrong. I seemed to be the lone voice. Fair enough. But my conviction isn't based on my opinion, it's based on the data itself.

Like most everyone else who works in and around the retail industry, I too read the media reports of retail store traffic trends and took them at face value. If it's being reported by major media outlets, then it must be reliable, right?

But here's the problem: I *am* in the retail traffic tracking business, and the store traffic data that I collected from many thousands of stores across North America and analyzed for my retailer clients often didn't comport with what the so-called indexes were indicating.

As a store traffic data analyst myself, I was aware of the many statistical factors that could account for why the slice of retailer data I had access to might not match a broader industry index. But this wasn't just a sample error issue. My primary concern was in how these indexes were being portrayed as representative of the market.

In early 2015, media reports about results for the 2014 holiday shopping season started to emerge, and references to store traffic trends were included in many of them. I found the results from three different so-called retail traffic indexes, and they all presented different findings. One index stated that store traffic was up, another suggested it was down, and a third stated that traffic was up but not as much as the other index.

I had seen enough. These indexes just don't make sense, and the way they were being presented in the media—literally cut and paste in some cases—was reckless and confusing.

I decided to lay out my case in an article, "Why You Should Take Retail Traffic Indexes with a Grain of Salt." It was published on March 30, 2015, by Retail Customer Experience, a widely read retail industry news website.[1]

I'm not exactly sure what I expected to happen because of my article, but I felt it was important to set the record straight. If it did nothing but cause some readers to be even a little more cautious about what these traffic indexes were and how to interpret them, then it was worth doing.

After the article ran, I received a call from the CEO of one of the companies that published a retail traffic index. I braced for a confrontation, perhaps even a legal threat. His reaction surprised me. "I saw your article on traffic indexes—I quite agree with your conclusions, Mark."

I received another interesting call after the article ran. This time it was the chief marketing officer (CMO) of a major mall operator. The call went something like this:

CMO: "Great article on traffic indexes."

Author: "Thanks."

CMO: "Every time we [the executive team] read a story about store traffic being down, we'd wonder about where the numbers were coming from and how accurate are they. You laid it all out in your article. They're not accurate!"

Author: "Well, technically, they may be 'accurate' for what they are, they're just not representative of the overall market . . . but they're being portrayed as if they are, and that's what's causing you the grief, right?"

CMO: "Exactly, it's causing us grief . . . because we have to continually address the 'traffic' question with tenants and Wall Street analysts . . . we don't see a traffic problem . . . our malls are performing well."

Author: "With all the misinformation about traffic, I'd suggest the best way for you to deal with the traffic question is to simply bring your actual data—fight a data argument with data—you do have traffic data for your malls, right?"

CMO: "Well . . . ah . . . no, not exactly."

Given that malls are essentially in the "traffic business," it behooves every mall operator to track traffic. While many malls do track traffic today, it still startles me to see malls that do not. Not having actual traffic data creates another source of confusion. In the case of the mall operator, his perception was that his malls were doing well—probably based on the sales data from his retail tenants. From the sales data, he inferred that traffic must be up. But that's not necessarily the case.

As I went on to tell the CMO, if you don't count visitor traffic in your malls, then you'll never know for certain if your traffic is up or down, and you'll have no way to defend your position when questions about visitor traffic come up—and they will come up.

The point is this: Without actual traffic data, there is no way for this mall operator—or any retailer—to truly know if traffic is up or down, or to what extent. Lots of retailers even today don't have traffic data, but they talk a lot about traffic based on inferences from sales data or by using sales transaction counts as a proxy for traffic.

While this type of unrepresentative store traffic index data is still being published today, thankfully, it seems some media are starting to avoid using these so-called indexes. It wouldn't surprise me if some media scrutinized the data a little more—like I did for the article I wrote—and realized that it's difficult if not impossible to verify the data. Because if pushed for details about the underlying data, I suspect that most of the traffic index providers would invoke "client confidentiality" to remain vague about specifically what retailer data is being used, along with their methodology and the veracity of their underlying data.

Confidentiality is a fair defense since store traffic data is highly sensitive data, but where then does that leave things with respect to a store traffic index?

Virtually everything in retailing is evolving and so, too, are ways in which shoppers are being tracked and constantly monitored. Along with new ways of tracking shoppers comes new attempts at creating a retail traffic index—but as you will see, these are also fraught.

## Satellites and Geolocation Tracking— Part of the "Alternative Data" Industry

When you think of brick-and-mortar store traffic tracking, the assumption is that the traffic counts are being captured in retail stores. And that is where most store traffic data is captured. But as it turns out, there are other ways to acquire store traffic counts, and for that, we'll need to turn to the world of "alternative data" to get it.

According to AlternativeData.org—an industry group composed of former buy-side and sell-side stock analysts, data analysts, and engineers passionate about how alternative data is changing fundamental investing—alternative data is data used by investors to evaluate a company or investment that is not within their traditional data sources like financial statements, Securities and Exchange Commission filings, management presentations, press releases, etc.

Alternative data helps investors get more accurate, faster, or more granular insights and metrics into company performance than traditional data sources.[2]

It's important to understand intentions here. The alternative data industry is not focused on helping the retail industry better understand market changes or trends. Instead, their business model is about providing investment community players—hedge fund managers, buy-side and sell-side stock analysts, and institutional investors—an edge in their investment decisions. While some of this data may benefit retailers, its primary role is to inform financial markets rather than improve retailer performance.

In fact, I'd wager that plenty of retailers have no idea that they're being monitored in these ways or how this data is being used by the investment community. Store traffic is an important signal in retailing that can help predict future performance, and the mad data scientists behind these alternative data providers are more than willing to supply this data—for a price.

## Counting Store Traffic with Satellites

My first real-world experience with alternative data came when I received a call from a vice president of a company that was tracking shopper traffic by analyzing satellite images of malls and major retailers' parking lots. From satellite images, they developed sophisticated algorithms to count the number of cars in the parking lots. From car counts, they estimated the number of shoppers each car represented, and by trending this data over time, they concluded that they had discovered an important signal of retail performance.

They did a brief demo of how their service worked and the type of insights they could deliver. I was impressed. The insights this company could extract from satellite images were amazing.

I learned that there are literally decades of satellite images that have been captured, and new ones are being captured every day. This firm figured out how to ingest large quantities of this satellite image data, compare these images to geo-specific locations they select (e.g., like a mall parking lot), and then use sophisticated algorithms to not only estimate shopper counts, but even more valuably to predict what the retailers' revenue may be in the upcoming quarter.

It was both creepy and compelling. I couldn't help but wonder where all this surveillance could lead.

As the discussion continued, the real motive for the outreach by this company became clear—they were looking for validation from an industry expert. More specifically, they wanted me to write a white paper or article to endorse their approach to tracking shopper traffic. They would then use this material as a selling tool to help them convince prospective clients that their service was effective.

In the end, I decided not to participate for one primary reason: I didn't think their traffic-counting method was accurate enough. I won't go into detail, but consider the practicalities of collecting traffic count data with satellite images.

First, satellite images can only be captured during certain times of the day. Obviously, there's no way to get a clear image at night or on cloudy days, so how would this limitation impact count accuracy? Their answer: "We have an algorithm for that."

Second, and even more importantly, was how they were using estimated shopper traffic counts to project a retailer's sales results. A retailer's sales can be significantly impacted by changes to in-store conversion rates (i.e., the activities that go on in the store, which a satellite can't see). So even if store traffic is trending down, it doesn't necessarily mean that sales will follow. This is a serious flaw in their model. After I sent my "no thanks" email, I never did hear from this company again.

While I don't think their approach to tracking shoppers to predict sales worked out, there are many really good uses for their satellite data and analysis beyond the retail industry. Tracking farm crop production, analyzing urban development trends, and monitoring manufacturing production and supply chain dynamics—the list goes on. Anything that can be spotted from a satellite seems to be fair game and big business.

But satellites are merely one form of alternative data. There are many data streams that fall into the alternative data category— and most of us already have the most ubiquitous one close by—the smartphone.

## How Does Google Know My Store Traffic?

I think most people would agree that the geolocation services that we have access to today have been positively life altering. Looking for the closest Starbucks? Do you want to know how long it will take to get to the airport? Or how far away your Uber is?

What about when you're interested in visiting a retail store or restaurant and you search it on Google? You'll now often see a little bar chart pop up that indicates popular times when people are visiting this location and how busy it is. These are helpful insights that come to us courtesy of Google's own geolocation tracking.

Geolocation tracking (also referred to as "geospatial data") makes these great services possible, and it is a big part of what makes smartphones so indispensable. They also happen to be an effective way to track shoppers and create traffic trend insights.

I'll spare you the entire history of smartphone tracking. For those interested, there is a substantial amount of academic and industry material readily available. But while the technical detail of how smartphone tracking works is beyond the scope of this book, a basic understanding will provide useful context for our discussion of how smartphones produce store traffic data.

Our smartphones are continually looking to connect, both sending and receiving signals. Some of these signals, like your Media Access Control (MAC) address, are unique twelve-character identifiers associated with your mobile device's network interface. However, modern privacy measures, such as the randomization of MAC addresses implemented in updated versions of iOS and Android operating systems, have made it more challenging for companies to acquire and use these signals for tracking.[3]

By applying techniques such as triangulation—a method of estimating a location by calculating distances from multiple Wi-Fi access points—companies can enhance tracking precision. This method is often used alongside GPS and Bluetooth data to improve accuracy.

According to Google, they create "popular times" and "busyness" insights by utilizing a combination of anonymized location data from mobile devices, Wi-Fi, and Bluetooth signals; historical data; user interactions; shared data from business partners; real-time data collection; and machine-learning techniques to create the insights.[4]

But there are limitations. For example, if Google can't acquire enough information about a particular location, it will simply not display a busyness chart for the location.

Notwithstanding the practical insights that Google provides in these popular times and live busyness charts, it's important to realize that these are only an indication of busyness and not precise store traffic counts that can be used for retail operations.

The fact is that Google doesn't know what your store traffic is, but it can provide a pretty accurate assessment of the relative, historical busyness level, which can be helpful for consumers looking to visit a retail store, restaurant, or other location of interest.

## What I Discovered Comparing Store Counts from Geolocation Tracking to Actual Store Traffic Counts

As of 2024, geolocation providers have become the source of retail traffic trends for the industry, and it seems the industry has embraced it. There are many dozens of firms in the geolocation space, but a few have emerged as leaders, in part because of the very compelling industry or retail sector reports they publish and propagate on traditional and social media.

These firms acquire smartphone location data through app integrations, data partnerships, and other sources, then they apply geospatial analytics to define an area of interest. For example, they can map every Starbucks location in the United States and analyze foot-traffic patterns based on aggregated and anonymized smartphone signals. The raw data is then processed using proprietary algorithms to filter noise, estimate movement patterns, and generate insights on customer behavior.

Specifics regarding the source of the smartphone signals or how these firms manipulate the raw data to draw their conclusions are hard to find, as this is considered confidential by these firms.

Today, retail traffic indexes by retail segment and/or by individual retailer are commonly published in retail trade publications and business press using geolocation data. And it was one such article that caught my attention.

The article was about the traffic trends for a national specialty retailer that just happened to be a client of mine. The article from the geolocation provider assessed the store traffic trends for the chain in detail and drew a number of conclusions. Since this retailer was my client, and I had years of actual store traffic data, I decided to compare the results presented in the article by the geolocation provider to what I knew was the ground truth based on accurate store-level captured traffic data, which is at least 95% accurate.

The results were surprising, but not what I expected.

## TOTAL AGGREGATED CHAIN-WIDE RESULTS—SHOCKINGLY ACCURATE

My assumption was that there was no way that traffic counts captured from geolocation signals could be as accurate as store-level captured traffic data. Think about it. Geolocation data is affected by constantly changing smartphone settings, user opt-outs, and other factors like signal quality and privacy restrictions. I couldn't imagine how the data could be reliably accurate for measuring store-level traffic.

I started by looking at the overall national picture of the results and was startled by what I discovered—the geolocation results were spot-on consistent with what the actual store traffic count data showed. In fact, the aggregated chain total traffic results matched my calculations to the decimal point. Wow! I didn't think that could be possible.

It's important to note that the geolocation report did not assess the actual traffic counts, but rather it focused on percentage change of the current year to prior years. This is no small point. When you track literally tens of millions of smartphone signals across the entire country and apply sophisticated statistical modeling, as was the case in this example, it seems that you can acquire apparently accurate trend insights. But there's a lot more to this story.

We then drilled down to the monthly trends, and that's when we started to see some variation. The following chart shows store-level captured traffic counts compared to the geolocation traffic counts by month for the chain in aggregate.

## 12-Month Total Traffic Trend

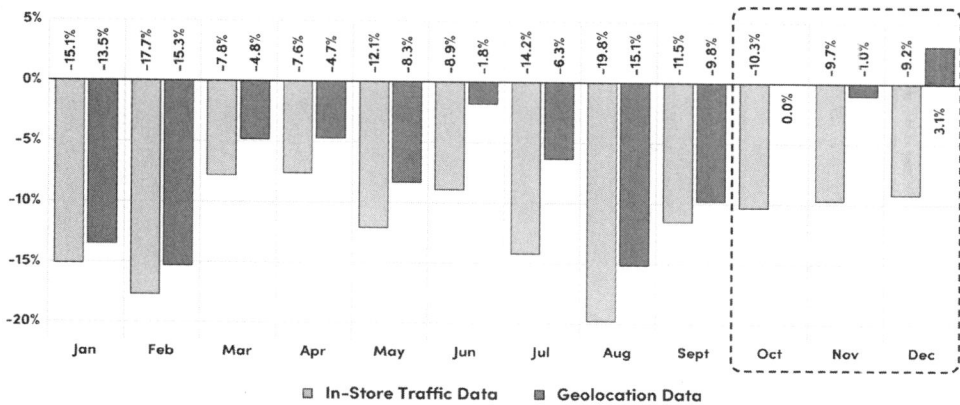

In-Store Traffic Data    Geolocation Data

As you can see, in some months the geolocation data was close to the store-level traffic data trends, though the geolocation data was never as precise as the store-level data. It's fair to say that the trends were directionally correct for most of the year.

However, as time went on, the variation became significant. For example, in October, actual store traffic was down 10.3%, but the geolocation data indicated that traffic was flat—that's a big miss. What was even more troubling was the December results that, based on geolocation data, showed that store traffic was up 3.1% when actual store-level-collected data revealed that traffic was down 9.2%!

Since the geolocation article included an assessment of a select number of state-level trends, we matched their analysis to the actual store-level data, and here's what we discovered.

## STATE-LEVEL TRENDS—SHOCKINGLY INACCURATE

Like the national results, the state-level trends only presented percentage change and not actual counts. The following chart compares the percentage change in total store traffic at a state level for a particular state compared to the actual store-level traffic count data.

## 6-Month Total Traffic Trend

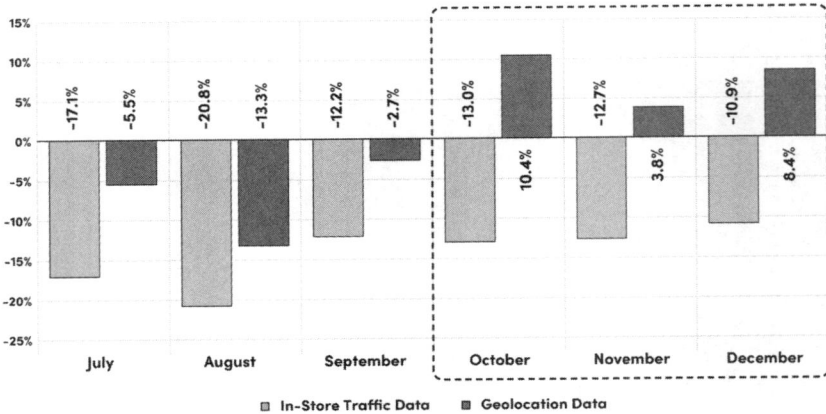

In-Store Traffic Data     Geolocation Data

As you can clearly see, in July, August, and September, the store-level traffic data and geolocation data are directionally consistent. Both data sets show that store traffic is down this year versus the two-year historical average. However, the orders of magnitude in the variation are disconcerting. For example, store-level data in July showed that traffic was down 17.1%, but the geolocation data indicated that it was only down 5.5%. The actions and decisions that management might take are very different if traffic is down 17.1% versus 5.5%. Orders of magnitude matter.

But the conclusions were even more dramatically problematic in October, November, and December, where the results are not even directionally consistent. In October, for example, the store-level data showed that traffic was down 13.0%, whereas the geolocation data indicated that store traffic was up 10.4%! This is a double whammy miss in terms of order of magnitude and directionality. The article went on to say that this retailer was experiencing a bounce back in traffic trend, which is not at all what the retailer was experiencing.

As a result of this analysis, I became much more skeptical of the geolocation traffic trend analysis, but I realized that this was only one geolocation provider's results, and perhaps others were more accurate. So we analyzed the results from an entirely different geo-location analytics provider.

In this next case, the geolocation provider claimed to have traffic count data right down to the individual store. I asked them if they would share a sample of their results for a particular specialty retail chain that was also a client of mine with hundreds of stores, so I had actual store-level traffic data to compare.

The following chart compares what the geolocation data shows for year-over-year (YoY) percentage change by month in aggregate for one store in the chain, compared to the store-level collected traffic data.

## YoY Results—2022 vs. 2021

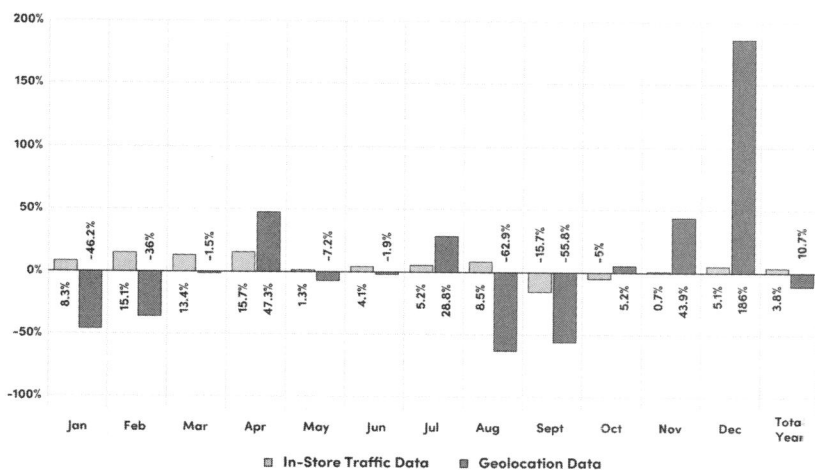

Compared to actual store-level traffic counts, the geolocation traffic results were alarmingly inaccurate both in order of magnitude and directionality. For example, the December YoY geolocation traffic count results showed a traffic increase of 186% compared to the 5.1% increase that store-level traffic counts showed. These results were so far out it's hard to imagine how any credible analytics firm could present these findings to a retailer with a straight face—and this firm was a very credible analytics firm based on their reputation!

## A Final Word About Geolocation Traffic Data

Notwithstanding my concerns about the accuracy of geolocation traffic counts at store level, I do believe that it offers valuable and new insights that heretofore were unobtainable by retailers, such as understanding general consumer movements to map trade areas. This is especially powerful when combined with demographic and other data sets.

Geolocation data can also provide insight into how your competitors' traffic may be trending relative to your chain. And one of the most pervasive uses for geolocation data is for store site selection. Retail real estate teams and property developers have been using geolocation data to inform site selection decisions for many years.

But there are several factors that retailers should be aware of when considering geolocation data to make store-level operational decisions.

1. **Variability of Underlying Geolocation Data:** Unlike traffic data collected at the store level using specially designed people-counting cameras, geolocation data comes from a multitude of smartphone apps, and the sources for the data are constantly changing. For example, when a smartphone manufacturer makes it easier for users to opt out of geolocation tracking, or when an app developer that was allowing their users' geolocation data to be used decides to no longer allow it, those actions impact the underlying data and results.

2. **Reliance on Statistical Modeling:** Since the underlying source data can change frequently, geolocation providers

must rely on statistical modeling to fill in the gaps. Less actual data and/or changing data means the underlying data is less stable, and ultimately, the conclusions will also be less accurate or reliable.

3. **Imprecision of Store-Level Data:** In my exploration of geolocation traffic insights, I had a conversation with one geolocation provider who informed me that the traffic trends they produce are based on a very small number of actual smartphone signals from the store. This explains why when you examine geolocation traffic data at the store level, the results are significantly off compared to those collected by actual people-counting devices in the store.

So then, does Google know your store traffic? The answer: kind of. Using smartphone signals allows Google to make some statistical guesses about how your store traffic is trending and what your busiest hours are. Geolocation data can provide very useful insights into trends at a chain level for large retailers with many stores.

However, as I have illustrated in this chapter, geolocation traffic data falls well short for making operational decisions at the store level where traffic count precision is essential for labor scheduling to the hour and improving conversion rate performance.

## 🛒 Chapter Takeaways

- Retail traffic indexes are widely reported in the media, but these indexes often come from analytics firms with limited data sets that are not representative of the entire market.

- Alternative data, like satellite images and geolocation tracking, is being used to estimate store traffic. These methods offer intriguing insights but lack the precision needed for decision-making at the store level.

- Google and other firms use geolocation data to estimate store traffic and busy times. While useful for general trends, this data is not reliable enough for operational decisions at the store level.

- Comparing actual store traffic data to geolocation data revealed significant discrepancies at the state level and especially the store level. This highlights the limitations of using geolocation data for store operation decisions.

## PRACTITIONER'S ADVICE

- Be cautious when interpreting retail traffic indexes reported in the media. Understand that these indexes may not be fully representative of the retail market and should not be the sole basis for business decisions.

- Use alternative data sources like satellite imaging and geolocation tracking in conjunction with other data sources. Do not rely upon them exclusively.

- Compare alternative data estimates with actual store traffic counts to ensure accuracy whenever possible. This is particularly important when making decisions that affect store operations, such as staff scheduling and measuring conversion rates.

- Prioritize first-party data collected directly from store-level traffic counters for operational decisions, as this data is significantly more accurate than alternative methods like geolocation tracking.

# CHAPTER 13

---

# AI, the Store of the Future, and Store Traffic

No one can predict the future, so any discussion about the future of physical stores should be viewed with a healthy dose of skepticism. While the future is uncertain, it's fair game to examine how artificial intelligence (AI) and other technologies may impact the physical store—and store traffic and shopper conversion.

Before we get bogged down in the realities of technology limitations, cost, and expertise constraints, let's imagine what the ultimate AI use-case might be for retail stores. If you were programming the ultimate AI-driven retail robot, what would its prime directive be? I would argue that for most retailers, the answer would be, "optimizing conversion rates in the store."

DALL·E

Meet AL (as in "algorithm"). He's the store associate of the future. AL knows everything. AL can find any product that you're looking for, process sales transactions, keep the store clean, and serve shoppers with the enthusiasm and passion of the best human store associate any retailer could hope to hire.

Could a robot like AL improve conversion rates in stores? Given the inconsistent and sometimes downright poor store experience that many retailers offer today, I would say a resounding yes! And while I suspect that day is years in the future, I have little doubt that robotic associates like AL will be serving real shoppers in stores.

As with all discussions surrounding new and nascent technologies and the impact they may or may not have in the future, with almost absolute certainty we will look back and ruefully smirk at how things evolved versus the ways pundits and especially the companies creating and promoting these systems said they would. As my late dad used to say, "Consider the source, son."

As I write this final chapter in early 2025, tech giants Google, Microsoft (OpenAI and ChatGPT), Meta, Amazon, and others are locked in a battle for AI supremacy. Virtually every industry is collectively thinking about the impact of AI—experimenting, creating, and applying AI use-cases in some way, shape, or form.[1]

While there is an almost endless list of potential AI use-cases for retailers, and because this book is all about store traffic and shopper conversion, let's narrow our focus to the ones that connect back to the physical store—and therefore to store traffic and conversion.

## AI Requires Data—Lots of It

Ultimately, AI requires data, and I argue that one of the most important data sets that can be used is store traffic counts. But before we get too carried away, let's do a quick reality check.

One of the great promises of AI is that it can improve forecasting and spot trends. However, in order to unlock these new insights, you need to combine store traffic data with myriad other data sources.

Just imagine all the external factors that can influence store traffic: the weather, marketing and promotions, competitor activity, local and national economic conditions, consumer sentiment, changing consumer demographics, shopper travel patterns, urban planning changes, and an incalculable array of social media sources.

And remember, since every physical store is completely unique, you will need to look at all these factors for every store. It's mind-boggling.

But even if you could identify and acquire all this data and verify that it comes from reliable sources, it would still be extremely challenging to assign weighting to each variable to create an algorithm that produces the store traffic forecast.

So while I very strongly believe in the potential AI offers, I also know from direct experience that retailers don't need AI to make better data-informed decisions. Store traffic and conversion data—data that many retailers already have or that any retailer could easily acquire—will enable them to spot traffic patterns and improve in-store conversion rates.

The retailers that use this data already have an advantage over retailers who do not. And since one of the significant benefits of AI is pattern recognition, then it is well suited to analyzing store traffic and conversion rate trends. As a data analyst, this is truly exciting.

However, as a practitioner, I also live in the world of practicality, and I don't believe that algorithms and AI layered on a poor store operating model or inaccurate underlying data will produce better outcomes. Retailers cannot algorithm their way to success.

## How Can AI Help Drive Store Traffic and Improve Conversion Rates?

Since January 2018, I have been a featured BrainTrust contributor on RetailWire.com, a leading information website that presents news stories and commentary from a diverse group of retail industry experts. As a BrainTrust commentator, I get a firsthand look at some of the most important, timely, and topical discussions in the retail industry, and in 2025, AI was at the top of the list.

As you read the headlines and articles, you might assume that AI is already running the retail industry and that every retailer is applying AI to great advantage and successful outcomes. But that's not necessarily the case in my experience working with retailers. Look past the hyperbolic headlines, oversized benefit claims, and public relations hype, and dig in to find the practical applications and real outcomes.

This is not to say that AI will not have the profound impact that pundits claim it will—there's little doubt in my mind that AI and automation will absolutely change retailing and how we conduct business in physical stores. In fact, it's already well underway. However, which AI use-cases will emerge as having real value and when these systems will become affordable, practical to implement, and manage are completely different and unanswered questions. And the answers will vary by individual retailer.

Let's start by briefly examining four of the most frequently cited AI use-cases for retailers and explore how they connect to the physical store through traffic and conversion.[2]

## ENHANCED CUSTOMER EXPERIENCE

AI-powered tools like chatbots and virtual assistants offer personalized shopping experiences, helping customers find products more efficiently and receive tailored recommendations, both online and in store.

Retailers have been using chatbots since the mid-2010s, but it wasn't until around 2015 when more sophisticated chatbots driven by large language models (referred to as LLMs in AI parlance), became better at understanding customers' questions and delivering useful answers.

However, for anyone who has ever interacted with a chatbot knows, as of 2025 this is still a work in progress. As much as these systems have improved, and AI has a lot to do with it, there's still much that needs to be done for a chatbot to match a skilled and motivated human representative.

If AI-driven customer service chatbots are more effective, then we should see an impact on in-store conversion rates. And that is the benefit many of the providers of these AI-based systems claim retailers will receive.

But if you don't track store traffic, and therefore cannot calculate your conversion rates, how will you ever be able to measure the impact a system like this has on in-store conversion rates? You can't.

## OPTIMIZED INVENTORY MANAGEMENT

AI-driven analytics claim to predict demand more accurately, reducing stock-outs and overstock situations. The theory is that this will help ensure that popular items are available when customers want them, leading to higher customer satisfaction and reduced inventory costs. Additionally, by better recognizing demand signals, AI-driven inventory systems should enable retailers to more effectively localize product mix by individual store, and this should certainly be reflected in higher conversion rates.

Every retailer should be interested in improving their inventory levels, and if AI can help do that, then this should become pervasive in the industry. I have little doubt that eventually it will.

While AI is better than humans at recognizing patterns and analyzing massive data sets that humans can't, these sophisticated systems still all require one important ingredient—data. Complete, reliable, and accurate data underpins all AI use-cases, and as I argue in chapter 8, store traffic and conversion data—especially stock keeping unit (SKU)-level conversion—are the foundational data needed to inform these systems.

It's important to remember that optimizing inventory isn't only about knowing what product should go to which store, but it also needs to physically get transported to the store. AI doesn't deliver product to the store, but autonomous delivery—which is underpinned by AI—is becoming a reality, and this should help enable optimized inventory.

This all said, you still need store staff to unload the truck, unpack the merchandise, and display the goods effectively. AI can help get the right product to the store, but this alone doesn't guarantee successful outcomes.

## DATA-DRIVEN MARKETING

Retailers can leverage AI to analyze customer data and create targeted marketing campaigns. The promise is that this will result in more effective promotions, personalized offers, increased customer loyalty, and ultimately sales.

As I described in chapter 9, the goal of retail marketing should be to drive sales opportunities to physical stores, and these marketing efforts should be measured by increases in store traffic and/or improvements in conversion rates by virtue of targeting and attracting more qualified buyers.

Another area where AI is having a tremendous impact is in how retailers are using it to help create marketing content faster, cheaper, and more effectively than they could have otherwise. When you consider all the marketing content retailers need to create, this is a meaningful and practical use-case.

So if AI can help more effectively target the right prospects and create more compelling marketing content, then this should translate into higher store traffic and/or improved conversion rates. While improving marketing effectiveness with AI may drive more shoppers to stores, the frontline team still needs to convert that traffic into sales.

## IMPROVED STORE OPERATIONS

The narrative around improved store operations generally focuses on how labor is allocated and applied in stores. The claim is that AI enables better staff scheduling and labor resource allocation by analyzing store traffic patterns and customer behavior. This leads to more efficient operations and a better overall shopping experience for customers.

I wholeheartedly agree with this claim, but you need store traffic data to accomplish this. I have been strongly arguing that retailers should be basing their labor allocations and staff scheduling on store traffic data for more than two decades, and many retailers have yet to do it. Will the pressure to implement AI cause retailers to finally do this? I hope so.

However, without complete and accurate store traffic data, I suspect these staff scheduling optimization AI models will be driven by sales transaction counts and potentially lead to the wrong conclusions and outcomes that fall well short of the expectations.[3]

There are numerous exciting AI-driven initiatives that I believe will improve store operations and store experiences, and one such example is the Store Employee AI Tool from Walmart. Here, AI is used to help the store associate answer virtually any question a shopper may have. I can't see how this wouldn't improve conversion rates.

As a retail traffic analytics practitioner, I have no doubt that AI can be applied in ways that would greatly improve how retailers allocate store labor and improve productivity, but AI does not (yet) serve customers directly in stores.

Physical stores are still operated by human beings interacting with other human beings who visit the store looking to buy something. As long as this human-to-human connection persists, AI will never be the panacea that it is often characterized as being.

Furthermore, whether it's AI or big data or any other innovation, it won't do a damn bit of good if your store operating model is broken. It's worth repeating: You can't algorithm your way to success.

## AI Won't Help If You Don't Do Anything Differently—Insights Versus Action

As much as the retail world is changing, some things remain the same, and one of those immutable laws is that you must take some action or behavior change based on the insights to produce different outcomes.

I'll digress to 2003 to illustrate. One of my very first store traffic reporting service clients was a single-location hardware store. The owner/operator, whom I'll call "Bob," was passionate about his store and wanted to use traffic insights to help him make better decisions.

Data and analytics were the AI of the time.

After being on my service for eight months, I called Bob and asked how he was using the store traffic insights I was providing. And here's how the call went:

> Author: Hi, Bob, it's Mark from HeadCount. I thought I'd call and see how you're using the daily reporting I provide.
>
> Bob: Well, Mark . . . the reporting is really interesting, but I'm going to cancel your service.
>
> Author: Sorry to hear, Bob, what's the problem?
>
> Bob: Well, I've been receiving your daily reports for months, and the trends aren't changing at all. So since

I now know the trends in my store, I don't need your traffic reports anymore.

Author: Well, I'm sorry to see you go, but I understand. Bob, before I let you go, may I ask what actions you took based on the traffic insights?

Bob: What actions I took? I didn't take any actions! I just keep seeing the same trends, week after week.

Author: OK, Bob. Good luck.

Unfortunately, too many retailers are like Bob. Whether the insights come from reporting or an AI-driven system, none of it will matter unless it is applied in some meaningful way to produce better outcomes.

Beyond the four use-cases that I described here, there are actually a multitude of AI-related initiatives going on in retail, and it's worth having a quick look at which retailers are implementing AI and which are not. If anything, it will provide a time capsule of AI evolution in retailing as of early 2025.

## Which Retailers Are Actually Applying AI?

Whether or not retailers are explicitly applying AI or not, it is being integrated into all varieties of store-related technologies and systems. From wayfinding, floor-cleaning, and shelf-scanning robots to digital shelf labels, the applications are many, and AI underpins how many of these systems work. Deploying them to relieve front-line personnel of mundane, repetitive tasks so they can focus on serving shoppers, delivering a better store experience, and improving conversion rates just makes good sense.

But as compelling as these systems sound, it's important to remember that it takes time and money to keep them functioning.

When it comes to anything technology related, it's understandable to feel like you're being left behind, and that's especially the case with AI. It seems as if virtually everyone is feeling behind because AI is moving so fast and in so many directions simultaneously.

Like almost all technological advancements in retailing, it's usually the largest retail enterprises that lead the way—as they should. They have the resources to hire AI experts to help them set a strategy and priorities, they can afford the technical knowledge required to implement and manage these systems, and they have pressure from Wall Street to deliver better financial results.

In this regard, AI is no different than any other technology retailers use—the largest firms are almost always leading the charge. But how are retailers applying AI based on their size?

Large retailers are hiring AI experts, building/refining systems, and implementing them in their businesses; medium and small retailers are leveraging third-party vendors to advance their AI aspirations since they often don't have the resources or budget to move forward; and independent mom-and-pop retailers I have encountered are either too busy focusing on serving their customers or not sure about where to begin their AI journey.

Let's have a closer look at each group.

## LARGE RETAILERS

There is widespread and advanced use of AI among the largest and most sophisticated retailers, with retailers like Walmart and Target at the forefront. They invest heavily in AI-driven technologies across various functions, including inventory management, customer service, and personalized marketing. For instance, Walmart uses AI to optimize its supply chain and predict product demand, apparently with remarkable accuracy.[4]

Walmart has also developed and deployed an AI-powered Assistant to empower store employees to find merchandise, make product recommendations, and generally enable their frontline store personnel to serve shoppers more effectively.

Not to be outdone, Target has also rolled out its own AI-powered chatbot, called "Store Companion," designed to assist store teams by answering questions related to store processes and procedures so that they can more effectively serve shoppers.[5]

## MID-SIZED RETAILERS

Mid-sized retailers tend to be more selective in their AI adoption, reflecting their resource and capability limitations. These retailers do not have the same resources as large retailers, but they can focus on specific areas where AI can offer the most immediate return on investment (ROI). This might include implementing AI for inventory management, dynamic pricing, or targeted marketing campaigns.

These retailers often start with one or two AI use-cases and expand as they see success. For example, they might initially use AI for demand forecasting before moving on to customer personalization or store operations.

## SMALL RETAILERS

It should come as no surprise that small retailers generally have lower adoption of AI tools, but according to some sources, that's changing.[6]

Some small retailers might only use basic AI applications, such as chatbots for customer service or simple data analytics tools for understanding sales trends. And instead of developing in-house AI capabilities, these retailers often rely on third-party platforms that offer AI features that are embedded into solutions like point of sale (POS) systems or customer relationship management (CRM) tools. This allows them to benefit from AI without having to make significant upfront investments in developing it.

This is how small retailers should approach AI—let the big retailers invest all the money, and the learnings and benefits will trickle down to any retailer willing to pay the money to access them.

## Small, Medium, and Large—All Retailers Have Their Challenges with AI

Regardless of the retailers' size and capabilities, all retailers seem to have challenges with technology in general, and it's not just AI-related initiatives.

The fact is even large retailers face challenges with integrating AI into legacy systems and scaling these solutions across all their stores. Mid-sized and small retailers often struggle more with these issues due to limited technical expertise and resources.

AI's effectiveness depends heavily on the quality and quantity of data available. Larger retailers typically have access to vast amounts of customer and sales data, which they can leverage for AI applications, while smaller retailers may not have sufficient data to fully capitalize on AI's potential.

In summary, while AI is being used across the retail industry, the extent and sophistication of its application vary among large, mid-sized, and small retailers. Large retailers are leading the charge, while smaller ones are more cautious, often focusing on cost-effective, third-party solutions.

## In the Store of the Future— Store Traffic Will Always Matter

In an interview for *Harvard Business Review* in 2007, Jeff Bezos, the founder and former CEO of Amazon, was asked what he saw coming in the future. His answer was curious.

"When I'm talking with people outside the company, there's a question that comes up very commonly: 'What's going to change in the next five to ten years?' But I very rarely get asked 'What's not going to change in the next five to ten years?' At Amazon we're always trying to figure that out, because you can really spin up fly-wheels around those things."[7]

This is exactly how all retailers should think about their store traffic.

Regardless of technological advances and AI, threats from online retailers, demand for new services by shoppers, and even pandemics, the act of visiting a store to discover new products and make a purchase is unlikely to change in the next ten years, and I'd argue for many decades to come. As long as this is the case, store traffic will be important.

As I described in this chapter, the promises of how AI and other technological advances can help retailers deliver a better store experience for shoppers and better business outcomes for themselves are truly exciting, but the realization of these benefits requires taking action or creating change, and that comes with a cost.

Connecting AI use-cases and other technology initiatives back to their impact on store traffic and shopper conversion is a reliable way to understand outcomes since virtually every operational decision made in a retail business connects back to store traffic in some way.

You might say, store traffic connects to everything in the physical store.

# 🛒 Chapter Takeaways

- AI has the potential to revolutionize retail by enhancing customer experience, optimizing inventory, improving store operations, and supporting data-driven marketing efforts.

- AI requires vast amounts of reliable, high-quality data to deliver useful insights. Store traffic and conversion data are key inputs for AI applications in retail.

- AI excels at analyzing large data sets to detect patterns, but human oversight and practical application of insights remain crucial.

- AI won't fix a broken store-operating model. Retailers cannot rely solely on algorithms to succeed. Actionable insights and sound operational practices are essential.

- Large retailers lead the way in AI adoption due to greater resources. Small and mid-sized retailers can benefit by leveraging third-party AI tools, but their challenges include cost, expertise, and integration with existing systems.

## PRACTITIONER'S ADVICE

- Remember that store-level AI-driven initiatives should ultimately aim to optimize in-store shopper conversion. Implementing technologies like chatbots or autonomous systems should enhance, not detract from, the customer's in-store experience.

- Start by collecting and analyzing store traffic and conversion data. This foundational step can provide valuable insights, even without complex AI applications.

- Act on data or AI-generated insights to improve outcomes. Simply having the information isn't enough.

- Focus AI investments on practical, high-impact areas like inventory management and targeted marketing campaigns, which can directly drive store traffic and help improve conversion rates.

- Ensure your investments align with the specific needs and capabilities of your business. Remember, AI is not a silver bullet, so avoid overreliance on trendy technology.

# Store Traffic Connects to Everything

S tore traffic is the lifeblood of retailing, and this holds true for every retailer regardless of size or category. From the most exclusive luxury retailers to warehouse clubs, from the smallest mom-and-pop store to the largest multinational chain, every retailer with a physical store receives visitor traffic. Ultimately, what the retailer does with that precious traffic is the difference between success and failure, longevity or a slow and painful demise.

The very best retailers make the most of every visitor who crosses the threshold of their store, and they understand that every visit represents an opportunity to delight a customer and make a sale.

Store traffic insights inform day-to-day operational decisions and enable retailers to better execute because they know how many shoppers are visiting and when. Furthermore, they can use conversion rates to pinpoint where service lapses may be occurring—right down to the hour of the day. That's what store traffic and conversion insights can do, but only if the retailer has accurate traffic data and uses it in a meaningful way.

Store traffic insights shouldn't be stuck in organizational silos, used only by whichever functional team "owns" them. The data and insights should be shared and leveraged broadly across most functional departments since they connect to virtually every operational decision that impacts the physical store. Store traffic data also provides the most reliable and quantifiable demand signal and contextualizes everything that happens in the store.

When a retailer talks about sales performance—good or bad—store traffic is almost always part of the discussion. Sales were down because of a decline in store traffic; sales were up because traffic was up. Store traffic, it seems, is both a cause for celebration and a curse.

As I noted in the opening chapter, while store traffic and sales are highly correlated, to say that store traffic is the key driver of sales is an oversimplification of the connection between store traffic and sales outcomes. Furthermore, it's impossible for any retailer to truly understand how well a store is performing unless they know what is possible, and traffic counts define the sales opportunity size.

It may be obvious to say that store traffic is important, but I will go a step further and call it a precious and nonrenewable resource. Precious? Nonrenewable? Why?

Consumers have so many options for where and how they buy goods that if you don't satisfy the shopper on the very first visit, there's no guarantee they'll ever be back—and that's what makes it nonrenewable. Even a single, relatively minor in-store service lapse can lead to the permanent loss of a customer. This may sound hyperbolic, but it's not. The stakes have never been higher for retailers.

If all retailers treated their store traffic like a precious, nonrenewable resource, I'd bet that the shopping experience would be significantly better and so too would conversion rates, sales, and customer experience.

Many retailers today are struggling, and for some of them, a decline in store traffic is certainly part of their problem. However, lower store traffic alone doesn't explain why some retailers are failing. Store traffic does a retailer no good unless it results in a sale—and this is precisely what conversion rates measure and why they, too, are important.

Retailers have become obsessed with technology and the threat of e-commerce competitors, especially Amazon. In fact, this obsession with technology and online competition is so acute that they seem to have forgotten what matters most—the shopper who is already in the store.

Brick-and-mortar retailers are not being beaten by e-commerce competitors or even by Amazon; they are beating themselves by not focusing on the shopper who visited the store but left without buying. The shopper they could have converted into a customer but failed to do so.

Perhaps shoppers are expecting too much from retailers today. Shoppers are *demanding* a better "store experience"—whatever that seems to mean to them personally. Maybe shopper expectations are just too high, too unrealistic when they cross the threshold of a retail store. Maybe retailers should stop trying to solve the unsolvable shopper conversion puzzle.

I don't think it's unsolvable. In fact, I'd argue that shopper expectations probably haven't changed much—in decades.

Do shoppers really want anything especially different today? Greet me like you're happy to see me in your store, not as an inconvenience; help me find what I'm looking for and answer my questions; take my money; and don't make me wait in long lines, then hard-press me to give you my email address and sign up for your company credit card or loyalty program.

Undeniably, shoppers and shopping have evolved. Shoppers are not only informed when they visit a store, but they're also armed with the most lethal shopping device known to humanity—the smartphone. And they're more than willing to use them, right on the spot, to check prices, to buy from an online competitor, or to post a scathing, one-star review on the plethora of social media at their disposal.

But this shouldn't be a war of wills. The shopper is not the enemy to be conquered, and the store manager and frontline team are not the opposing force, strategically deployed to subvert the shopping experience and create barriers to buying. But that's exactly how many shoppers feel today.

Retailers need to pay serious attention to the people who visit their stores but leave without buying. Think about it. These shoppers made the effort to *physically* visit the store—these are potentially the retailers' very best fans. But you would never know it by the service that is so often experienced and retold by shoppers. It seems that many retailers don't fully appreciate just how precious these visitors are or that visiting a brick-and-mortar store is a real commitment given the demand for consumers' attention that exists today—online and in innumerable, nonretail experiences.

People need to buy things, but they no longer need to do this in your brick-and-mortar store. The retail industry has been permanently transformed by this because for some shoppers, online is virtually the only way they will buy now. That's why every retailer must be able to also sell their goods online and do so in a way that complements and supports their brick-and-mortar store experience, not create confusion and conversion friction as so many seem to do.

And as much as online has impacted and transformed the retail industry, the passage of time has also proven that brick-and-mortar stores aren't going away anytime soon.

Any store operating model that doesn't place the shopper—and shopper conversion by extension—at its center is misguided at best and reckless at worst. Instead of reducing purchase friction and making it easier for shoppers to buy, these misguided retailers seem to make it worse—creating barriers to buy and causing shoppers to walk out in disgust and leave empty shopping carts in their wake.

What some disenfranchised shoppers may find surprising is that retailers *really* do want to make shoppers happy—they *really* do want every shopper to buy and have a delightful and satisfying shopping experience. These retailers are well-intended, but many seem to do the wrong things at the wrong times. Good intentions aside, retailers who are oblivious to store traffic and conversion rates are destined to struggle.

When you really dig into store traffic and conversion rates as I have, you discover that brick-and-mortar retailers have a significant advantage over online retailers—even Amazon—but only if they play to their strengths.

Focusing on store traffic and conversion rates is not just a strategy to outperform competitors, deliver better results, and thrive, it's become a matter of survival for some retailers. And while it's true that retailing in physical stores has proven to be remarkably resilient against the online onslaught, tumultuous change, and even pandemics, plenty of individual retailers and chains are struggling.

Every hour of every day, shoppers visit stores intending to make a purchase but leave without buying. Knowing when and how many store visits they receive and exactly when conversion rates are sagging can help any retailer deliver a better store experience and improve business outcomes.

Store traffic is indeed a gift, and a precious one at that. It is my sincere hope that all retailers start treating it accordingly.

# Acknowledgments

First, I want to acknowledge the hundreds of retailers across more than twenty countries who have trusted my team and me with their precious store traffic data. Their willingness to engage with us has been the foundation of my work, and this book is a testament to those partnerships.

While my name is on the cover, this book is the result of years of dedication from my team at HeadCount. I can't acknowledge everyone by name, but several have made significant contributions, including Donald Anderson, James Cummings, Tim Keen, Corine Matsuda, Darryl Martin, Stephanie de Boer, Mike Sweeny, and Terry Thomas. A special thanks to Brant Menegozzo for his excellent work in reviewing and refining all the data elements and charts in the book.

I'm also grateful for the support and advice of my board of directors: Daniel Finkelman, Bruce Johnson, Paul McElhone, PhD, Doug Bell, and Bruce Alton. Special thanks to Doug Cox.

A heartfelt thank you to the talented team at Greenleaf Book Group for their expertise and guidance in bringing this book to life—especially Jen Glynn, my editor Chrissy Wolfe, and Jared Dorsey for their dedication and attention to detail.

To RetailWire and the dozens of BrainTrust colleagues, including Art Suriano, Jeff Sward, Gary Sankary, Paula Rosenblum, Craig Sundstrom, Georganne Bender, Shep Hyken, Bob Phibbs, and Lisa Goller. Your daily insights continue to challenge and inspire me. And a special thanks to Neil Saunders for writing the terrific foreword for the book.

To my dear friends and confidants, Ross Marasco, Blaine Bertsch, Tom Dodd, and Paul Ingram—your encouragement and support have meant the world to me. And to Mike and Donna Marasco—thank you for your generosity in allowing me to work on this book from your beautiful home in Phoenix.

Finally, to my family—Cole, Taylor, Terry, Marlane, Darren, and Roni—your love and support mean everything to me.

# Notes

## Chapter 2: How to Convert More Store Visitors

1. US Census Bureau, "Quarterly Retail E-Commerce Sales, 2nd Quarter 2024," August 19, 2024, https://www2.census.gov/retail/releases/historical/ecomm/24q2.pdf.

2. "Amazon Conversion Rate Statistics: Key Facts and Stats to Know," Push-Pull, August 8, 2022, https://pushpullagency.com/blog/amazon-conversion-rate-statistics-key-facts-and-stats-to-know/.

3. HeadCount Corporation, "Estimated In-Store Conversion Rates by Category Based on Proprietary Retailer Data, 2015–2024," (proprietary data based on analysis of actual retailer performance).

4. *The Real Reasons Shoppers Aren't Returning to Your Stores*, ServiceChannel, 2021, https://servicechannel.com/resources-download/reports/state-of-brick-and-mortar.pdf.

5. HeadCount Corporation, *Exit Survey of Non-Buyers*, unpublished proprietary retailer data.

## Chapter 3: Labor

1. "How to Develop an Effective Retail Labor Performance Management Program," UKG, accessed January 2, 2025, https://www.ukg.com/resources/white-paper/how-develop-effective-retail-labor-performance-management-program.

2. "Store Labor Productivity Analysis," Umbrex, accessed January 2, 2025, https://umbrex.com/resources/how-to-analyze-a-retail-company/store-labor-productivity-analysis/.

3. Bryce Davies, "How Retailers Can Build an Accurate Labor Model," UKG, April 25, 2023, https://www.ukg.com/blog/workforce-management/how-retailers-can-build-accurate-labor-model.

4. *Labor Management–Understanding the Basics*, Columbus Consulting, accessed January 2, 2025, https://www.columbusconsulting.com/wp-content/uploads/2021/02/CCI_InsightSeries_LaborManagementBasics.pdf.

## Chapter 5: CRO

1. "Top Conversion Rate Optimization Agencies in 2024," Feedbax, accessed January 2, 2025, https://feedbax.io/conversion-optimization.

2. "Guide to eCommerce Conversion Rate Optimization: 20+ Proven Tips for Success," Admetrics, accessed January 2, 2025, https://www.admetrics.io/en/post/ecommerce-conversion-rate-optimization.

## Chapter 6: Store Team

1. Anonymous Reviewer, "Review of [Retailer Name Withheld for Confidentiality]," Yelp, May 20, 2020.

2. HeadCount Corporation, "Analysis of Online Reviews of [Retailer Name Withheld for Confidentiality]," proprietary research, February 2020.

3. Sheila Stafford, "How Retailers Can Turn the Tide on Employee Exodus," *TotalRetail*, August 27, 2024, https://www.mytotalretail.com/article/the-retention-revolution-how-retailers-can-turn-the-tide-on-employee-exodus/.

4. "Pull vs. Push Reporting: Leading KPI Development," Kestrel Management, accessed January 2, 2025, https://kestrelmanagement. com/pull-vs-push-reporting-leading-kpi-development/.

## Chapter 7: Did It Work?

1. "2024 Attendee Demographics," NRF 2025: Retail's Big Show, accessed January 2, 2025, https://nrfbigshow.nrf.com/ about/2024-attendee-demographics.

## Chapter 8: Merchandising

1. Rachel Hand, "Sell-Through Rate: Formula and 2024 Trends Explained," ShipBob, last updated November 22, 2024, https://www. shipbob.com/blog/sell-through-rate/.

2. Darrel Rigby, "Localization: The Revolution in Consumer Markets," Bain & Company, accessed January 2, 2025, https://www.bain.com/ insights/localization-revolution-in-consumer-markets/.

## Chapter 9: Marketing

1. Statista, "Revenue in the Advertising Market in the United States from 2020 to 2030 (in Billion US Dollars)," *Statista Advertising & Media Outlook*, accessed January 3, 2025, https://www.statista.com/ forecasts/1435654/revenue-advertising-advertising-market -united-states.

2. Yaqub M., "46+ Online Shopping Statistics: The Facts & Trends," BusinessDasher, October 24, 2024, https://www.businessdasher.com/ online-shopping-statistics/.

3. Leyla Ezgi Dinc, "CPM Trends 2024: What's High vs. Low in Advertising Costs?," *Enhencer Blog*, accessed January 3, 2025, https:// enhencer.com/blog/understanding-cpm-trends-what-is-considered- high-vs-the-low-in-2024; "Is Online Advertising Expensive? Online Advertising Costs in 2025," Top Draw Inc., October 9, 2024, https:// www.topdraw.com/insights/is-online-advertising-expensive/.

4. Elise Dopson, "What Facebook Ads Cost in November 2024," *Shopify Blog,* November 13, 2024, https://www.shopify.com/ca/blog/facebook-ads-cost; Artyom Dogtiev, "Cost Per Click (CPC) Rates (2024)," Business of Apps, July 2024, https://www.businessofapps.com/ads/cpc/research/cpc-rates/; Leyla Ezgi Dinc, "Google Ads CPM Benchmarks for 2024 Explained," *Enhencer Blog,* August 27, 2024, https://enhencer.com/blog/google-ads-cpm-benchmarks-for-2024-explained.

5. Mark Hamstra, "Businesses Large and Small Tap Multibillion-Dollar Retail Media Network Trend for Growth," *CO by US Chamber of Commerce*, March 2024, accessed January 3, 2025. https://www.uschamber.com/co/good-company/launch-pad/how-retail-media-networks-fuel-growth.

6. Statista, "Largest Daily Newspapers in the United States in the Six Months to September 2023, by Average Print Circulation (in thousands)," *Statista,* February 2024, accessed January 3, 2025, https://www.statista.com/statistics/272790/circulation-of-the-biggest-daily-newspapers-in-the-us/.

## Chapter 10: Amazon and New Shopper Demands

1. Bobby Marhamat, "Five Things Businesses Should Know about BOPIS," *Forbes Business Development Council, Forbes,* May 11, 2021, https://www.forbes.com/sites/forbesbusinessdevelopmentcouncil/2021/05/11/five-things-businesses-should-know-about-bopis/.

2. "Buy Online, Pick Up in Store (BOPIS) Statistics," *Capital One Shopping Research,* last updated, November 18, 2024, accessed January 3, 2025, https://capitaloneshopping.com/research/buy-online-pick-up-in-store-statistics/.

3. John Nash, "Retail CX Predictions for 2025: Personalization Takes Center Stage," Redpoint Global, December 6, 2024, https://www.redpointglobal.com/blog/retail-cx-trends-and-predictions-for-2025-personalization-takes-center-stage/.

4. *Future Stores Trends Report 2022*, Publicis Commerce, accessed January 3, 2025, https://www.publiciscommerce.com/insights/future-stores-trends-report-2022.

5. Jenny McTaggart, "Grocery Tech: A Look at the Past Century's Innovations," *Progressive Grocer*, March 30, 2022, https://progressivegrocer.com/grocery-tech-look-past-centurys-innovations.

6. Emmeline Taylor, "Supermarket Self-Checkouts and Retail Theft: The Curious Case of the SWIPERS," *Criminology and Criminal Justice* 16, no. 5 (2016): 552–567, doi: 10.1177/1748895816643353; Maggie Davis, "69% of Self-Checkout Users Think It Makes Stealing Easier—and 15% of Shoppers Admit to Purposely Doing So," LendingTree, November 17, 2023, https://www.lendingtree.com/debt-consolidation/self-checkout-survey/.

7. Matt Smith, "New Checkout Experience Seeks to Eliminate the Wait and Add Options at the Register," News, Walmart Corporate, June 30, 2020, https://corporate.walmart.com/news/2020/06/30/new-checkout-experience-seeks-to-eliminate-the-wait-and-add-options-at-the-register; Anna Gordon, "Walmart Rolls Out Major Changes for Customers. What to Know," *Time*, April 19, 2024, https://time.com/6968997/walmart-stores-self-checkout-cuts/.

8. Cory Mitchell, "Amazon Effect," *Investopedia*, July 17, 2024, https://www.investopedia.com/terms/a/amazon-effect.asp.

9. Jeff Spross, "What Caused the Retail Apocalypse?," *The Week*, May 9, 2017, https://theweek.com/articles/697378/what-caused-retail-apocalypse.

10. US Census Bureau, "Quarterly Retail E-Commerce Sales, 2nd Quarter 2024," August 19, 2024, https://www2.census.gov/retail/releases/historical/ecomm/24q2.pdf.

11. Sara Lebow, "Amazon Will Surpass 40% of US Ecommerce Sales This Year, Despite Slower Growth," *eMarketer*, April 17, 2024, https://www.emarketer.com/content/amazon-will-surpass-40-of-us-ecommerce-sales-this-year.

12. Mohammad Yaqub, "Amazon Statistics: The Ultimate Numbers Must Know in 2024," Contimod, November 5, 2024, https://www.contimod.com/amazon-statistics/.

13. Amazon, "Amazon Hub Locker," Amazon, accessed January 3, 2025, https://www.amazon.com/b?ie=UTF8&node=13853235011; "Thousands of Retailers across the Country Are Using Amazon Lockers to Drive More Foot Traffic to Their Locations. Now You Can, too," PayHereNetwork, accessed January 3, 2025, https://www.payherenetwork.com/amazonlocker/; Staff Writer, "Lockers—Amazon Hub, USPS & Temperature Controlled," Kiosk Industry, April 3, 2024, https://kioskindustry.org/lockers/.

14. "Amazon's 1st High-Tech Grocery Store Opens to the Public," CBC, January 22, 2018, https://www.cbc.ca/news/science/amazon-go-grocery-store-1.4497862.

15. Mark Ryski, "Why Amazon Go Is a 'No-Go' for Most Retailers," *Retail Insider*, February 23, 2018, https://retail-insider.com/retail-insider/2018/02/why-amazon-go-is-a-no-go-for-most-retailers/.

16. Steve Holtz, "Amazon to Close 8 of Its Cashierless Convenience Stores," *Supermarket News*, March 3, 2023, https://www.supermarketnews.com/grocery-technology/amazon-to-close-8-of-its-cashierless-convenience-stores.

## Chapter 11: Your Traffic Data

1. Mark Ryski, "Mall Audits of Traffic Counter Penetration in Select Shopping Malls, December 2022 to April 2023," unpublished research conducted by the author.

2. Owen Kell, "People Movement & Location Analytics in the Retail Sector: Applications, Opportunities & Market Prospects – 2017 to 2022," Intelligent & Green Systems Ltd., accessed October 31, 2024, http://www.igsystems.co.uk.

3. Metro, "The Evolution of People Counters: How Do They Work?" *Metro XP*, March 14, 2022, https://metroxp.com/the-evolution-of-people-counters-how-do-they-work/.

4. Zac Amos, "Top Data Challenges Facing Modern Retailers," *Open Data Science*, June 26, 2023, https://opendatascience.com/top-data-challenges-facing-modern-retailers/.

## Chapter 12: Traffic Indexes

1. Mark Ryski, "Why You Should Take Retail Traffic Indexes with a Grain of Salt," Retail Customer Experience, March 30, 2015, https://www.retailcustomerexperience.com/articles/why-you-should-take-retail-traffic-indexes-with-a-grain-of-salt/.

2. "What Is Alternative Data?" AlternativeData.org, accessed January 4, 2025, https://alternativedata.org/alternative-data/.

3. Petra Borisovas, "Tracking and Tracing with MAC Addresses," NordVPN, June 22, 2023, https://nordvpn.com/blog/track-mac-address/.

4. Google Support, "About Popular Times, Wait Times & Visit Duration Data," Google Support, accessed January 5, 2025, https://support.google.com/business/answer/6263531; Matt D'Zmura, "Behind the Scenes: Popular Times and Live Busyness Information," *The Keyword*, Google, October 15, 2020, https://blog.google/products/maps/maps101-popular-times-and-live-busyness-information/.

## Chapter 13: Future & AI

1. Cade Metz and Keith Collins, "How ChatGPT Kicked Off an A.I. Arms Race," *New York Times*, February 3, 2023, https://www.nytimes.com/2023/02/03/technology/chatgpt-openai-artificial-intelligence.html.

2. Bobby Marhamat, "7 Strong Use Cases for AI in Retail," *Forbes,* September 4, 2024, https://www.forbes.com/councils/forbesbusinessdevelopmentcouncil/2024/09/04/7-strong-use-cases-for-ai-in-retail/.

3. Vikram Chatterji, "Data Quality: The Real Bottleneck in AI Adoption," *Forbes*, February 1, 2023, https://www.forbes.com/councils/forbestechcouncil/2023/02/01/data-quality-the-real-bottleneck-in-ai-adoption/; Yuri Gubin, "The Hidden Risks in AI: Why Data Quality and Integrity Are Non-Negotiable," *Forbes*, October 14, 2024, https://www.forbes.com/councils/

forbestechcouncil/2024/10/14/the-hidden-risks-in-ai-why
-data-quality-and-integrity-are-nonnegotiable/.

4. Walmart Corporate, "Walmart Reveals Plan for Scaling Artificial
   Intelligence, Generative AI, Augmented Reality, and Immersive
   Commerce Experiences," Walmart, October 9, 2024, https://
   corporate.walmart.com/news/2024/10/09/walmart-reveals-plan-
   for-scaling-artificial-intelligence-generative-ai-augmented-
   reality-and-immersive-commerce-experiences; PYMNTS,
   "Walmart's AI Helps Create 'Ready-for-Anything' Supply
   Chains," *PYMNTS*, https://www.pymnts.com/supply-chain/2024/
   walmart-ai-helps-create-ready-for-anything-supply-chains/.

5. Lindsey Wilkinson, "Walmart Rolls Out Generative
   AI-Powered Assistant to 50K Employees," *Retail Dive*,
   August 30, 2023, https://www.retaildive.com/news/Walmart-
   generative-AI-tool-My-Assistant/692402/; Nicole Silberstein,
   "Target Launches Gen AI Chatbot for Store Associates
   Chainwide," *Retail TouchPoints*, June 20, 2024, https://www.
   retailtouchpoints.com/topics/data-analytics/ai-machine-learning/
   target-launches-gen-ai-chatbot-for-store-associates-chainwide.

6. Michelle Kumar and Justin Antonioli, "Small Businesses
   Matter: Navigating the AI Frontier," Bipartisan Policy
   Center, April 29, 2024, https://bipartisanpolicy.org/report/
   small-businesses-matter-navigating-the-ai-frontier/.

7. Jeff Bezos, "The Institutional Yes," interview by Julia Kirby and
   Thomas A. Stewart, *Harvard Business Review*, October 2007, https://
   hbr.org/2007/10/the-institutional-yes.

# About the Author

**MARK RYSKI** is a recognized authority on store traffic and shopper conversion. He is the author of *When Retail Customers Count*, the first book ever written dedicated to these critical retail metrics, and *Conversion: The Last Great Retail Metric*.

His insights have been featured in *Forbes*, the *Wall Street Journal*, *Financial Post*, *Chain Store Age*, and other leading business and retail publications. He is also a featured "BrainTrust" contributor on RetailWire.com, where he provides expert commentary on retail trends. In 2025, RETHINK Retail named him one of "The Top Retail Experts (TRE)."

Mark is the founder and CEO of HeadCount Corporation (headcount.com), a company specializing in store traffic and shopper conversion analytics. For over twenty years, HeadCount has helped retailers—from independent stores to large-scale chains in more than twenty countries—understand their traffic and improve shopper conversion. Clients span virtually every major retail category, including malls.

Early in his career, Mark worked in retail himself—as a department store sales associate, a sporting goods store manager, and later, in a computer retail business where he became marketing manager and first recognized the untapped power of store traffic data.

Mark can be reached at mark.ryski@headcount.com.